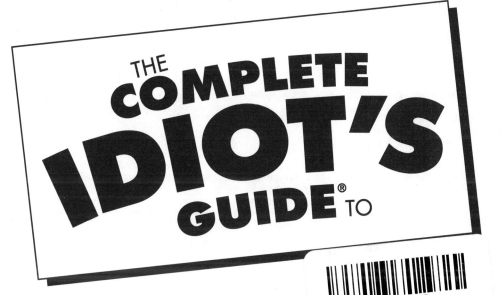

THE COMPLETE IDIOT'S GUIDE® TO

Grilling with Ted Reader

by Ted Reader, Barbara Grunes, and Virginia Van Vynckt

Prentice Hall Canada

A Pearson Company
Toronto

alpha
books

Canadian Cataloguing in Publication Data

Reader, Ted
  The complete idiot's guide to grilling with Ted Reader

Includes index.
ISBN 0-13-086720-9

1. Barbecue cookery. I. Grunes, Barbara. II. Van Vynckt, Virginia. III. Title.

TX840.B3R418 2000   641.7′6   C00-930121-6

© 2000 Pearson Education Canada Inc.
Toronto, Ontario

Adapted from The Complete Idiot's Guide to Grilling © 1999 by Barbara Grunes and Virginia Van Vynckt

ISBN 0-13-086720-9

Editorial Director, Trade Division: Andrea Crozier
Acquisitions Editor: Nicole de Montbrun
Copy Editor: Matthew Kudelka
Production Editor: Lori McLellan
Art Direction: Mary Opper
Cover Image: Hal Roth
Interior Design: Nathan Clement
Production Manager: Kathrine Pummell
Page Layout: Pixel Graphics
Illustrator: Kevin Spear

1 2 3 4 5 WC 04 03 02 01 00

Printed and bound in Canada.

Visit the Prentice Hall Canada Web site! Send us your comments, browse our catalogues, and more.
www.phcanada.com.

Contents at a Glance

v

Contents

vii

Foreword

When Ted first told me he was working on an 'idiot's' guide to grilling, I told him not to be so hard on himself; after all none of us is perfect. When Ted explained to me exactly who the idiot in question was, I soon realized what a tailor-made project this was for him because, simply put (after all, Ted may be reading this) Ted Reader was made for the grill, uh, made to grill. He lives to grill, he loves to grill, to barbecue, to add a lick of smoke and a luscious sizzle to everything from mammoth steaks and spuds to plump little quail and honking great turkey legs. Even in his powder blue 1973 convertible Mustang fastback, the wind blowing through his stylish locks, his eight-track blaring Vic Damone, he is thinking 'grill'. In fact, if there was a way for him to fire up the barbie while driving, he'd have another grill installed on that car.

But all guys like to grill, don't they? Put a guy outdoors on a summer patio or deck, slap a cold one in his hand and before you can say 'let's fire up the grill', the deck's on fire. Call it primal instinct or he-man heroics, there's something about fire outside that seems to get their culinary juices flowing. Ted Reader, my buddy and grill chef extraordinare, is definitely one of those guys. But, unlike your average grill man or backyard barbecue meister, Big Bold Ted understands the art of grilling. He 'gets it', rather like Charles Oakley gets basketball or Eric Clapton gets the guitar.

Ted maintains—and I believe him—there is almost no food that can't be grilled. You name it, at one time or another, he's grilled it—and grilled it well (except for my porterhouse which must be medium-rare). Even things that no one would dream of slapping on a grill. For a cookbook on specialty grilling Ted and I co-authored, he came up with a procedure and recipe for grilling 's'mores', those campfire treats beloved by kids. Yeah, right Teddy, I said when he eagerly told me about the concept. Sure, blackened graham wafer-wrapped marshmallow chocolate gooeys on the grill—yum. There's no way. Uh, way! He not only proved me wrong (if you want to find out how, you'll have to buy this book), he proved it deliciously. And that's Ted. He imagines, conceptualizes and finally creates recipes that are imaginative, do-able and absolutely bang-on—which pretty much sums up *The Complete Idiot's Guide® to Grilling with Ted Reader*. Here he has beautifully and simply combined his ongoing love affair with food and grilling in one perfectly clear, foolproof, A-Z fashion that will prove itself over and over. I'm not a betting gal, but I'm willing to wager this book will become your personal guide to grilling whether you're a dab hand who needs some new material or a grill novice who only gets fired up in traffic. (Now can I have a free copy, Ted?)

So, if you're standing in a bookstore trying to decide which grill book is for you, the decision has just been made for you. This is it. Quit stalling, take it to the checkout, pay the money, take it home and fire up the grill. Ted Reader is here to show you how—and how!

Kathleen Sloan

Author of *Rustic Italian Cooking*, *The Global Grill*, co-author (with Ted Reader) of *The Sticks & Stones Cookbook* and co-author (with Tony Aspler) of *The Wine Lover Cooks*.

February 2000

Introduction

Just moved to the suburbs and planning to buy your first grill? Or perhaps you already have a grill, but every time you use it, you feel as though the food is burned, your hair is singed, and you'll be divorced if your spouse doesn't quit offering useful advice on how to stack the coals. Maybe you can grill basic stuff, but need some recipes and tips to get you out of that hot-dog rut. Or you're pretty proficient at the actual grilling, but need some help in getting organized and planning, so you don't end up running the equivalent of a marathon between your refrigerator and the grill.

You're no idiot, of course, but the vast array of grills, accessories, utensils, woods, charcoals, sauces, and spices—not to mention terminology—is beginning to make you wonder if this whole barbecuing thing isn't beyond you. Or at the very least, a lot more work than it's cracked up to be.

Relax. This book is for you. By the time you finish reading The Complete Idiot's Guide to Grilling, you will know just about everything there is to know about choosing a grill and other equipment, selecting foods for grilling, and cooking them to perfection. You'll be able to put together the sort of casual outdoor parties that everyone loves, and wow your guests with entire menus cooked on the grill. You'll be able to turn out juicy steaks, "wood-fired" pizzas, roasted vegetables, and even grilled desserts with ease.

With our help, you can be confident that when you shell out the money for steak or seafood or exotic vegetables, they'll arrive on your guests' plates grilled to perfection. You'll soon win the kind of acclaim reserved for those who are deemed not "complete idiots," but accomplished pros.

Before You Get Started

Hold your fire! Before you take a match to the coals, we recommend that you read The Complete Idiot's Guide to Grilling all the way through. There's a lot more to grilling than just slapping a piece of chicken on the grid. You need to learn how to best organize your kitchen, eating and grilling spaces, storage—and time—so you don't waste effort and charcoal.

What's What

Read these boxes for definitions of important terms.

Hot Tip

Look here for information on how to accomplish a task more efficiently or make a food taste better.

Don't Get Burned!

These boxes caution about potential hazards, or mistakes that could ruin your meal.

Tasty Tidbit

These are interesting morsels of extra information we thought you'd enjoy reading.

A meal is only as good as its ingredients, so you also need to know how to select the best foods for grilling. Also, you need to know how to prepare them so that grilling enhances rather than obliterates their flavours.

Even beginning grillers will have fun practising with various rubs, marinades, and sauces to find the ones that hold the greatest personal appeal. Learn to understand the workings of the grill so that you'll know how best to use its dry, intense heat to advantage.

Although grilling recipes tend to be fairly simple, some do require more sophisticated techniques and/or equipment. If you're a novice griller, start with the most basic recipes—those we have marked "easy"—and gradually expand your repertoire. Remember, grilling is the cooking method most associated with summertime fun. After reading this book, you'll be so at ease with it that you'll be grilling year-round. The goal is to create great grilled fare, and also to have a good time.

What You'll Find in This Book

Part 1: For Starters explains how to set up grilling, eating, and food preparation spaces to best advantage, details grills and accessories, and lists what you'll need in your pantry.

Part 2: Getting Warmer tells you how to start a perfect charcoal fire and keep it going.

You'll learn how to cook over direct and indirect heat, and how to keep you, your family, and your yard safe from everything from flying sparks to food poisoning. We'll also clue you in on how to plan and host successful outdoor parties, and tailor menus to appeal to different tastes.

Part 3: Ladies and Gentlemen, Start Your Grills tells you everything you need to know about marinades, rubs, and sauces; explains the basics of selecting, preparing, and cooking meats, poultry, seafood, vegetables, and grains, and shares great ideas for "recycling" grilled leftovers.

Part 4: Hot Stuff: The Recipes is an assortment of tested recipes that run the gamut from appetizers to desserts. Whether it's the perfect barbecue sauce or the most luscious shellfish, you'll find it here.

We've included three appendices, which will tell you how to troubleshoot various grilling problems, help define common grilling terms for you, and point you to resources for equipment and further advice.

Extras

We've also sprinkled various sidebars throughout the book, which highlight information we especially want you to have.

Acknowledgments

A Smokin' thanks to Nicole de Montbrun and Catherine Dorton of Prentice Hall Canada for their wonderful support and encouragement in putting together this version of The Complete Idiots Guide to Grilling. Awesome! Thank you to Teresa Stahl of Weber-Stephens Products Company Canada. Your support of me on "Cottage Country" and throughout all of my grilling endeavours has helped make these recipes delicious. And lastly, a really big thank you to Pamela for being once again my greatest critic and love.

Trademarks

All terms mentioned in this book that are known to be or are suspected of being trade-marks or service marks have been appropriately capitalized. Alpha Books and Macmillan General Reference cannot attest to the accuracy of this information. Use of a term in this book should not be regarded as affecting the validity of any trademark or service mark. The following trademarks and service marks have been mentioned in this book:

Weber	Kamado
Kingsford	Big Green Egg
Nature's Own	

Dedication

To my wonderful parents Astrida and Alex Reader, whose love is so great and whose encouragement is positive and supportive. You bring out the best in me!

Part 1

For Starters

In grilling more than almost any other kind of cooking, organization is vital. With the right foodstuffs, tools, and equipment on hand, you'll discover that barbecuing is a breeze.

We begin at, well, the beginning. Before you start cooking, you need to set up your food preparation and eating spaces, buy a grill if you don't have one (or clean the old one if you do), collect all the accessories and utensils you need—and maybe a few that you simply want—and make sure you have all the provisions to make grilling and entertaining a success.

Chapter 1

The Smell of Success

In This Chapter

➤ The meaning of barbecue

➤ Setting up a pleasant outdoor eating area

➤ Organizing cooking and storage spaces

Why do we love grilling and barbecuing so much?

When asked that question in surveys, most people say it's because the food tastes great and because they like to eat outdoors.

But you knew that, didn't you?

We think another reason that North Americans love grilling is that we don't have to cook that way. Instead of a chore, grilling is a sport, an art, a hobby. Folks who wouldn't be caught dead lighting a stove and cooking an omelet will fire up the coals and nurse a brisket for 12 hours.

Yet another reason to love barbecuing is that it touches something fundamental in us. Archaeologists reckon that early humans probably stumbled onto cooking meat by accident, when a forest fire charbroiled the animals they'd been using for food. People have been cooking all sorts of foods over fire ever since. Barbecuing over fire is the oldest form of cooking, and truly universal. Heck, in a lot of countries they still cook most of their meals that way.

Tasty Tidbit

The word barbecue dates far back in North American history, and has been a staple in cooking for many people throughout the world. The definition of barbecue is essentially to cook foods over dry heat. Whether it be meat or poultry, fish or vegetables, the act of barbecuing is a primal feast of flavours where foods are cooked over wood, charcoal, gas, or electricity. Generally performed outdoors, barbecuing and grilling have become one of the most popular culinary events throughout North America.

In modern North America, what we like to barbecue depends on who you talk to. Some surveys put chicken on the top; others vote for hamburger. Steaks are second in line, with hot dogs not too far behind.

One thing is for certain: North Americans are particularly fanatical about styles of barbecuing. Cooking foods over fire is the subject of almost religious-like reverence and intensely heated debates. Everyone seems to have their favourite method, as well as their favourite menu choices—the fun part is discovering your own.

Canadians love to grill. We are as adventurous as any Americans when it comes to the barbecue and grill. But Canadians, even though willing to experiment with flavours, have learned a lot about the barbecue and grill from our friends to the south—the all-mighty U.S. of A., a place that lives to barbecue. Each region of the United States has a definitive flavour of barbecue. North Carolinians swear by their pig pickin's. New Englanders have their clambakes, a cooking method that dates back to the original inhabitants of the region. As you move westward, to Memphis and St. Louis, ketchup predominates and vinegar lessens, and "sloppy barbecue"—fatty ribs glistening with sauce, pork piled high on a sandwich with coleslaw—takes over. In the Midwest, chicken joins the ranks of popular barbecue foods.

What's What

There's a difference between grilling and barbecuing, at least to true fans of these culinary arts. *Grilling* means cooking food fairly quickly over medium-hot coals. Most of the recipes we offer in this book are for grilled foods. *Barbecuing* means slow-cooking foods over a low fire. For our purposes, *smoking* is basically barbecuing, with the use of wood chips or chunks to create extra flavour. Most Canadians spend time grilling rather than barbecuing. For one thing, it is faster, and with the number of cold months in Canada it is easier to grill that to barbecue. Our friends to the south love to barbecue, which is an art form. An expression in taste. Not to say that as Canadians we do not take pride in what we do—we just don't do it as often.

Finally, when you move far enough west to, say, Texas, an honest-to-gosh barbecue will feature beef rubbed in a mixture of seasonings and served as is. Sauce on the side is strictly optional, and don't you even think about drowning the meat in it.

Go even farther west, to California, and suddenly grilling takes on an almost European flavour, with vegetables and pizzas and polenta starring alongside the meat, and with smoke provided by dried grapevines and bits of recycled wine barrels. In the northwestern United States, salmon is the choice, lightly seasoned in spices and smoked over the delicate sweetness of alder. Go even farther west, to Hawaii, and the pig reappears, as the star (and main course) of the luau.

In Canada there are many similarities to the United States. In Ontario and Quebec, ribs are usually boiled or braised first to make them tender and succulent. These are usually glazed with a sweet red barbecue sauce, whereas in Calgary ribs are usually dry and smoky and the sauce tends to be darker and rich with smoke. On the West Coast, Pacific salmon is a big favourite, and so is planked salmon, where the delicious salmon is smoked on a plank of cedar or alderwood. In the Northwest Territories there is an abundance of venison and elk, which is grilled and smoked, as is Arctic char. On the East Coast we find our friends grilling the ever-succulent Atlantic salmon. Lobster, scallops, and cod are also favourites on the grill. Canada is an country with a dynamic selection of flavours. So next time you're in Windsor, try the ribs at Tunnel BBQ, and when in Montreal try the smoked meat from Swartz's Deli. When at the Calgary Stampede have some smoky beef ribs, and if you ever get a chance, try a little taste of plank salmon from chef Ted Reader.

What's What

One of the most classic—and probably earliest—of the American barbecues is a Carolina *pig pickin'*. Pork is slow-cooked, then pulled into shreds with forks and moistened with a vinegary sauce that probably owes its origins to English-style ketchups, and piled high on buns. North Carolinians make a plain vinegar sauce; South Carolinians add mustard; in western Carolina they add a touch of ketchup.

While regional food styles may vary widely, the love of cooking outdoors spans the continent. More than three-quarters of North American households have a barbecue grill, and every year more than 4 million cookouts are held throughout the United States, Canada, and Mexico. Not surprisingly, families barbecue more often than single people. After all, if you're going to fire up the grill, you might as well cook enough for three or four or more. That's not to say that single people don't appreciate the grill as well—what better way to prepare a whole bunch of grilled foods for the week, from leftover steaks for sandwiches, to grilled chicken breast for a spectacular Caesar salad?

Getting It Together

The joys of grilling are obvious. The frustrations are less obvious—until you find yourself standing at the grill and realizing that you're out here and the salt and your basting brush are inside.

A little thought to getting organized can keep grilling from becoming a real hassle. You'll often need to prepare food in the kitchen and bring it outdoors to cook, and still have the energy left to carry the dirty dishes back inside. If you don't have everything you need at the ready, you'll be running inside while the shrimp kebabs cook—which, of course, is not a good idea.

That's why successful grilling depends so much on getting yourself, your work and storage spaces, and your serving/entertaining area in order.

Tasty Tidbit

You probably won't be surprised to learn that more men than women grill (64 percent compared with 36 percent, according to Weber), but in almost one-quarter of Canadian households (22 percent), outdoor cooking is a shared activity. I wonder who is in charge of clean-up!

If you're wealthy (and/or in the restaurant business), you can stop reading right here. Call your contractor and designer and have them design and build you one of those lovely outdoor kitchens. While you're at it, hire a chef to do the cooking.

If you're like most of us, you gaze longingly at those ads for outdoor kitchens and $5,000 grills, and try to figure out how you can approximate it with your beat-up old kettle and something nice in, say, recycled plastic. The good news is that while you cannot bask in luxury, you can put together a tidy, pleasant eating area and efficient cooking space for not that big an outlay.

Eating/Entertaining Space

Ideally, you already have a decent deck or patio, or the wherewithal to build one. Of course, if you live in a condo or townhouse with a little balcony, you're probably planning to eat inside, or hosting a smaller gathering.

The major things you need in the eating area are comfort, a shield against the elements, and the ability to serve and clean up easily. The eating area needs to be as close to the kitchen as possible—or even in the kitchen or dining room, if outdoor seating is simply an impossibility. If you can, screen in the deck or patio; it's so much nicer to enjoy a good meal and conversation if the mosquitoes aren't making hash of you and if you don't have to swat flies off your steak. If your deck is large enough and not screened, you can burn citronella torches to help keep mosquitoes at bay; just make sure the smoke isn't going to get in your guests' eyes.

You also want the eating area to be near the grill, but not close enough that your guests choke on the fumes. Take into account the prevailing winds, and which way they're most likely to blow in late afternoon. One of the pleasures of grilling food is the anticipation that the smoky aromas incite—but that doesn't mean you want to smoke your friends.

Since most barbecues tend to take place in the afternoon or evening, try an awning or roof to protect the eating area if it has a western or southern exposure. It can be very uncomfortable to eat while you're steaming in your sweat, or squinting to make out your partner across the table. It can also spell the end of a party when the thunderclouds roll in just as you're serving the Cornish hens with a flourish. If an awning or roof is out of the question, a big umbrella's the next best thing.

The actual eating arrangements need to be comfy as well. Those molded plastic chairs are OK for emergencies, but can get pretty uncomfortable during a three-hour party. Padded chairs or benches and, if you can afford it, a glass-topped or other easy-to-clean table make sense. If you're likely to be entertaining older people most of the time, skip the picnic tables of the kind where you have to crawl over the bench. After the age of 40 or so, legs don't bend quite as easily.

Unless the table you have for guest seating is large, you'll need an extra table or cart for serving. Get an enclosed one if possible; then you can store plates, silverware, pitchers, and other serving utensils in it.

Hot Tip

When you're shopping for a food storage or preparation cart, don't confine your search only to barbecue or cookware shops. Workshop carts designed for tools might offer better storage options. You'll find them in home-building centres. If the top surface isn't conducive to food preparation, just set a cutting board on top of it.

The cart really should be on wheels so that you can load it with dirty dishes and wheel it into the kitchen, clean it off, load up the clean dishes and wheel it back out to the patio. (Needless to say, this doesn't work if you have stairs.)

Cooking/Prep Area

This one's easy, you say. My 'cooking area' is the grill.

Well, yes. But there are several factors to keep in mind. For a start, there's safety. First things first: The grill must be outdoors. (Don't even think about using anything but a small electric tabletop model in the house.) At the same time, it must be reasonably sheltered from the wind. It has to be on firm, flat ground with little or no vegetation. It can't be too close to the house, yet it has to be close enough that you don't feel you're travelling to outer Mongolia to turn the steaks. It should be situated where it won't blow smoke through the windows and into the house, or constantly in the guests' faces.

Getting a bit more complicated, eh?

Once you figure out where the grill goes, then you have to take care of storage and work space.

If you've got one of those everything-but-the-kitchen-sink gas grills with condiment racks, enclosed storage, and pullup side tables, you're probably all set. At the other end of the spectrum, if you've got a no-frills kettle, you can buy tool racks, work tables, and condiment shelves that hang over the side of it. You might find it more handy, though, to just buy a tall, rolling, enclosed cart and slap a cutting board on top of it.

Hot Tip

If you have a sheltered spot for them (or extra room in the cart), keep salt, pepper, and a few other basic seasonings right by the grill.

Another possibility is to build in storage. You're in luck if there's a sheltered nook or cranny near the grill where you can put up hooks, or shelves and doors, or all three. You'll need ample space to hold the barbecuing tools, pot holders and mitts, grill screens, thermometers, kitchen towels, and all the other accessories.

Keep your charcoal and smoking woods in a dry place. Unless you live in a dry climate, that usually means keeping them in the garage, or even in the house. To make it easier to haul them around, you can put the bags in a wheelbarrow.

If you're into gardening as well as grilling, try growing containers of herbs such as rosemary and thyme right on the deck or outside the patio. It's so satisfying to snip off a few leaves of fresh basil or rosemary to sprinkle right on the grilling chicken or fish.

Hot Tip

While it's tempting to store your carving knives near the grill, don't do this if children—yours or someone else's—would have access to them.

Serving Utensils

For outdoor dining, plastic is the way to go for dinnerware and glasses. These days, you can get plastic cups and glasses in a rainbow of stunning, casual colours that look great in an outdoor setting. In fact, you can buy a set just for outdoor entertaining; if you have a good enclosed serving cart, keep it there.

For really casual parties, you can use paper or disposable plastic plates. Do make sure they're sturdy. Just envision the tandoori chicken somersaulting into your boss's lap, and you'll agree that the extra cost is marginal.

When it comes to silverware, plastic doesn't cut it, literally. Real flatware just works better unless you're hosting a big party and need 50 forks and knives. Plastic is fine for the kids, but give the adults real stainless. If you can, it's also great to have a second set of forks and knives just for outside dining. This will lessen the chance that your good forks end up in the flower garden. Be sure the flatware is stored where it'll stay clean.

Make sure you have plenty of serving platters and bowls. A couple of meat platters stored near the grill can keep you from running back and forth to the kitchen. You'll also want a pitcher or two for iced tea, lemonade, sangria, or juice.

If you have a wood picnic table, you'll want to protect it from grease stains and spills. Vinyl tablecloths are ideal. You can buy reusable ones in pleasing patterns or, for less work, throwaway ones in bright colours.

There's no need for cloth napkins. The paper ones come in festive patterns and colours, and can be tossed in the trash.

Hot Tip

For casual outdoor parties, who cares if the silverware's fancy or the plates match? Hit the garage sales or discount outlets, and you should find flatware for next to nothing. Check out similar sources, or party-supply stores, for plastic dishes, serving platters, and whatever else you need.

Have lots of fun when barbecuing and grilling. You are only limited by your imagination of flavours.

Love, Grill, and Eat—a motto to live by.

The Least You Need to Know

➤ Vegetables are too seldom chosen for the grill, and can inspire great creativity.

➤ Barbecuing and grilling are not the same.

➤ Barbecuing is a truly universal form of cooking.

➤ Your eating space should be comfortable.

➤ Cooking and storage spaces should be designed with the goal of having the cook run back and forth between the kitchen and the grill as little as possible.

Chapter 2

The Unmistakable Grill

In This Chapter

➤ Types of grills

➤ Cleaning and maintaining your grill

➤ Smokers and how they work

As civilization evolved, so did grilling equipment. People discovered that meat tasted better if it wasn't covered with ashes, so they stuck it on sticks. Then they realized that meats could be cooked on flat stones heated in the fire. After that, they cooked it in grills woven of green wood. On the other side of the world, grillers cooked meat more quickly by cutting it into chunks and sticking it on sword and dagger blades. Finally, people started putting the fire in clay jars, brick ovens, and fireplaces.

The modern grill essentially is still little more than a glorified, enclosed campfire. Of course, that's like saying the automobile is an internal combustion engine on wheels. In case you haven't noticed, the grill has gone upscale. In fact, the market for upper-end grills has been spreading like wildfire. Suddenly, those stainless-steel outdoor kitchens are no longer just for the very rich.

Of course, increasing choices bring increasing confusion. While you'll still find plenty of charcoal kettles in North American backyards, you'll also see gas grills, ranging from your basic box-and-burners-on-wheels to gleaming wonders that could double as restaurant kitchens. Even if you're not quite ready to trade in the car for a new grill, you'll still find plenty of decisions confronting you. Should you buy charcoal or gas? What's the difference between lava rocks and flavouring bars? Does it matter what the cooking grid is made of? And how do you maintain the grill once you've lost the owner's manual in that jumble of papers in the kitchen drawer (or is it the garage)?

What Kind of Grill?

Before you even head out to the store, there are a few basic questions to ask yourself:

➤ How often do you barbecue? Twice a summer? You'll want a very basic charcoal grill. Every other weekend during the spring, summer, and fall? Look for a more deluxe charcoal grill or a medium-range gas grill. If you're the type who stands out in the cold grilling the Thanksgiving turkey, you want the best grill—either gas or a genuine smoker-type grill—that you can afford.

➤ If you currently have a grill, how and when do you use it? If you think you would grill more often if only you didn't have to lug around the charcoal and clean out the ashes, it may be time to switch to a gas grill. If you're constantly juggling to find room for the chicken and steaks, you'll need a larger cooking grid.

➤ Which is more important to you: flavour or convenience? Honest-to-gosh charcoal-grilled flavour comes only from charcoal. If you're the sort who can tell that there's a touch too much alderwood in the salmon, you won't be happy with gas. On the other hand, if you're tired of cursing at briquets that don't light and long for a turn-it-on-and-go experience, you should definitely consider a gas grill.

➤ What size grill do you need? If 90 percent of your barbecuing will be for you and your spouse, a tabletop model may suit you fine. If "grilling" usually means entertaining 40 of your closest friends, you'll need the biggest cooking surface you can afford.

➤ Where do you do most of your barbecuing? If nearly all of it is on your patio or deck, you want an average to large-size grill. If you're a roaming, in-the-park griller, you'll find a tabletop model useful. And of course, if you're one of those super-serious sorts who enter every barbecuing contest in the country, you're talking something that can be hauled on a trailer.

➤ Are there any restrictions on grilling where you live? If you live in a condo or apartment, you may not be allowed to have an outdoor grill at all—in which case, you should get a stovetop grill. Or you may be confined to a small electric grill.

➤ Which niceties do you want? Add money if you want a cart or side table (well worth paying for, in our opinion), warming baskets or shelves (nice, but you can live without them), a grease catcher (something else that's important), wood instead of plastic shelves, and so on.

What's What

Cooking grids are made of different materials:

➤ Chrome-plated. Foods tend to stick, and the grid can rust.

➤ Stainless steel. Most common. Doesn't hold heat well, but is rustproof and easy to clean. Foods can stick.

➤ Porcelain-enameled steel. Nonstick and easy to clean. Doesn't hold heat well.

➤ Cast iron. Holds heat well; great for searing meats. Heavy, and prone to rust. Must be kept oiled if it's not porcelain-coated.

By the way, in a Barbecue Industry Association survey, these were the features that gas-grill owners rated as most important: a large cooking surface, shelves, side burners, grease catchers, and a fuel gauge. Charcoal owners voted for ash catchers, smoking capability, and shelves.

Charcoal Grills

Although gas is catching up, in sheer numbers the most popular grill is still the kind that burns charcoal. Most households that have a grill at all own a charcoal one—including more than half of the folks who own gas grills as well.

Choosing One

Although charcoal grills come in all shapes and sizes, the most popular shape is the kettle, introduced in the 1960s by Weber. Its rounded shape allows for good airflow. You pile coals on the bottom grate and cook food on the top grid. The temperature is determined by the heat of the coals and by the vents, top and bottom.

Nearly all kettle grills have a baked enamel finish and ash catchers underneath to make cleanup easier. You can buy tables and carts that the grill fits into to make two side shelves. Extra features include adjustable racks, bigger ash catchers, lids that tuck in a pocket on the side of the grill, and hinged cooking grids (standard on newer models). They come in various sizes, from 14 1/2 inch (37 cm) diameter tabletop models to huge models designed to grill for a crowd. Far and away the most popular sizes, though, are the 18 1/2 inch (47 cm) and 22 1/2 inch (57 cm) diameter kettle grills. On the former, you can easily cook enough chicken breasts or hamburgers to feed six to eight people.

Although you'd never guess it from the sea of kettles on backyard decks, charcoal grills do come in other shapes. Some are shaped like horizontal barrels; others, like rectangular boxes. Many of these non-kettle grills are designed for serious barbecuing, and may feature extra-large cooking surfaces, heavy-gauge steel construction, adjustable racks, and the ability to smoke or grill in the same box. Highly popular, these are the kinds of grills you'll see at the annual church picnic.

Another grill is the brazier, a round, shallow grill without a lid that once was found everywhere in suburbia but has largely vanished, except for a few small models (see Tabletop Grills).

Some charcoal grills allow you to adjust the cooking grid. Big, commercial-size grills often have a pulley allowing you to raise or lower the rack. Home grills may just have brackets inside in two different places so that you can choose where to put the rack. Unless you're a serious barbecuer (in which case you'll probably have a serious, smoker-type grill), adjustable racks probably aren't that important. Nearly all food is grilled 4 to 6 inches (10 to 15 cm) from the coals, which is just where the standard rack sits.

Pros and Cons

The advantage of charcoal is that, for aficionados, it's the only way to get that true, smoke-kissed, wood-grilled flavour. It's also inexpensive. The initial grill costs anywhere from $115 to $300. Deluxe kettle models can run $600 and up, but that includes a gas ignition system and a deluxe cart. Charcoal is cheap, too, even if you use the pure hardwood charcoal we recommend. (See Chapter 5, "Fire and Smoke.")

Charcoal grills are reliable. Since there are no moving parts, ignitions (except in a few high-end grills), and other potential trouble spots, they last practically forever with little maintenance. Buying one is as simple as running down to the hardware or discount store and looking for the best price. The only choice you have to make is size and, sometimes, shape.

The disadvantages of charcoal grills? They are dirtier than gas—you have to clean up the ashes. They can be a hassle to get started, controlling the cooking temperature is much more of an art than a science, and they're easily affected by the whims of weather, as anyone who's tried to grill during a cold rainstorm can attest. They tend to require more hands-on attention, especially for indirect cooking, in which you have to replenish the coals every 45 minutes or so. However, this makes little difference for most types of grill foods, which cook up relatively quickly (precisely why planning ahead is so important).

Finally, a charcoal grill's very simplicity limits the extras you can have. Forget side burners. You've got either heat or no heat.

Cleaning and Maintenance

Besides choosing and installing your grill, it's important to maintain it and keep it clean.

For kettle grills, at the end of the season use a brass-bristled brush to clean off the cooking rack and any flaking, baked-on grease on the inside of the kettle lid. Never use the brush on the outside; it'll scratch the finish. You also can use very fine (000) soapy steel wool.

Empty out all the ashes. Get a big bucket of warm water with some dish soap in it and a big sponge. Sponge down the grill with soapy water, inside and out. Then just hose it down completely to rinse it off. Let it sit outdoors in the sun until totally dry, then stick it in the garage or another covered storage space away from the elements. If you have a canvas or vinyl grill cover, use it to keep off spider webs and dust. When it's time to pull the grill out for the season, all you'll need to do is dust or hose off the outside.

If you have a porcelain-enamel coating on the outside, never paint, wax, or use a metal brush on the exterior. Don't use caustic cleaners, such as bleach or dishwasher detergent, on either the inside or the outside of the grill. They can ruin the finish.

If you live in one of those climates where you can grill year-round comfortably in the outdoors (though for hard-core grillers, weather is no obstacle), clean your grill this way a couple of times a year.

For day-to-day maintenance, the most important thing is to keep the ashes emptied. If they build up, they can obstruct airflow through the vents.

You should clean off the cooking grid every time you get ready to cook. It's easiest to just burn the gunk off. Stick the cooking grid over the coals while they're still red hot, and cover the grill for about 5 minutes. Then scrape the residue off the grid with a brass-bristled brush.

Every once in a while, you may want to scrub down the grid with hot, soapy water, then give it a good rinse.

Clean the brass-bristled brush by soaking it in hot water to which you've added a bit of dishwasher detergent. Be sure to rinse well; dishwasher detergent residue can give your chicken a pretty foul flavour.

Gas Grills

Gas grills are becoming more popular every year. They've come a long way from the "scorch it" school of cooking. They're more expensive than charcoal grills, but not outrageously so. You can easily spend thousands for a top-of-the-line grill, but you also can get a perfectly decent grill for $300 to $450.

While the high-end grills generally do a great job, price is not the only indicator. The best way to buy a gas grill is to ask various friends and colleagues for recommendations.

Ask them what kinds of foods they grill most often, and what they like and don't like about their grills.

Choosing a Grill

Nearly all gas grills run on liquid propane. The tank sits underneath the grill. You no longer need tools to assemble most of them, but check. Some models also have a natural-gas hookup, so if you have a gas line handy, you can utilize this. Obviously, your grill isn't portable, so make sure it's where you want it.

Gas grills work pretty much like stoves. Fuel flows through a flexible hose into the grill, and you push a button or turn a knob to produce a spark. Some newer grills have electronic ignitions, like gas ranges. They usually require a battery to run, but are more reliable than grills with the old ignitions.

Most gas grills have two or three burners. Some cheaper models have only one, while upper-end models may have six or more. Some have one burner with individual controls for each side, which you can count as two burners. Because it's important to good grilling to be able to move the food off direct heat, we recommend a grill with at least two burners or burner controls. The ones with three burners give better cooking control, but may cost a bit more. Most burners are made of stainless steel and should last a long time, usually the life of the grill.

Gas grills use various types of heat distributors, which sit atop the flame and also act as flavouring elements. Some use metal plates or bars; others use briquets made of ceramic or pumice, a porous stone. These materials help distribute the heat evenly from the burners, and as the juices from the food drip onto them, they create smoke, which helps give grilled foods a charcoal flavour. Briquets or lava rocks need to be turned occasionally, and are more subject to flare-ups. Bars shaped like upside-down Vs do a good job of letting grease run off, reducing the chance of flare-ups. Plates that cover the bottom of the grill are best at keeping flare-ups to a minimum.

Obviously, the heat distributors catch a lot of grease and smoke buildup, so if you keep the grill a long time, plan on replacing them sooner or later. As long as they don't get chipped, porcelain-enamelled bars are easy to clean and hold up well.

Cooking grates on gas grills may be the standard skinny rods found on typical charcoal grills, or wide bars set close together—the best for keeping foods from dropping through. Porcelain-coated steel is easiest to clean; stainless steel holds up well. Cast iron can rust if you don't season it properly (follow the manufacturer's directions) and keep it coated with oil. An adjustable rack is a nicety that allows you to raise or lower the food above the coals.

Paying more for a gas grill will get you a sturdier cart, better performance at grill-roasting and slow cooking, and more optional features. One of the most popular of these additional features is a side burner that lets you cook side dishes while you grill other foods, or reheat the marinade to enhance the flavour of your grilled food while keeping food safety in mind. Other upgrades include a warming rack (to keep one batch of foods hot while you grill another); shelves (a great convenience); fuel gauges; electronic ignitions; smoking boxes (to hold wood chips); extra burners; larger work surfaces or storage space; condiment racks; and stainless steel finishes.

Burners come in various shapes and materials. The most common burner shape is an "H." Some are oval; others are long, thin rectangles. If you need to replace the burners, make sure they're the same shape as the original. Aluminized steel, similar to galvanized steel, is used in less expensive grills. Porcelain-coated steel is sometimes used, but most common is stainless steel in varying thicknesses. Some grills have cast iron burners, which must be oiled so they don't rust. Cast brass, which lasts the longest, is used on some very expensive grills.

To clean the burners, use the wire grill brush to scrape off corrosion or oily residue. If any of the holes are clogged, you can open them with a metal paper clip bent straight. If the burners are really corroded, you should replace them.

Always keep long matches handy; if the igniter goes out, you'll have to light the grill manually. Check the instruction book for directions.

Pros and Cons

Gas grills have several advantages over their charcoal counterparts. They're cleaner, are less of a hassle to start, heat up faster, and are less dependent on weather. It's no coincidence that people with gas grills are more likely to cook year-round (64 percent, compared with 41 percent of charcoal-grill owners).

The disadvantages are that gas grills can be a pain to assemble, they're generally more expensive than charcoal grills, and you have to deal with replacing the propane tank. Like all gas appliances, they can pose a danger if not installed and maintained properly.

Perhaps the biggest disadvantage, to true barbecue aficionados, is that you don't get the same flavour. Gas grills flavour foods by juices dripping onto the briquets or flavour bars, so they're actually more like broilers than real barbecues.

Cleaning and Maintenance

To keep gas grills in good working order, follow the manufacturer's instructions. Models that use pumice or ceramic briquets will often require that you turn them occasionally to clean them. Another important thing with a gas grill is to check that the fuel pipe does not get clogged. Some gas grills have insect guards to keep your friendly neighbourhood spider from building webs or nests in your gas pipe.

To clean the cooking grid, turn the burners to high, close the lid, and wait until the grill stops smoking, about 5 to 10 minutes. Then use the wire brush to scrape off the residue.

When the grid cools down, you can remove it and clean it with warm, soapy water.

Keep the bottom tray and grease catch pan clean. This will help prevent grease fires, and also discourage visits from four-legged neighbourhood critters.

Fairly often, you should change the liner for the catch pan. If the grill lid has smoke stains, use fine soapy steel wool to clean it off. Don't scrub too vigorously; a light touch will do it. (Note: To clean a cover over the side burner, use warm soapy water and a sponge, never steel wool.)

If you have porcelain-coated metal bars as heat distributors, most of the residue will burn off. Just scrub them every now and then with a brass-bristled brush. If your grill has lava rocks or ceramic briquets, you need to turn them every now and then to clean them, and occasionally replace them. Follow the manufacturer's instruction booklet.

Clean the outside of the grill occasionally with warm, soapy water, and try to clean up grease spills immediately, preferably while the grill is still slightly warm—not hot! Don't use harsh cleaners, which can ruin the finish.

If you have cast iron cooking grids, lightly oil them after cleaning to keep them from rusting.

Electric Grills

Electric grills range from the high-end, indoor cooking grates found on fancy cooktops to outdoor grills that plug into a handy outlet. They're still pretty rare compared with gas and charcoal grills; very few Canadian households have an electric grill.

Because they don't tend to get as hot as gas or charcoal grills, electric grills often feature nonstick cooking surfaces.

Pros and Cons

In general, grilling mavens don't like electric compared with gas and charcoal. They don't get as hot. They don't come in the assortment of sizes (and often tend to be small). They're more expensive to run.

They are, however, a good choice—and often the only choice—if you live in a 23rd-floor apartment with a small balcony, or if you go camping a lot with your RV. They also are cleaner than both charcoal and gas.

Cleaning and Maintenance

You clean electric grills like any other electrical appliance. Obviously, you cannot submerge or hose down any of the electrical parts. But the cooking grid can be cleaned with soapy water. Wipe down the grill now and then with a cloth.

Tabletop and Portable Grills

Tabletop grills come in charcoal, gas, or electric versions. The electric ones can be used indoors. They don't offer much of a cooking surface and are good for cooking only quick cuts, but they're very portable, which makes them great for picnics and camping.

What's What

One of the most famous of the tabletop grills is the Japanese *hibachi*. A small, rectangular grill, it has a stand, rather than legs, so it won't tip over, and a fairly heavy cooking grid that can be adjusted by fitting it into notches on the side.

If you're tight on space (grilling on that balcony, for example), a tabletop grill might be all you want. Note that they're really only suitable for grilling enough for one to two people.

Of course, you can also just buy a grill pan—a heavy pan with evenly spaced ridges that produce grill marks on food—and use it on your stove.

Specialty Grills

Two specialty grills with devoted followings are the Kamado and its cousin, The Big Green Egg. Both are inspired by the *kamado*, a ceramic cooker that originated in China 3,000 years ago and is popular in Japan, where U.S. servicemen discovered it after World War II. Their manufacturers and devotees say the extra-thick ceramic walls and bell (or egg) shapes of these grills provide more precise control over cooking temperature.

The Kamado is larger and prettier than The Big Green Egg—its outside is decorated with tiles in various colours. It also has thicker walls. But essentially, these grills are very similar to each other.

Cooking in clay retains moisture, so a water pan is not needed. The manufacturers also claim that because of the insulation provided by the thick clay walls, you get a wider range of temperatures, from very low to very high, which makes the Kamado-type grill suitable for both slow smoking and searing.

The disadvantages? Both grills are pretty expensive, not widely available, and very heavy—the large Kamado weighs 248 pounds (112 kg). Ceramic can weaken or even crack if you drop it or if you splash water on it when it's hot.

Another specialty grill, which is still pretty rare, is the pellet grill. Pellet stoves, which are popular in parts of the western U.S.A., burn small pellets made of wood, compressed sawdust, and fillers. Pellets burn more efficiently than whole wood, with fewer emissions and less smoke. A couple of stove manufacturers have started making these types of grills. They're similar to convection ovens. The pellets are fed through a hopper and ignited.

True barbecue aficionados, the people who roam the country from one grilling contest to another, often construct their own grills. Some of these contraptions are wondrous to behold.

Build-Your-Own Pits

For true grilling rituals, such as cooking for a crowd, you usually have to build your own grill. Some folks dig an actual pit—this is easy to do if you're grilling clams on the beach—but that may not always be possible or desirable. Instead, you can build your own grill on the spot with cement blocks. The dimensions depend on how big the pig, lamb, or side of beef is, or how many you're roasting, but it should be at least 3 blocks wide by 5 blocks long, and 18 inches (46 cm) deep. You make a cooking grid out of metal rods inserted into the cement blocks, and top that with a metal screen to hold the meat.

You must start with real wood (often oak) and burn it down until it's mostly charcoal before you can start cooking. Needless to say, pit barbecuing is not something you do on the spur of the moment—though it does make for a great party.

You can build a simple barbecue box in the backyard using this method. If you have trouble visualizing it, you can buy plans at home-building centres and some hardware stores.

Smokers

A word about jargon here: What manufacturers and most of us call "smoking" is actually what most true barbecue fans (and there are a lot of them out there) call "barbecuing." When you order the baby back ribs or pulled pork at your favourite barbecue joint—you know, the one with all those fragrant trailers or the smoke shack out back—you're getting meat that is cooked in a long, slow process that involves smoke. You can't duplicate this at home on a standard grill. You have to use a smoker, or a deep grill that's capable of both grilling and smoking.

"Real" Wood Smokers

These are for serious barbecuing, the kind that involves cooking a brisket or three turkeys for 25 of your closest friends. They're used mostly for large cookouts. If you are a serious barbecuer, the kind who roams the country looking for contests to win, this is what you need.

These babies weigh a minimum of 200 to 300 pounds (90 to 135 kg), and some much more. There's one big difference between a smoker and the standard grill: the firebox is separate from the cooking area. It's off to one side. The cooking chamber has a chimney in it. A baffle between the firebox and the cooking chamber forces the smoke and heat underneath the food before it escapes out the chimney. The food cooks slowly in this "bath" of smoke and heat. The firebox may have a lid that can be raised, turning it into a grill. Some wood smokers also have a water chamber beneath the cooking grid(s), which helps keep foods from drying out.

The advantage to this kind of smoker is that the slow, gentle cooking makes meats taste out of this world. The disadvantage is that you need a trailer to haul these smokers around, and you may have to experiment a lot to master this type of cookery.

Water Smokers

The most common smokers for home use are water smokers, which come in charcoal, electric, and (less commonly) gas versions. They're shaped like a big upright cylinder on legs. The bottom is the firebox, where you put the charcoal and/or wood chunks. Above that or next to it is the water pan, and the food sits on a rack above that. Some smokers have two racks, which gives them a bigger capacity. The food is tightly covered and often spends hours, rather than minutes, in the smoker. As the water boils, it creates a flavourful, smoky steam that bastes the food as it cooks.

Choosing One

This is pretty easy since there really aren't that many different water smokers and they're pretty basic. Your basic choice is usually between charcoal or electric, and various capacities. Some smokers have only one rack, others have two. Most have a door in the side so that you can easily feed in additional charcoal.

Pros and Cons

Water smokers are easier to use than wood smokers. However, wood smokers impart a better flavour. Electric smokers are easier to use, since you don't have to keep replenishing charcoal.

Cleaning and Maintenance

Again, follow the manufacturer's directions. Since a smoker is basically a specialized charcoal grill, the cleaning and maintenance is much the same. (For an electric smoker, consult the owner's manual.) Because the water pan is permanent, it should be cleaned frequently in hot, soapy water so it doesn't get all grimed up.

The Least You Need to Know

➤ Charcoal gives a more "authentic" flavour to barbecued foods, but gas is more convenient.

➤ Cleaning and maintaining the grill is as important as choosing the proper one.

➤ For long, slow barbecuing, you need a smoker.

Chapter 3

The Extra Touch

In This Chapter

➤ Tools that are essential to good grilling

➤ Tools that are helpful but not necessary

➤ "Toys" for the griller with money to spare

➤ Kitchen tools to make food preparation easier

You didn't really think you would just buy a grill and be done with it, did you? Like any other sport, grilling requires an assortment of specialized equipment. Some of it is absolutely vital to smooth grilling and outdoor entertaining, and some is merely helpful. Then there's the category of grilling "toys," fun items that you don't need at all—at least until you've convinced yourself (and your spouse) that you really, truly cannot grill without them.

Nearly all of these accessories are inexpensive and readily available in supermarkets, cookware stores, discount or department stores, hardware stores, and/or home-building centres. For less common accessories or those, such as rotisseries, that are specific to certain grills, you might have to look in a shop devoted to barbecuing supplies, or contact the manufacturer of your grill.

The Core Collection

This handy list of all of the must-haves of grilling includes several items already in your home that you'll simply not want to forget when planning your grilling session.

Hot Tip

Most barbecue tool sets come with one pair of tongs. But you'll need a second set. That way, you'll have one pair of tongs for the coals, and one for the food.

Tools

Why can't you just use your kitchen tongs and spatula? Because their handles are too short to offer you protection against the searing heat of hot coals. Barbecue utensils have extra-long handles. They're cheaper by the set: fork, tong, spatula. Get a good stainless steel set with flameproof plastic or composite handles. Wood handles tend to scorch and can look ratty when they're kept outside for any length of time.

One handy variation on the spatula combines a spatula and tongs. The top lever is tongs; the bottom is a spatula.

Pot Holders and Mitts

To keep your hands away from the heat, you should use barbecue mitts—extra-long, flame-retardant "mittens" that protect your hands and lower arms from the coals' intense heat. Because the mitts can be fairly clumsy, you'll also want a pair of extra-thick pot holders with a flame-retardant coating.

Hot Tip

Haven't gotten around to getting a grill screen yet? You can mimic one by folding foil to make a double thickness, and punching holes all over it with a fork or knife. Set the foil on the cooking grid, and the food on top of that.

Grill Screen

A flat, portable metal grid designed to sit atop the grill's cooking grid, the grill screen has mesh or holes set closely together. It's designed to keep small foods such as sliced onions and shrimp from taking a nosedive through the wires of the grid and into the coals. Most grill screens have handles and nonstick surfaces, which makes them easy to move around and clean. A variation on the flat grill screen has deeper, sloping sides, similar to a wok's, making it easier to turn or toss foods.

Grill Brush

You can clean the cooking grid with wadded foil, but a grill brush works much better. It has stiff metal bristles that easily scrape cooked-on grease off the wires of the grid. There's no need to spend a fortune on this implement—it's going to get pretty grimy, and you'll just want to replace it anyway at some point.

Basting Brushes

You should also have at least two brushes for basting food. Having more than one allows you to baste different foods with different sauces at the same time. Among those we find useful:

➤ An all-purpose basting brush with a long handle and wide, angled bristles. This makes it easy to spread sauces over large amounts of food.

➤ A basting mop. Made of cotton string attached to a wooden handle, these brushes are basically a miniature version of your kitchen mop. They're ideal for slathering foods with thin sauces, like those wonderful vinegar-based sauces that are essential to a Carolina pig-pickin'.

➤ A round brush for brushing small game birds and long skewers of meat and kebabs and for dabbing a bit of sauce into hard-to-reach cavities.

Whichever brushes you buy, be sure to clean them thoroughly in hot, soapy water, both to keep them from getting gummed up and to prevent the growth of bacteria.

Skewers

It's one of the unwritten laws of grilling: sooner or later, you will cook kebabs. That means you will need either wooden or metal skewers to thread through the chunks of meats and vegetables. The most common wooden skewer is the bamboo skewer. Bamboo skewers are inexpensive, have a rough surface that grips food well, and can be discarded when you're through with them. However, they do have to be soaked in water for 20 to 30 minutes and drained before you use them so that they don't catch fire.

> **Hot Tip**
>
> Appalled by the prices the cookware store wants for decent basting brushes? Check out long–handled, narrow paintbrushes at the local hardware store for an alternative. Don't get the really cheap kind, though—they'll shed bristles into your food.

Another underused wooden skewer is the grape vine. You can find these in specialty food shops, or if you live in a wine region go directly to the winery. In the springtime, wineries spend a great deal of time pruning the grape plants, and there will be an abundance of pruned vines around. They make great skewers and can also be used as smoking chips, to add flavour to your foods.

Metal skewers can be used over and over again, and usually are longer, so they'll hold more food. They are slippery and don't grip foods well, so the meat tends to spin when you turn the skewer. Also, the exposed surfaces get very hot during cooking.

If you make kebabs often, you might want to spring for double skewers, which look like giant bobby pins and help keep the food in place, or even a kebab rack, a whole set of skewers set in a rack, with a rod in the middle that turns them. Or, you can just thread the meat and vegetables on two skewers, instead of one, to keep them from slipping off.

Tasty Tidbit

Shish kebab originated in the Middle East, probably with meat skewered on swords.

Food Thermometer

For thicker cuts of meat, a thermometer is the best way to tell if the food is really cooked through. Some meat thermometers are intended to stay in the food during cooking, but they tend to get gunked up with grease and hard to read. We recommend an instant-read thermometer. You stick it in the cooked food, wait for about a minute, or until the needle stops moving, and get a reading. Some grills come with thermometers.

Knives

You'll also need at least one good knife, and preferably three or four. These are not just for grilling, of course, but are essential kitchen tools. The best knives are made of forged carbon steel. They hold up well as long as you keep them dry. If they stay wet, they can rust.

What's What

Choose the right knife for the job. *Chef's knives* have thick, heavy blades and are all-purpose chopping and slicing utensils. *Carving knives* have very long, fairly thin blades and are strictly for slicing. *Boning knives* have thin, curved blades designed to cut meat off the bone. *Paring knives* have short blades suitable for peeling and other detail work.

Cutting Boards

You'll need at least one good cutting board, in acrylic or solid wood. Besides having a cutting board in your kitchen, you might want to keep a second one handy to the grill.

For best results, use a board with a trench around the outside to collect juices. Just be sure to clean the cutting board thoroughly with hot, soapy water (or in the dishwasher, if it's acrylic) after each use.

At one point the experts said that acrylic boards were safer against collecting harmful bacteria from raw meats, but there is now some disagreement on this subject. Apparently, knife ridges in acrylic can host bacteria just as well as wood. Whichever you choose, it's important to keep your board clean by washing carefully it after each use.

Charcoal Dividers or Holders

These help keep briquets in a neat pile and stop them from tumbling into the drip pan when you're cooking over indirect heat. Some are simply standup racks that sit between the water pan and the charcoal; others are actual containers that you fill with charcoal. Obviously, you can skip these if you have a gas grill. Many charcoal grills come with these racks as standard equipment.

Fire Starters

If you have a gas grill, the fire starter is that little spark which ignites the propane when you turn that handy knob. If you have a charcoal grill or smoker, you'll need one or more of these:

➤ Charcoal chimney. This ingenious but simple device offers a very efficient way to light charcoal. Basically, it's a metal can with a shelf inside and a heatproof handle outside. You fill the top with charcoal and the bottom with wadded-up newspaper, and light the newspaper. As it burns, it ignites the coals in the bottom, which in turn gradually ignite the coals above them.

➤ Electric starters. These glowing wands are very efficient for lighting coals, and are very tidy. You just put the starter in the grill, pile charcoal on top of it, and plug it in. Obviously, this kind of starter will do you no good unless you have an electrical outlet near the grill.

➤ Long fireplace matches. To light the charcoal, and to light your gas grill if you need to do so manually. Don't use regular matches, which aren't long enough to keep your hands free of any flaring flame. As an alternative, you can use a utility lighter, which works like a cigarette lighter, but has a long wand that allows you to

Tasty Tidbit

The charcoal chimney started out life as a coffee can. Generations of Boy Scouts and cowboys knew that if you punched holes around the bottom part of a coffee can, filled the can with charcoal and lit it, you'd have glowing coals in no time.

light the coals without getting your hands too close to them. Some lighters have a child-resistant guard.

Work Table

If your grill didn't come with one, better get one. You'll need something handy for carving meats, cutting into chicken to see if it's done, slicing foods into serving portions, and so on. For kettle grills, you can get a work table that hooks onto the side of the grill. Or, get a small, freestanding table.

Ice Bucket and/or Cooler

This is not directly related to grill-cooking, of course, but since by its nature, most grilling is done for outdoor parties, you can either have something to store ice in, or run back and forth to the freezer—and who needs that? A cooler can be used both for ice and for storing cans of soda and such, but an ice bucket adds a bit more class.

Don't Get Burned!

If your tray has a smooth surface, things can slide right off, especially if you need to go up or down stairs to get to the deck or patio. Get a piece of the bumpy vinyl that's used to keep dishes in place on shelves or to keep throw rugs from slipping, and cut a piece to fit the inside of the tray.

Tray

Carrying foods and dishes in and out of the house gets old fast. A large tray makes the toting much easier.

Tool Holder

One popular tool rack has three or four hooks, and hangs from the side of the grill. While these are handy, they do tend to lift up when you tug a tool off. A better bet, if possible, is to use screw-in hooks and hang the tools in a place handy to the grill.

Drip Pans

You'll need these for indirect cooking on charcoal grills, to keep the food moist and away from the coals. Disposable cake pans are ideal for this. They're not too sturdy, so use two of them, one nested inside the other. The bigger the surface area, the better. We recommend the 12 by 8 or 13 by 9 inch (3.5 L) foil cake pans for most purposes.

Aluminum Foil

You'll need this to wrap delicate foods such as fish or vegetables, and to cover already-grilled foods while you finish cooking the rest of the batch. It also can come in handy if you've misplaced your grill brush. Crumple the foil into a ball and use it to scrub the grease off the cooking grid. (Caution: don't do this when the grid is hot.)

Small Watering Can

The spout makes it easy to replenish the water in the drip pan without splashing water on the hot coals. You'll need this only if you're using a charcoal grill or a smoker.

Spray Bottle

Fill it with water and keep it by the grill so that you can easily put out minor flare-ups. Again, you'll need this only if you grill over charcoal.

Scoop for Briquets

A large plastic flour scoop is ideal. With a scoop, you don't have to plunge your hands into the charcoal bag, getting soot up to your elbows.

Garbage Bags

This is something that's easy to overlook. There you are, standing at the grill, holding a greasy, wadded-up paper towel or ball of foil, and realizing that there's no place to toss it. And of course your guests need someplace to throw away the paper plates. Actually, it's not a bad idea to have a small wastebasket or garbage can designated just for outdoor parties. Put it somewhere where it won't collect water when it rains (or turn it upside down when it's not in use). And be sure to change the bag after every grilling/eating session, or you'll have raccoons or other "friends" rooting around on the deck.

Fire Extinguisher

If you've set the grill away from flammable objects and take care in grilling, the chance that you'll need a fire extinguisher handy is about nil. However, you should definitely have one in the kitchen. And if your kitchen is handy to the grill . . . well, it's nice to know the extinguisher is there, just in case.

Nice, But You Can Live Without Them

Hinged Cooking Grid

These look like a standard round cooking grid, except that they're hinged on two sides. They make indirect cooking much easier. You simply lift up the hinged ends of the grid and drop more into the fire. Hinged grids are standard on many new charcoal grills.

Grill Lifter

This implement is designed to slip under the wires of the cooking grid and lift it up so that you don't have to handle it when it's hot. Frankly, we think a combination of a barbecue mitt and a barbecue fork (slide it under a handle) works fine. A hinged cooking grid is even handier.

Smoker Box

This metal container holds the wood chips you use to impart flavour to foods. It sits in the base of a gas or electric grill. It contains the ashes so they can't clog the starter.

Cart

If your grill doesn't come with one, consider buying one. It makes moving the grill around, as well as storing the charcoal, easier.

Rotisserie

If you often cook whole chickens or other poultry, roasts, and other big pieces of meat, a rotisserie can come in handy. It turns the meat as it cooks so that it roasts more evenly. You must have an electrical outlet handy. Be sure to get a rotisserie designed for your make of grill, so that it will fit.

What's What

A *rotisserie* consists of a long rod, or *spit*, with prongs on either end to hold the food in place. At one end is a small motor, which rotates the rod with the food on it, helping larger cuts of meat and poultry to cook more evenly.

Food Holders

Vertical roasters are small racks that keep a chicken or an ear of corn upright. A horizontal rack is designed for roasts. Neither type is essential, but they help cook meat evenly, and in the case of the vertical roasters, you don't have to turn the meat or vegetables while they cook.

Warming Rack

This fits on the side of a charcoal or gas grill over the cooking grid. It's ideal for warming hamburger buns and quick-cooking vegetables. A lot of grills come with warming racks as standard equipment. Bear in mind, though, that a hamburger bun can also be heated quickly right on the grill, toasting it up and adding attractive grill marks.

Cooking Bags

Reynolds Aluminum makes heavy-duty foil bags that you fill with meats and vegetables, then place on the grill. They eliminate cleanup and are especially suitable for more delicate foods that might not stand up that well to direct grilling.

You also can buy perforated aluminum bags that contain wood chips and sugar. You put the meat inside the bag and lay it on the grill. The chips and sugar flavour the meat, and the sugar also helps brown it.

Burger Press

If you've got a thing about perfectly round (or square) burgers, better get one of these. At least one burger press puts spiral grooves in the meat, which supposedly make it cook faster. It will also keep the kids from fighting over the bigger burger.

Oven Thermometer

If your grill or smoker does not have a built-in thermometer, setting an oven thermometer on the cooking grid can give you at least a rough idea of the interior temperature.

Grill Baskets

These hinged, long-handled metal baskets make turning more delicate foods, such as fish or vegetables, easier. They come in different shapes, with square being the most popular. A fish basket is a grill basket shaped like a fish. As the name implies, it's for grilling fish, especially whole fish. There's nothing more frustrating than having your perfectly grilled fish fall through the grid.

Condiment Shelf

This hangs from the side of the grill and holds barbecue sauce, ketchup, salt and pepper, and whatever.

Flashlight

Sooner or later, you'll probably be grilling in the dark, whether you intended to or not. If your deck or patio (or fancy grill) doesn't have a light that will illuminate the grilling area, having a flashlight handy is essential. Of course, if you want to get fancy, you can clip a halogen light to the grill table.

Vinyl or Canvas Grill Covers

These can help keep dirt, leaves, and bird droppings off your grill. That is, if you remember to put them over the grill once it's cooled down.

Grillers' "Toys"

Poultry Shears

Few folks outside of the food professions have these, but they can come in handy if you have a sudden urge to butterfly your own Cornish hens. (Butterflying your poultry speeds the cooking time—see Chapter 12, "Birds of a Feather," for details.)

Barbecue Glasses

For toy value, these rank up there with those onion-flower makers you see on TV. They're goggles designed to keep the smoke out of your eyes while you grill. For those who lack that final grill accessory, and enjoy the serious look of "grill expert" that the goggles naturally impart to the wearer.

Silly Aprons and Hats

You don't need these at all, but hey, they're a tradition. What's suburban barbecuing without silly slogans on Dad's apron? Also recommended are the logo T-shirts your cousins sent you from their last vacation.

Cast Iron Griddle

This can be nice for fajitas and such, but unless you're into making pancakes on the grill, you really don't need one.

Heat-Resistant Gloves

The gloves come in two varieties, one for picking up food and one for picking up a hot grill by the handles. A little more nimble than those oversize mitts, they can come in handy when you're cooking a large cut that is easier to turn with your hands, such as a whole turkey or a roast. They're also good for turning metal skewers.

Baking Tiles or Stone

For those times when you want to recapture that woodburning pizza experience. Baking tiles are basically thick, unglazed, high-fired quarry tiles; baking stones are, indeed, made of a light stone. You'll want these if you plan to make pizza or similar breads on the grill. Some cookware stores sell baking tiles and a grilling screen as a set.

Pizza Peel or Paddle

This is basically a long-handled giant spatula, made of all wood or of metal and wood, used to transfer pizza or focaccia to the grill and to remove it when it's done. Again, you only need this if you like to grill pizza or other breads.

Light Strings

Somewhere along the line, some savvy marketing type realized that Christmas lights needn't be confined to the holidays. You can buy lights in the shape of pumpkins, ears of corn, chiles, fish—you name it. Definitely not essential, but they add a festive atmosphere to evening parties.

Citronella Candles or Torches

If you don't have a screened-in patio, these can help keep mosquitoes at bay, more or less. And they're much trendier and smell nicer than bug-repellent spray. Just make sure the smoke won't be blowing in your guests' faces.

The Least You Need to Know

➤ Regular kitchen tools don't cut it for most barbecuing purposes—get grilling utensils.

➤ Along with standard grilling accessories, don't forget the other, easily overlooked indispensables, such as garbage bags, foil, and a good knife.

➤ You need only a few "core" accessories, but there are plenty of other tools and gadgets that can make grilling easier or more fun.

Chapter 4

The Proper Provisions

In This Chapter

➤ Basic food preparation

➤ Spices, and what they go with

➤ Buying and storing perishable foods

Now that you've got the grill and all the accessories set up, all you need is the food. If you like to fire up the barbecue but have never turned on the oven, bread flour probably isn't high on your list of priorities. So we've confined the list to the sorts of foodstuffs you're most likely to use in grilling and smoking. We've also added a minisection on food preparation, in case you're a kitchen novice.

Herbs and spices play a big role, since they are frequently used as both seasonings and *aromatics* on the grill.

What's What

An *aromatic* is a herb, spice, or other ingredient that you sprinkle onto the coals or into the drip pan to perfume the smoke and enhance a food's flavour.

The Griller's Spice Rack

Spice and smoke—ah, what a combination. Barbecue means spice: the rub on a beef brisket, the secret ingredients in a barbecue master's sauce. Here are some you may find useful.

Allspice

A bit like cloves, but not as sharp and a bit sweeter. Allspice is a key component in Jamaican cooking and in jerk, a Jamaican rub for grilled meats.

Basil

Sweet-sharp and with undertones of anise, basil goes with almost anything. Use it fresh if possible. Dried basil is not bad, but just doesn't have the full flavour.

Bay Leaves

A wonderful aromatic tossed onto the coals, or placed in the cavity of a whole chicken or fish. Remember to remove the bay leaf before eating, though, because it is inedible.

Chives

This mildly onion-flavoured herb was born to go with fish and potatoes.

Hot Tip

Dried herbs and spices make wonderful aromatics for grilling. Soak them for about 5 minutes, squeeze out the moisture, and sprinkle them either directly on the coals, or in the water pan if you're cooking over indirect heat. Watch out for seeds such as mustard and coriander, though; heat makes them pop.

Cilantro

This is the fresh, leafy herb; coriander is the seed of the same plant. It has a very assertive minty-peppery flavour that is commonly found in Southeast Asian, Mexican, and U.S. Southwestern cooking. Great in salsas, with potatoes, corn, most meats, poultry, and fish. Use it fresh; it loses a lot of its flavour when dried.

Cinnamon

Although it's usually associated with sweets (just think cinnamon rolls), cinnamon is used for savoury dishes in the U.S. Southwest and in some parts of the Mediterranean. It's lovely with beef. Toss some cinnamon sticks onto the coals for a delicious smoke, or use them as skewers.

Coriander

Citrusy-peppery, this fairly assertive spice is good with poultry, and also makes a good aromatic. A key ingredient in Montreal steak spice.

Cumin

Sharp and a little musty, cumin is used around the world. In the United States, it's probably used most heavily in the Southwest, where it helps give sauces and rubs that distinct "Tex-Mex" flavour. It is commonly a flavour component of chili.

Dill

With its grassy-citrus flavour, dill seed or fresh dill was born to go with fish, but its also nice with lamb and poultry.

Fennel

This licorice-tasting spice is nice with fish or pork sausages (it's a key seasoning in Italian sausage), or sprinkled over the coals or in the water pan. It is a seed that closely resembles cumin. Remember that fennel the spice is not the same as fennel the vegetable; the latter is a celerylike bulb that is popular in Italian cooking.

Garlic

Ah, where would the world be without it? Fresh garlic is superb when it's roasted on the grill (see Chapter 14). Don't toss garlic on the coals, though, because it turns acrid when it burns. You can put fresh, granulated, or powdered garlic in the drip pan when you smoke foods or cook them over indirect heat.

Green Onions (Scallions)

Supermarkets label them "green onions," but they're actually scallions. (Green onions are more bulbous on the bottom.) These are good in marinades and are fabulous brushed lightly with oil and grilled until they're lightly charred and softened.

Marjoram and/or Oregano

The pizza herb, and it's great with any tomato-based sauce. It also enlivens poultry, especially with lemon, and goes well with mushrooms. Don't toss it on the coals; it smells remarkably like another herb that is illegal.

Hot Tip

One delightful way to use herbs, especially fresh ones, is to finely chop them and mix them with a bit of softened butter to make herb butter. A dab of herb butter is wonderful on fish.

Mint

Fresh spearmint or peppermint makes a lovely seasoning for fish, lamb, poultry, and yogurt- or citrus-based sauces.

Onions

Like garlic, onions are wonderful roasted on the grill. They also turn acrid when burned, so leave them off the coals. You can put fresh, granulated, or powdered onion in the drip pan when you smoke foods or cook them over indirect heat.

Parsley

Peppery but pleasant, it enlivens nearly any dish. Italian (flat-leaf) parsley has a stronger flavour than curly parsley. Use it fresh; it doesn't retain much of its flavour dried. It doesn't do much as an aromatic.

Pepper (black)

It adds a pungent-hot-fragrant note to just about anything, but is especially nice with more assertively flavoured foods such as beef and salmon. It's great in rubs.

Pepper (red)

An extra dose of fruity heat. Don't sprinkle red pepper on the coals; the smoke may burn your eyes. But do use it in rubs and sauces. Remember to wash your hands before touching your face.

Tasty Tidbit

Greek fishermen use rosemary to preserve their catch. Scientists say those fisherman have the right idea—and rosemary is indeed a preservative. All the more reason to use it in that marinade.

Rosemary

Piney and sweet, this is a wondrous herb, both as a flavouring agent and as an aromatic. It goes with pork, lamb, poultry, vegetables, and fruit. Use it on the food and on the coals. With the needles pulled off, a twig of rosemary also works great as an impromptu kebab skewer. If it's very dry, remember to soak it in water for 20 minutes before using it this way.

Sage

It has a strong but pleasant smoke, making it a good aromatic. Flavour-wise, this grey-green herb has a strong, almost medicinal flavour that's great with "autumn foods" such as pork, poultry, tomatoes, mushrooms, and squash. Sage is a common ingredient in the stuffing for the Thanksgiving turkey.

> **Tasty Tidbit**
>
> Some Native Americans in the Southwest burn sage (actually, a relative of the culinary herb) to purify their surroundings. It does have a cleansing, incenselike aroma.

Shallots

This member of the onion family grows in bulbs like garlic and tastes like an onion with garlicky undertones. Shallots are superb with anything, and essential to Southeast Asian–style pastes and marinades.

Spice Blends

Blends of various spices or herbs can be quite convenient. Some popular ones for grilling include Cajun-style blend, Italian seasoning, chili powder, herbes de Provence, fines herbes, and lemon pepper.

Tarragon

Another anisey-flavoured herb, French tarragon is sweet and delicious with fish, poultry, and most vegetables. You also can toss it onto the coals, or into the water pan with white wine.

Thyme

Pungent and minty, this small-leafed herb goes nicely with beef, pork, poultry, tomatoes, and mushrooms.

Oils, Vinegars, and Condiments

Balsamic Vinegar

Traditionally, this vinegar was aged for years in barrels in Modena, Italy, until it turned dark, sweet, and utterly delicious. Nearly all the "balsamic vinegar" you buy in North America nowadays is actually balsamic vinegar mixed with red wine vinegar. (It's easy to spot genuine balsamic vinegar: it costs way, way more than you're ever likely to pay for a bottle of vinegar.) However, even this pale imitator is a very nice vinegar. It's good with all foods, either in the marinade or sprinkled on them just before serving.

Rice Vinegar

Its low acidity makes this an ideal vinegar for marinating more delicate foods. If you can find it (some Asian markets carry it), aged rice vinegar is truly mellow and delicious.

Wine Vinegars

White wine, red wine, and sherry vinegars are, of course, made from wine. Any of them are suitable for marinades.

Flavoured Vinegars

Vinegars flavoured with fruits or herbs make great marinades, and also are lovely sprinkled lightly on foods before serving. Try blueberry vinegar on fruit kebabs, or a dill-garlic vinegar on fish. Yum.

Olive Oil

For marinades, any regular olive oil, or virgin olive oil (a cold-pressed olive oil that's more acidic and slightly less flavourful than extra-virgin), is fine. For salads and finishing sauces, you might prefer the full, fruity flavour of extra-virgin. Olive oil is good for brushing lean foods such as chicken breast or fish so they don't stick to the grill or dry out during cooking.

What's What

Extra-virgin olive oil, from the first pressing of olives, is low in acid and rich in flavour. Drizzle it over foods such as cooked fish or vegetables. Virgin olive oil is also made from the first pressing, but is higher in acidity. Plain olive oil, which is fine for marinades and general cooking, is a blend of refined and extra-virgin or virgin olive oil.

Sesame Oil

Pressed from sesame seeds, this comes in two varieties: a clear yellow oil that's fine for cooking, and a dark reddish oil made from toasted sesame seeds. The latter has a robust, nutty flavour and is usually drizzled on foods as a condiment.

Canola Oil

A clear, flavourless oil that's popular because it's the lowest in saturated fat of all the vegetable oils. It tends to have a fishy odour when it burns, which of course makes it ideal for fish but a bit less desirable for foods such as fruits. You can buy blends of canola and other vegetable (usually corn) oils.

Vegetable Oil

A flavourless, all-purpose oil that's usually made of soybeans. It's fine for marinades and for brushing foods.

Nonstick Cooking Spray

This mixture of oil and propellants is the quickest way to coat the cooking grid or grill screen with oil. If you're a purist, you can use special spray bottles that you fill with your own olive oil. Spray it on your grill and grill screens while they are cold, before you turn on the grill. Do not spray it on your grill while the fire is going.

Hot Tip

For a quick sauce that's your very own, jazz up store-bought barbecue sauce by adding chopped chiles, a little more Worcestershire, a splash of extra vinegar, some chopped fresh onions or garlic, or whatever you have a taste for.

Barbecue Sauce

Face it—plenty of times you won't have the time or inclination to make your own. Experiment with different brands till you find the one with the flavour you prefer.

Hoisin Sauce

Another dark, fermented sauce, this sauce made of soybeans is sweet and makes a great Asian-style barbecue sauce for fish, pork, or poultry. Add a touch of honey to hoisin to make a great glazing sauce.

Ketchup

Well, you need something for your burgers. Ketchup also is the base for most homemade barbecue sauces.

Maple Syrup

This is a great addition to store-bought barbecue sauces. It adds a touch of sweetness to balance the acidity of some sauces.

Mayonnaise

You'll need it for the leftovers and all those sandwiches. Also, add some chopped pickles or pickle relish, some capers if you like, and voilà—tartar sauce.

Mustard

Many supermarkets carry a treasure trove of mustards. The sharp bite of mustard perks up marinades and makes the condiment a great companion to beef, pork, poultry, and, especially, sausages. Don't forget—if you serve hot dogs, the mustard had better be yellow. Look for Dijon, Grain, Sweet and Spicy, Honey Mustard, and many others to add life to your recipes.

Salad Dressing

You'll need something to put on the salad, of course. Plus, ready-made salad dressings make great emergency marinades. Your in-laws are arriving a day earlier than planned? Pop a couple of chicken breasts in Italian dressing, marinate, and slap them on the grill.

Soy Sauce

Rich, dark, and salty, this sauce can be thought of as an all-purpose condiment. Use it in marinades and pastes and as a table seasoning. Don't confine it just to Asian foods. It's wonderful on hamburgers.

Teriyaki Sauce

Soy sauce mixed with sugar, wine, and seasonings. It's a very popular sauce for grilled foods. Use it in marinades, or just brush it on the food during grilling.

Worcestershire Sauce

This fermented sauce of English origin is a must in most barbecue sauces. It rounds out the ketchup, sugar, and vinegar with an intriguing tang.

The Perishables

Because of its very simplicity—the best grilled foods taste of themselves, with a hint of seasoning and a wisp of charcoal—grilling requires top-notch ingredients. The grill is no place to try to resurrect that chicken breast that's been sitting in the back of the freezer for a year. Fresh meats are better than frozen, though frozen are acceptable, and you should always select the freshest fish, poultry, and seasonal vegetables.

As for meats and poultry, those that are best for the grill are tender without being overly fatty (fat causes flare-ups). Remember, however, that very low-fat meats can easily dry out on the grill, so be careful not to overcook.

Don't Get Burned!

Buy meats, poultry, fish, and other perishables last, just before you're ready to check out of the supermarket. And don't stop to run other errands on the way home. That way they'll still be cold when you get them home.

Storing and Handling Foods

To keep perishables at their very best, keep them well-wrapped (except for live crabs or shellfish, which need to breathe) and store them in the coldest part of the refrigerator—usually the bottom shelf. Use them as quickly as possible, or freeze. Don't refrigerate or freeze them too long; they'll spoil, or at the very least suffer in flavour and texture.

Table: How Long Can You Keep Them?

Food	Refrigerate (40°F or 4°C)	Freeze (0°F or -17°C)
Meats, raw (steaks, roasts)	3 to 5 days	6 to 12 months
Meats, cooked	3 to 4 days	2 to 3 months
Poultry, raw	1 to 2 days	6 to 12 months
Poultry, cooked	3 to 4 days	4 months
Hot dogs (beef, pork, or poultry)	2 weeks	1 to 2 months
Hot dogs, opened package	1 week	1 to 2 months
Ground meats, raw	1 to 2 days	4 months
Ground meats, cooked	3 to 4 days	4 months
Fish, raw	1 to 2 days	1 to 6 months*
Fish, cooked	2 to 3 days	Don't freeze
Shellfish, raw	1 day	1 to 2 months
Shellfish, cooked	2 to 3 days	Don't freeze

Lean fish, such as cod, will keep for 6 months; somewhat more fatty fish, such as trout or bass, for about 4 months, and very fatty fish, such as salmon, for only a month or two. Never refreeze fish that has been previously frozen and thawed; it will turn mushy.

43

Food Prep 101

If you're a novice, here are a few definitions of basic terms you'll encounter in this book's recipes.

Boil: To cook a liquid on medium-high or high heat until the liquid is very active, with large bubbles breaking the surface.

Chop: To roughly cut food into fairly small pieces, using a chef's knife or food processor. To chop onions, peppers, and similar vegetables, lift and drop the blade of the knife rapidly, using a bit of a rocking motion.

Core: To remove the woody or seedy centre of a fruit, such as a pear, apple, or pineapple. If you don't have a special tool called a corer, the easiest way to do this usually is to cut the fruit in half lengthwise, and cut out the core.

Dice: To cut a food into little cubes, about 1/2 inch (1 cm) or smaller. It's neater than chopping and is often used for hard foods such as carrots. To dice, you slice the food one way, then the other way to make small squares.

Grate: To shred a food such as ginger or cheese by rubbing it against the holes on a grater. Used interchangeably with shredded.

Marinate: To tenderize and flavour meats by soaking them in a liquid, usually a mixture of acid and oil, for a long time—anywhere from an hour to overnight.

Mince: To chop into very fine pieces. Garlic, ginger, and herbs are often minced.

Oil or spray: To coat a food or the cooking grid lightly with a vegetable oil (use a brush or a paper towel for this), or to spray it with a nonstick cooking spray.

Don't Get Burned!

Keep your knives well-sharpened. Contrary to what you might think, dull knives are actually more dangerous—because they don't cut as easily through the food, you have to use more force when cutting, so they're more likely to slip.

Peel: To remove the skin of a fruit or vegetable. The easiest way to peel hard vegetables such as potatoes or carrots is to use a vegetable peeler. The easiest way to peel soft fruits such as peaches or tomatoes is to put them in boiling water briefly, then slip off the skin (see Chapter 14). We also use peel to refer to the colored part of the rind in citrus fruits, commonly referred to as zest.

Pit: To remove the large seed in a fruit such as a plum or peach. Cut the fruit in half lengthwise, then pry out the seed.

Process: To grind, chop, or blend foods in a blender or food processor.

Simmer: To cook foods at just below a boil. The liquid will have small bubbles coming to the surface but will be "calmer" than a boiling liquid.

Slice: To cut crosswise or lengthwise through a food to make thin, fairly large pieces.

Trim: To cut off and discard parts of a food that you don't normally eat. That includes such things as the woody bottoms of asparagus, the ends of green beans, or the fat and gristle on meats.

Turn: To use a spatula or tongs to flip a food onto its other side.

The Least You Need to Know

➤ The right herbs, spices, and condiments can make the difference between a so-so grilled dish and a great one.

➤ Choose the freshest meats, fish, and poultry, and refrigerate or freeze them no longer than recommended.

➤ Chopping is rough; dicing is neater; mincing is small.

Part 2
Getting Warmer

So you've got your grill. You've got your accessories. You've got a cupboard full of flavoured vinegars and boutique barbecue sauce from somewhere in the heart of Texas, and a refrigerator that's just waiting to receive the best of the best in meats and vegetables.

Now the learning begins in earnest. In this section, we show you how to build a great fire, prepare your grill for direct and indirect cooking, keep your family and your food safe, plan successful outdoor parties, and gracefully juggle the demands of cooking for varied tastes, including low-fat and vegetarian.

Chapter 5

Fire and Smoke

> ### In This Chapter
>
> ➤ Types of charcoal
> ➤ Getting the fire lit
> ➤ Keeping it at the proper temperature
> ➤ Putting out the fire

When it's time to light a charcoal fire, you quickly realize why we label grilling an art rather than a science. Many a weekend barbecuer has stood around cursing as the coals don't light (then get too hot), or the wind comes up, or humidity turns the fire into a wimpy, smoking mess.

However, with a little practice, and some attention to coal and grill temperature, and the help of good charcoal and accessories, you'll find that it is quite simple to keep frustration to a minimum.

First, here's a quick lesson in Wood Combustion 101. Of course, most folks don't grill over plain wood, but pure charcoal is nothing more than burnt hardwood.

How Wood Burns

The hardwoods used in barbecuing are made up primarily of wood fibres (cellulose, hemicellulose, and lignin), extractives (tannins, starches, resins, oils, dyes, alkaloids, and sugars), and ash. Green wood is mostly water, which is why it smokes rather than burns. It's the extractives that give various woods their distinctive characteristics and that make pecan wood smell like, well, pecan.

When wood is heated, it releases water and volatile gases such as carbon monoxide, sulfuric acid, carbon dioxide, hydrocarbons, hydrogen, acids, ketones, alcohols, aldehydes, and tar, which comes from the sugar residues.

What's What

Hardwood is the solid, compact wood of various, usually deciduous trees. Hardwoods commonly used in grilling include oak, cherry, maple, hickory, and mesquite. *Softwoods* come from conifer trees such as pine, spruce, fir, and cedar. They contain a lot of resin, making them unsuitable for barbecuing, although you can use small twigs for kindling.

If oxygen is present and the temperature is high enough, the volatiles burn off. This is why you should light the briquets or charcoal, then let them burn to ash with the grill uncovered. When temperatures are too low or when there is not enough oxygen for the volatiles to burn off completely, the wood smoulders and gives off creosote, an icky, oily substance that will give foods a bitter flavour.

This is why if you are starting from scratch with dried wood (as you might if you're pit-barbecuing or cooking foods in a large smoker), you must burn it down to embers before you start cooking.

Once it's dried, hardwood consists of about 20 to 25 percent moisture, 50 to 55 percent volatile compounds, and 25 percent char.

Commercial hardwood charcoal is produced by heating wood for several days in closed ovens to get rid of noxious fumes, water, and just about everything except the pure char—that dry, black, porous stuff we know as charcoal. (The coal in this case is a misnomer, and manufacturers of pure charcoal often prefer to label it charwood.) Char has few volatile compounds and only about 3 percent moisture. It burns cleanly, with little smoke.

Of course, damp wood produces plenty of smoke. That is why you soak wood chips or chunks in water before you put them on the coals.

All About Charcoal and Briquets

Charcoal briquets are not pure charcoal. They do contain charcoal that has been ground to a powder, but may also contain binders, cardboard, borax, actual coal, limestone, sawdust, and other materials, even motor oil. The better-quality briquets contain a high percentage of charcoal to other ingredients, which is why they catch faster and burn better. This is one area where you get what you pay for.

We highly recommend pure hardwood charcoal for grilling. It imparts no "off" flavours to the food, and burns very well. But we realize that it is not as widely available as briquets, and costs more. Good-quality briquets are acceptable for most grilling purposes.

Instant-lighting briquets have been soaked in lighter fluid and have that unpleasant petrochemical smell. We recommend avoiding them and using a charcoal chimney to get the charcoal started.

Whatever type of charcoal you use, store it in a cool, dry area such as the basement or garage. When charcoal absorbs moisture, it can be hard to light. If you live in a dry area such as the Southwest, you can probably keep it outside, but you should still cover it. If you buy charcoal in large bags and have to store it some distance from the grill, put the bag in a wheelbarrow or cart to make transporting the charcoal easier. And don't forget a large scoop, so that you don't have to dig the charcoal out with your hands.

The lighter fluid in instant-lighting charcoal can evaporate, so keep the bag tightly closed.

For tailgate parties and other occasions, you can buy briquets in a bag that's meant to be ignited right along with the charcoal. These are expensive but convenient.

Tasty Tidbit

Back in the good old days, charcoal wasn't something you trucked out to buy for weekend parties—it was a cooking necessity. Charcoal vendors used to roam the streets and sing ditties to attract customers. One common chant from 19th-century Philadelphia:

Charcoal by the bushel

Charcoal by the peck

Charcoal by the frying pan,

Or any way you lek!

Tasty Tidbit

Some guy named Kingsford invented the charcoal briquet, right? Nope. It was none other than Henry Ford, better known as the inventor of the mass-produced automobile. Ford used wood in the Model Ts, and started burning the scrap to make industrial charcoal at his plant in Kingsford, Michigan. To reduce storage and shipping costs, he compressed the charcoal into briquets. The supply was greater than the demand, so Ford tried selling the briquets to the public at car dealerships. The business never truly "caught fire," though, until the Kingsford Company acquired it.

Don't Get Burned!

Pouring coals from a charcoal chimney to the charcoal grid creates sparks. Put the rim of the chimney as close to the grid as possible, and pour the coals slowly and gently, standing as far back as you can. Be sure to wear long mitts to protect your hands and forearms.

According to Kingsford, makers of charcoal briquets, a 5 pound (2.2 kg) bag of charcoal contains 90 to 100 briquets, a 10 pound (4.5 kg) bag between 180 to 200, and a 20 pound (9 kg) bag 360 to 400. As a rule, the company says, allow about 30 briquets per pound of food you're grilling.

Starting the Fire

First, sweep any old ashes out of the grill so they won't block any of the air vents.

Be sure to burn the coals with the lid open until you're ready to cook. This feeds plenty of oxygen to the fire to keep it going, and also allows any volatiles to burn off.

There are several ways to light the fire:

➤ Kindling method. Pile some kindling—wadded-up newspaper that has had 1 teaspoon vegetable oil added to it, a few pine cones or some twigs—in the bottom of the grill. Mound the coals in a pyramid shape atop the kindling, leaving some gaps for air to come in and so you can light the kindling. Light the kindling material with a long-handled match or utility lighter. Once it catches, it will heat the coals and get them started. This method works for wood as well as charcoal fires.

➤ Charcoal chimney method. Fill the chimney with briquets or lump charcoal. Place wadded-up newspaper in the bottom of the chimney, and light it in a couple of places through the air holes, using a long-handled match or utility lighter. When you see that the charcoal on top is alight, carefully pour the charcoal out into the grill.

➤ Electric starter method. Plug in the starter, place it in the bottom of the grill, and arrange the briquets atop it in a pyramid shape. When the starter glows red and ignites the coals, remove it and unplug it (be sure you put it on a fireproof surface until it is thoroughly cool).

➤ Solid starter method. These white cubes are made of a nontoxic wax. Pile the charcoal in a pyramid, tuck some of the starter cubes between the charcoal pieces, and light.

➤ Lighter fluid method. This is our least favourite method, because lighter fluid gives off obnoxious fumes. Also, if you don't burn the coals long enough to get rid of the residue, it imparts an unpleasant flavour to your food. Plus, using lighter fluid is illegal in some localities because of its polluting emissions. Pile the charcoal in a pyramid. Squirt the equivalent of about 1/4 cup (50 mL) of lighter fluid onto the coals and let sit for a minute, then light with a long match or utility lighter. Never squirt lighter fluid onto coals that are already burning.

➤ Just plain coals method. You simply pile the charcoal or briquets up in a pyramid and light them. Unless you're using instant-lighting coals (which have been saturated with lighter fluid), this method is the least reliable.

When Is It Ready?

Charcoal goes through three stages before it's ready for cooking. First, it's literally aflame. Then the flames die down but the charcoal is still glowing red hot. Finally, the charcoal is mostly covered with ash and will have only a slight glow. That's what we call medium hot, and it's the proper temperature for most foods.

Since charcoal grills, unlike ovens, don't have handy little lights that go off when they're preheated, you'll have to use your eyes and your hands to tell when the charcoal is ready for cooking.

First, you should look at the coals. Then, for a further check, you can hold your hand, palm down, about 1/2 an inch (1.5 cm) above the cooking grid, or about 6 inches (15 cm) above the coals. Count off how many seconds ("one thousand one," "one thousand two," and so on) you can comfortably hold your hand there. Here's what you're looking and feeling for:

Tasty Tidbit

According to the Barbecue Industry Association, sales of grills stayed steady from 1987 to 1997. In the same period, however, sales of charcoal briquets climbed by 14 percent and the number of "barbecue events" doubled. In other words, people have been buying grills all along, but in the 1990s they've actually been *using* them.

➤ Glowing or red hot coals. The coals will still be very red and glowing. You will be able to hold your hand over the grid for only about 2 to 3 seconds. The charcoal is still too hot for cooking most foods, but is ideal for searing meats.

➤ Medium-hot coals. The coals will still have a bit of a red glow, but they'll be about 70 percent covered with a medium-thick layer of gray ash. You'll be able to hold your palm over the grid for about 4 to 5 seconds.

➤ Cooling coals. The coals will be thickly covered with gray ash. You'll be able to easily hold your hand over the grid for 5 seconds or longer. At this stage the charcoal is too cool for most cooking, but OK for warming foods, or gently grilling fruit for dessert.

Of course, if you have a gas grill, this process is much easier; just read the thermometer.

Keeping It Going

If you're cooking over direct heat, you shouldn't have any problem getting all your cooking done well before the coals die down. If you're slow-cooking foods over indirect heat, though, you will have to add some lit charcoal to the fire every 45 minutes or so, to keep the fire fuelled.

Generally coals are ready anywhere from 20 to 45 minutes after lighting. Really narrows it down, doesn't it? But the fact is, coals are very dependent on temperature, humidity, wind, what you use to start them, and so on. With a little practice you'll have no trouble whatsoever telling when the coals are ready for grilling.

Don't Get Burned!

Never pour water on a flare-up in a gas grill. Water can make a grease fire spatter dangerously. It also can wet the ignition, making it impossible to light the gas until the igniter dries out. If the fire flares up, cover the grill to smother it.

Preheating Gas Grills

For a gas grill, you always want to preheat it before cooking. Set all the burners on high and close the lid. Heat for 10 minutes, or until the thermometer registers 500 to 550°F (260 to 288°C).

Open the lid, which will immediately start to lower the heat. Some manufacturer's directions call for turning off a burner or two, but we've found it usually works better, at least in a three-burner grill, to turn all the burners to medium, unless we're cooking over indirect heat. Each grill is different, however, so experiment to see what seems to work best.

Table: How Many Briquets?

Generally, for direct grilling, you need enough briquets to extend 1 to 2 inches (2.5 to 5 cm) beyond the food. Or follow these guidelines. For indirect grilling, remember that you need to pile half the briquets on either side of the drip pan.

Grill size	Indirect grilling	Direct grilling
14 1/2 inches (36 cm)	30 (15 per side)	25
18 1/2 inches (46 cm)	40 (20 per side)	30
22 1/2 inches (56 cm)	50 (25 per side)	35
26 1/2 inches (66 cm)	60 (30 per side)	40

Where There's Smoke, There's Flavour

Smoking woods and aromatics won't cook your food. Rather, they're designed to create a fragrant smoke that enhances foods so they get that distinctive barbecued or smoked flavour.

You can use a wide variety of herbs, spices, and woods to create a nice smoke (see the table below for some ideas). You can buy wood chips or chunks in hickory, mesquite, pecan, and oak, as well as more offbeat "flavours." You should soak wood chips for 20 minutes in cool water, or wood chunks for an hour. Drain them well, then put them on the coals. In a gas grill, you can put them on the ceramic briquets or other heat dispersers, but it's even better if you put them in a smoking box, to keep ashes from clogging the burners.

If you're using fresh herbs in a recipe, toss the stems or leftovers onto the fire. They won't give as strong a flavour as dried herbs, but will perfume the smoke a bit.

You can mix and match woods, or woods and spices, to get different flavours. Try oak with a fruit wood, for example, or mix mesquite with sage or cumin.

Be careful not to put too much smoking wood on the fire. It can make foods bitter.

"Shop" in your garden for woods. When you prune the grapevine or lilac bush or maple tree, save some vines or branches for grilling. Most herbs, especially the woody types such as thyme and rosemary, can be used as aromatics. (Do make 100 percent sure that the twig you use is not from a poisonous plant—it's possible the smoke could make you sick.)

Putting It Out

The easiest and safest way to put out the fire is to cover the grill, close the top and bottom vents, and let the coals burn out. Let the ashes

Hot Tip

Next time you have corn on the cob, put the cobs out in the sun to dry. Once they're completely dry, store them in a paper sack that's out of the reach of raccoons and other curious creatures. Next time you barbecue, tuck the cobs among the lumps of charcoal. They produce a sweet smoke that gives foods a fabulous flavour.

Don't Get Burned!

Be careful what you use as aromatics. Chile peppers can be fairly potent when burned. Garlic and onion turns acrid. Pine is very resinous and gives off a greasy smoke that can lend an unpleasant flavour to foods. Some shrubs, such as dogwood, are too flowery and can literally "perfume" the food.

Part 2 ➤ *Getting Warmer*

cool for at least 48 hours before you dispose of them. Natural charcoal ashes can be used in the garden or compost heap. (It's probably best not to do this with the ashes from briquets, which may include petroleum products.)

Any lumps of charcoal that did not burn completely can be saved for your next grilling session. Just add them to the new briquets.

Don't use water to put out the fire, either by dumping water into the grill or by dumping the coals into a pan or bucket of water. This can create potentially dangerous hot steam. And dumping water into ashes creates a mildly corrosive paste that's bad for the grill's finish and definitely a pain to scrape up.

The Least You Need to Know

➤ Pure charcoal burns cleanly and gives the best flavour, but good-quality briquets are acceptable for most purposes.

➤ The coals are medium-hot, the preferred temperature for most foods, when they are covered with ash and you can hold your hand over the grid for 4 to 5 seconds.

➤ For extra flavour, use smoking woods or other aromatics, such as herbs.

56

Techniques That Really Cook

You're smart enough to realize that you don't grill-roast a whole chicken the same way that you grill a hot dog. But how, exactly, do you grill them? Besides, roasting a chicken or turkey on the grill seems pretty complicated.

Relax. With this book to guide you and a bit of practice, you'll realize that grill roasting a turkey, or just about anything else, is not complicated at all. It simply requires a slightly different technique. Before long, you'll be able to grill anything short of a whole suckling pig. Actually, if you have a large enough grill, or a pit and a bunch of willing neighbours and friends, you can even do that.

Directly to the Point

By far the most popular method of grilling is over direct heat. That means just what

Hot Tip

For most grilling, you should completely open both the top and bottom vents. However, if it's a very windy day, or if you're having a problem with the coals flaring up a lot, partly close the bottom vents.

you think it does: You stick the piece of meat, fish, chicken, vegetable, pizza, or whatever grilled fare you've a mind to try on the cooking grid, right over the hot coals. When it's browned, you turn it over and cook the other side.

This method is ideal for chicken breasts, thin hamburgers, fish fillets, Portobello mushrooms, and other foods that will cook in 20 minutes or less. It's also great for precooked foods, such as hot dogs or sausages, that you want to just char a little. Thin foods will brown nicely on the outside, but not burn, before they are cooked through in the centre.

You can sear really thin foods on an uncovered grill. But most foods cook more evenly if you keep the grill covered for most of the cooking time. Open the vents in the lid and in the bottom of the grill.

Although we talk about cooking food directly over the coals, foods with any fat on them, such as chicken breast with the skin, actually fare better if you set them slightly off centre, away from the coals. That way, the fat is less likely to drip into the fire and cause flare-ups, which can burn the food and, possibly, you. It's also important to cover the grill when cooking fatty foods. By putting the lid on, you feed a bit less oxygen to the fire, thus making it less likely to flare.

The way you arrange the coals also affects cooking and the likelihood of flare-ups. For very thin and/or quick-cooking foods—for example, precooked sausages that you're just charring, or cutlets—keep the coals slightly mounded for very hot heat, and put the food directly over them. For slightly thicker cuts, such as boneless chicken breast and thick beef patties, put the coals in a single layer. If the food seems to be charring too quickly on the outside, move it off centre so that it's not over the hottest coals.

Nearly all foods are grilled over medium-hot coals, which means the coals are no longer red-hot and glowing, but mostly covered with a layer of white ash. One exception is steaks or other foods that you want to sear before cooking through. They should be

What's What

To *sear* a meat, you cook it quickly on both sides over very high heat. This forms a crust on the surface, which helps seal in the juices.

seared over red-hot glowing coals. Then finish cooking the meat over medium-hot coals. One easy way to accomplish this is to separate the coals slightly, with most of the still-glowing ones on one side of the grill, and the mostly ashy ones on the other, before you set the cooking grid in the grill.

If flames are licking out of the coals, never place the food directly over them. Wait until the flames have died down. If flames shoot up while you're grilling, move the food to one side and cover the grill. A notable exception is marshmallows—some connoisseurs like them really black and gooey.

Indirectly Speaking

We know several folks who like to grill their Thanksgiving turkeys. It's a great way to free up the oven for all those side dishes, and with some care the turkey turns out moist, juicy, and slightly smoky—in a word, luscious. These people know the secrets of indirect grilling, or grill-roasting.

When you grill-roast, you're basically using your grill like an oven. The standard covered kettle-shaped grill works quite well as an oven. It gets plenty hot and provides lots of air circulation around the food. Do note, though, that your grill must have a lid for you to use the indirect method.

Hot Tip

If you do a lot of grilling, a hinged top rack can come in handy. Its sides lift up, making it a cinch to add extra coals when you're cooking over indirect heat.

Indirect cooking is ideal for larger foods such as beef roasts, whole chickens, and turkeys, that would char to a crisp over direct heat long before their insides were done.

To keep foods moist, add a drip pan to the grill. Place the drip pan—you can use a couple of disposable foil pans nested inside each other—in the middle of the grill, on the bottom rack. Fill the pan half full of water. If your grill is 18 1/2 inches (46 cm) in diameter, pile about 18 to 20 coals on each side of the drip pan; if it's 22 1/2 inches (56 cm), use 24 to 26 coals. Add or subtract a few coals if your grill is larger or smaller than that. If your grill came with two charcoal holders or dividers, by all means use them. They'll keep the coals from spilling all over (like into the water pan).

Light the coals. When they are covered with a

Hot Tip

Got an old cake or bread pan that's too battered or grease-stained to use for baking? Turn it into your drip pan for the grill. Reserve it just for that purpose, and wash it in hot, soapy water between uses.

thick layer of ash, replace the top rack and put the food in the centre of that, over the drip pan. The drippings from the meat or poultry will drip into the pan, flavouring the food and keeping the coals from flaring up.

To perk up the flavour of grill-roasted foods, you can toss some soaked wood chips or dampened herbs such as rosemary sprigs on the coals. Or, you can put wine, broth, or water with dried herbs in it in the drip pan.

If you have an extra grill or a charcoal chimney, you can light the coals before you pile them in the grill. The advantage of this is that the coals will be burning evenly on both sides. Be sure to very carefully pour the coals where they're needed, and not into the drip pan.

Hot Tip

Soak wood chips in cool water for 20 to 30 minutes and wood chunks for 1 hour before adding them to the coals. This keeps them from burning up, and creates more smoke.

Don't Get Burned!

Baked (and, presumably, grilled) potatoes wrapped in foil can be a source of botulism. Apparently because the foil traps moisture, the potato does not get hot enough to kill the bacteria. There's no danger as long as you eat the potato while it's still hot, or if you refrigerate it.

Unlike your oven, your grill relies on fuel that burns down. This means that for longer roasting, you need to feed fresh coals to the grill every 40 to 45 minutes. There, doesn't that make you appreciate those nineteenth-century women who cooked three meals a day on a woodstove?

To replenish the coals, gently lift the food off the top rack and onto a plate. (This assumes you do not have a hinged grill rack; see "Hot Tip.") This is preferable to trying to pull up the rack and the food; there's something really heartbreaking about watching your half-cooked capon slide head (well, neck) first into the grass. With the food safely aside, remove the rack. Wear thick, extra-long barbecue mitts on both hands, and gently lift the rack by its handles. Set it on or prop it against a level, heatproof surface. If you're cooking a 20-pound (9 kg) turkey, better get someone to help you lift it and the rack.

Some recipes require low heat. If you're using a charcoal grill, keep the heat low by using fewer coals, waiting until they are ashen, and adding only enough coals periodically to keep the fire going. In a three-burner gas grill, it may mean turning two of the burners off and keeping the remaining burner on medium.

Cooking indirectly on the gas grill is much easier. Just follow the manufacturer's directions. Usually, that means preheating the grill to about 500 to 550°F (260 to 288°C), with the lid down. Two of the burners (on a three-burner grill) or one burner (on a two-burner grill) are turned to medium, and the other burner is off. The food is placed over the burner that's turned off. You may have to experiment a bit, perhaps turning off two burners instead of one, for example, to find a "comfortable" temperature for indirect cooking.

If your gas grill has only one burner, without dual controls you can't cook foods by the indirect method.

Rotisserie Grilling

This is the way those roasted-chicken restaurants cook their birds to a golden turn. It's a great method for whole poultry or large poultry pieces with the skin, as well as for large beef, pork, or lamb roasts, because as the bird turns, it bastes itself with its own fat. It also cooks more evenly. You can use a rotisserie over direct or indirect heat. Rotisserie attachments are sold for gas and charcoal grills.

The first thing you'll need is an electrical outlet handy to the grill so that you can plug in the rotisserie. Put the meat on the spit (rod), carefully fastening the forks in place. The meat can be anywhere from 5 to 10 inches (12.5 to 25 cm) from the heat, depending on how slowly you want to cook it. Start the rotisserie and check to make sure the meat or poultry isn't loose or wobbling. If it's rotating unevenly, take it off the spit and start over.

Cook the meat, occasionally checking on it and the coals, and replenishing the charcoal as necessary.

Planking

Plank grilling is one of the oldest methods of cooking in North America. The Haida Indians found that cooking on cedar or alderwood quickly added a wonderful smoky flavour to salmon while keeping the fish tender. Plank grilling is a relatively easy method of cooking. When you do not have the time to babysit a smoker for hours on end, planking can give you similar results in a fraction of the time.

First you need to purchase untreated aromatic wood. Hardwoods work best (alder, maple, oak, cherry, apple, hickory, mesquite, or pecan). And of course cedar is traditional. You can find these woods at your local lumberyard or specialty wood shop. Sometimes you may have to special-order the wood or use what you can get. When purchasing your planks, ask for untreated wood, no more than 1 inch (2.5 cm) thick, 8 to 10 inches (20 to 25 cm) wide, and 10 to 12 inches (25 to 30 cm) long. Purchase a number of planks at a time, as you will find that once you start to plank you won't want to stop.

Once you have your planks, you will need to soak them in water for at least 4 to 6 hours. This will help keep the planks from igniting on your grill too quickly; also it will provide the moisture needed to create the flavourful smoke.

This method of cooking provides a generous amount of smoke. When planking, you will be cooking with the grill lid closed so as to keep the heat and smoke inside the grill. Exercise caution when opening the grill lid so as not to get smoke in your eyes.

When planking, you will not need to turn or move the food. Just set your favourite food on a preheated plank, close the lid, and set your timer. You will need to check the food occasionally while it's cooking. Reduce the heat if the plank ignites. Use a spray bottle of water to put out the flames, and close the lid and continue to cook. It truly is easy and delicious.

Hot Tip

Obviously, you don't want to add unlit coals to your fire. You can use a charcoal chimney to heat more coals (set it on a heatproof surface, such as concrete). If you frequently cook over indirect heat, you might want to buy a small, cheap tabletop grill and use it just for lighting those extra coals.

Cooking in Embers

This is down-and-dirty cooking, the way our ancestors did it. While the cavemen and women cooked wild boars right in the fire, you've probably only explored this culinary avenue with marshmallows.

Cooking in embers also works for some dense foods, usually vegetables, where you want long cooking and a smoky undertone. You wrap the food in foil and place it directly in the coals. Potatoes and sweet potatoes are great cooked this way.

Smoking

You might think you can't really smoke foods at home. It's true that making, say, bacon, is an art best left to the professionals. But if you want to smoke a little fish, poultry, or meat, all you really need is a water smoker. This is a tall, narrow grill shaped like a silo. The coals sit in a pan at the bottom of the smoker. Over them lies a water pan, and the food sits directly over that, with a lot of air above it to give the smoke room to rise. The combination of hot air, smoke, and steam cooks the food.

To smoke foods, you first light the charcoal, then wait for it to burn down to ash. You cook the food the same way you grill by the indirect method, adding another 12 to 14 coals, plus additional wood chunks, to the fire every 30 to 45 minutes. Most smokers have a door on the front so you can easily add more coals.

Unlike grills, water smokers have a permanent drip pan that slides into brackets.

The usual temperature range for smoking is 200 to 250°F (95 to 120°C), with 225°F (107°C) being the optimum. Don't peek at the food too often; you'll only increase the cooking time.

Sprinkle soaked wood chips over the coals to help perfume the smoke and flavour the food. Don't go overboard on the wood chips, though, or the smoke flavour will be overpowering. Often 2 to 3 cups of soaked chips is about right, but for best results follow the individual recipe or the smoker manufacturer's directions. To further enhance the flavour, you can use cider or wine in the pan instead of water, or use water and add a handful of dried herbs.

Although we don't recommend starter fluid for any grilling, we especially caution against using it to light the coals in a smoker. The smoke gets more concentrated in the smoker than it does in a grill, and starter fluid can leave an unpleasant aftertaste. For the same reason, we strongly recommend using pure charcoal in your smoker rather than briquets.

If you're really serious about barbecuing (smoking), you can use a wood smoker. Use either real hardwood charcoal or actual wood (three sticks is about average) for the fuel. The air intake (vent) on the firebox should stay open to release smoke; close it partway if the fire is too hot or flaring up frequently. A wood smoker will cook food more quickly than a water smoker.

Tasty Tidbit

Commercial smoking is a more complex process than home-based water smoking. Take traditional ham. It starts with fresh pork, which is cured with a rub of salt, sugar, and spices, or brined (soaked in water with salt, sugar, and spices). It is then hung in a smokehouse for several months (if it's made the old-fashioned way) or several weeks (more likely these days). It picks up flavour from the rub or brine and from the wood used to smoke it. Processors either cold-smoke foods at 70 to 90°F (21 to 32°C), or hot-smoke them at 100 to 190°F (38 to 88°C). Commercially smoked foods may or may not be fully cooked—check the label.

Done to a Turn

Okay, so you've got the grill going—now, how do you handle the cooking? Here are some general tips that apply to grilled or barbecued foods in general. You'll find more tips, geared specifically to certain foods, in Chapters 10 through 14.

➤ Don't overcook. While you do want foods to be cooked through, grilling is a dry heat. Overcooking lean foods, especially, is a good way to ruin their flavour and texture. Remember, foods continue to cook after they're removed from the grill. When in doubt, it's better to undercook a bit; if the food turns out to be underdone, you can put it back on the grill. Once it's over-cooked, there's not much you can do except drown it in sauce.

➤ Lightly brush very lean foods such as skin-less chicken breast or vegetables with a bit of olive oil before grilling, to help keep them moist.

Hot Tip

If your smoker is getting a bit hotter than you like, or if you need an extra-low temperature to smoke something like cheese, add a few ice cubes to the water pan.

Don't Get Burned!

It's best not to salt meats, poultry, or fish before grilling. Salt draws out the natural juices, further drying out the food.

➤ Baste foods, especially if they're lean. Baste the food every 5 minutes or so during cooking with the marinade or barbecue sauce. If you have soaked raw meat, poultry, or fish in the basting sauce, you should quit basting it at least 5 minutes before the expected end of cooking, so that the food will get hot enough to kill any bacteria on the surface.

➤ Plan ahead, so that you know the cooking times for various foods and can grill them in succession or simultaneously, as appropriate. For more on time-tables, see "A Grilling Timetable" in Chapter 8.

➤ Soak bamboo skewers in cool water for 20 to 30 minutes before using them. This will help keep them from charring or even catching fire, burning the food along with them.

➤ Turn foods grilled over direct heat at least once, and more frequently if the fire's a bit too hot or if the food has a sauce on it. The exception is delicate fish, which should not be turned at all.

What's What

Basting is a fancy name for brushing or drizzling a liquid over a food as it cooks. You can baste with a kitchen brush, a clean paintbrush (with bristles that don't shed), a spoon, or a bulb baster, which is a tool designed for the purpose. The bulb baster works only with thin liquids. Use a brush or spoon for thick liquids such as barbecue sauce.

➤ To make kebabs, cut the meat, poultry, or fish, and your vegetables or fruit, into chunks about 1 to 1 1/2 inches (2.5 to 4 cm). Thread the skewer through a chunk of meat. Alternate the meat with vegetables (if you're using vegetables). Alternating, say, beef with a cherry tomato, then a piece of pepper, then a piece of onion, then another piece of meat, makes for an attractive arrangement. Don't cram the ingredients too tightly on the skewer; you want a touch of air circulation so the meat will cook. Because the skewer can push surface bacteria into the centre of the meat, kebabs, like hamburgers, should be cooked until they're no longer pink in the centre.

➤ Drain marinated foods thoroughly, and brush any sauce on grilled foods toward the end of the estimated cooking time. The sugars, garlic, and other ingredients in sauces can burn, while the oils in marinades can drip into the fire and cause a flare-up. Usually the sauce is added to smoked ribs and meats during the last 30 minutes of grilling. For chicken, the sauce is brushed on during the last 10 to 15 minutes; for steaks and chops, just the last 5 minutes, and for sausages and hot dogs, the last 5 minutes.

Don't Get Burned!

When you pull up the lid of your charcoal grill during cooking, lift it to the side. When you lift it straight up, you can create a draft that draws ashes up onto the food.

➤ Keep the vents open during grilling to feed oxygen to the fire. You can adjust the bottom vents if necessary, but the top vents should always stay open to release the smoke. Remember, metal vents get hot! Use barbecue mitts or pot holders to adjust them.

The Least You Need to Know

➤ Quick-cooking foods should go directly over (or very near) the coals.

➤ Thicker cuts, roasts, and foods that need longer cooking should be roasted away from the coals, over a drip pan.

➤ For any but the thinnest cuts, keep the grill covered for even cooking.

Chapter 7

Safety First

In This Chapter

➤ Cooking and eating safely outdoors

➤ Handling and storing perishables properly

➤ Making sure foods are cooked through

➤ Reducing any risks associated with high-heat cooking

Cooking and food safety are always important, of course. But they can be especially important when grilling. Because grills deal with open flames (in the case of charcoal, anyway), get very hot, and are out in the open, they pose greater risks than the average kitchen appliance.

Food safety can be a big concern, too. The foods you are most likely to grill are meats, poultry, and seafood—foods that are at higher risk of bacterial contamination. Toss in the fact that grilling is more art than science, and it can be harder to make sure foods are cooked through as much as they should be.

To top it off, you're usually eating grilled foods outdoors. Which means foods sitting outside, maybe in the hot sun. And yellow jackets buzzing around the food. And kids buzzing around the grill.

So, here's all that stuff you'd rather not hear about, but need to know. Once you've had a little experience, though, this stuff will be second nature.

Grills First

Grills are wonderful. They also can be very dangerous. Not only do they get very hot, but unlike stoves, they don't have safety knobs to keep kids from playing with them. So it's important to follow some basic safety rules:

➤ Pick a level spot away from dense vegetation. That's especially true for smaller or lighter charcoal grills, which can tip easily.

➤ Never use a grill inside the house, garage, or any other enclosed space. Grills can give off carbon monoxide, a poisonous, colourless, odorless gas.

➤ Don't put the grill too near the house. If it's too close to a window, it could send fumes and sparks into the house.

➤ Try to keep the grill out of the way of where the kids usually play and run through the yard, or where guests are likely to be walking.

➤ Never leave the grill unattended if there are young children around. You should also keep an eye on pets, which may be attracted by the food smells.

➤ Don't wear loose, long sleeves or flowing clothing when you grill.

➤ Try not to use a charcoal grill when it's really windy. Besides the fact that it's difficult to light the fire and the food may not cook well, the wind can whip the flames and sparks around—or, in a real gust, possibly knock the grill over. If you've already started grilling when the wind gets gusty, close the bottom vents most of the way.

➤ Keep a spray bottle of water nearby in case of a minor flare-up. Note: This applies only to metal charcoal grills and when planking. Never use water to put out a flare-up in a gas grill, or in a ceramic charcoal grill. In fact, the method should be used only as a last resort in charcoal grills, since water mixed with ashes makes quite a mess. Always try to smother the flare-up first by covering the grill and closing the vents.

What's What

Propane is a colourless, flammable (but of course) gas that's a component of petroleum and natural gas. It burns more cleanly than gasoline, and, unlike natural gas, can be toted around, making it the ideal fuel for gas grills and camp stoves.

➤ Never use kerosene, gasoline, or other liquids in place of charcoal lighter fluid, or try to run a gas grill on anything other than the fuel it's designed for. The results can be explosive.

➤ Never dump out the coals while they're still hot. Cover the grill and close all the vents, and let the coals cool for at least 48 hours before you dump them.

➤ If your gas grill flares up, turn all the burners off and move the food to another area of the cooking grid, away from the flames. Once the flames die down, light the grill again. Never use water to put out a fire in a gas grill.

Don't Get Burned!

You do know you should never, ever squirt starter fluid into lit charcoal, right? If you're like most impatient grillers, you've probably done it anyway. Do not do it again. The flame could travel back up the stream of liquid and burn you.

➤ Do not line the bottom of a grill, especially a gas grill, with foil. This can collect grease, which might catch fire.

➤ If you have a gas grill, it's a good idea to check it for leaks whenever you remove and reconnect the propane tank. Consult the owner's manual to see which connections you should check, how you should check them (usually you brush on soapy water and look for bubbles), and what to do about it if you find a leak. When in doubt, don't try to fix it yourself; turn off the gas and call the company that made the grill.

➤ If you have any reason to believe the fuel lines are clogged or leaking or the gas jets aren't working properly on your gas grill, and simple maintenance or cleaning procedures don't help, do not operate the grill until you have checked with the manufacturer.

➤ Keep the grilling area clean; it can attract unwanted critters. Usually this means mice, cats, and maybe raccoons, but depending on where you live, it could also include mountain lions or bears.

➤ Exercise caution during that unwelcome ritual at cookouts and picnics throughout much of North America: the swarming of the yellow jackets. Earlier in the summer, these yellow-and-black-striped insects prefer a diet of bugs, but in late summer and early fall, they start foraging for other foods, especially sweets. Yellow jackets alone are responsible for about half of the "bee" stings annually in North America

If you're planning a cookout in August or September and have been having problems with yellow jackets, consider eating inside (if you don't have a screened-in patio). Another possibility is to put out traps, although they help only somewhat; the wasps will still make a beeline for the food and drink. There's little you can do other than ducking out of their way as much as possible. Swatting at them will only make them mad.

Yellow jackets like to fly into open soda cans, attracted by the syrupy liquid. More than one person has been stung in the throat after drinking from a soda can with an unexpected inhabitant. If yellow jackets are likely to visit your cookout, pour the soda into cups. It won't stop the wasps from swarming around your cola, but at least you'll be able to see them.

Fending Off the Bad Bugs

Don't Get Burned!

Juices from raw meat and poultry can drip onto other foods in your shopping cart. To prevent this, immediately drop the package of meat or poultry into one of the plastic bags supplied in the meat department.

Grilling is not the most precise of cookery methods. You can never be exactly sure when a food will be done, because the timing depends on humidity, wind, air temperature, how many coals you use, how cold the food is, how hot the coals are, and so on. This is why it is very important to remember that the cooking times in this book (or any other grilling book) are simply guidelines. Never rely on time alone to make sure a food is cooked through.

Since you want your guests to remember your Canada Day picnic for all the fun they had, and not for the fact that they lived in the bathroom for five days afterward, it pays to handle and cook foods properly. Here's the scoop on food safety:

Keep It Clean

➤ Store meats and poultry in the refrigerator away from other foods, and put a paper towel under the package to absorb any leaking juices.

➤ Never put cooked food on a platter that held raw food. If you use a paring knife to cut into a chicken breast that turns out to still be pink, wash the knife in hot soapy water before using it to cut into the chicken again.

➤ If you marinate raw meat, poultry, or fish, and want to also serve the marinade as a sauce, either set some aside before you add the rest to the meat, or in a saucepan bring the marinade to a boil for a full minute before reusing it. Don't count on the vinegar or other acid to kill germs; at most, it'll just slow them down. You can use the marinade or sauce to baste the meat during cooking, but stop basting at least 5 minutes before you expect the food to be done, so the outside gets hot enough to kill bacteria.

➤ Wash all produce thoroughly. That especially applies to berries, lettuce, and other items you're likely to eat raw, unless you buy already trimmed and washed vegetables in a bag.

Keep It Cold (or hot)

➤ Keep meats, poultry, or seafood in the refrigerator until it's time to put them on the grill.

➤ Defrost foods in the refrigerator, under cold water that you change every 30 minutes, or in the microwave. Because microwave defrosting warms up foods, don't defrost foods that way unless you plan to cook them immediately.

➤ Once you grill foods, serve them immediately, or refrigerate them. Cooked foods, including meats, salads, coleslaw, and the like, should not sit out longer than one hour on a fairly warm day. (Dry foods, such as breads or cookies, are OK for longer periods.)

Cook It Through

You bring the nicely browned chicken to the table, only to discover it's still pink inside. The next time, you try to compensate by adding another 5 minutes to the grilling time, and wind up with stringy chicken that your guests politely chew, and chew, and chew.

How you tell whether a food is done without being cooked to death depends, not surprisingly, on the type of food. Wiggling a drumstick works great with a whole chicken, but not too well with chicken breasts.

After some practice, you'll get better at telling when a food is most likely done. Meats, fish, and poultry tend to firm up and lose that "squishy" feel when they're cooked through. Clams and similar shellfish advertise their doneness by opening their shells. Foods like shrimp turn colour. For more on judging when individual foods are cooked through, see Chapters 11 through 14.

To take the guesswork out of the process, use an instant-read thermometer. Many grills, especially gas grills, come with a thermometer. Note that you do not stick an instant thermometer into the food while it is cooking—it can break. Instead, you put it in the cooked

Hot Tip

When are foods considered cooked through? Here are the minimum temperatures:

Beef steaks, lamb chops	145°F (63°C)
Pork, kebabs, ground beef	160°F (71°C)
Poultry (dark meat)	180°F (82°C)
Poultry (breast)	170°F (77°C)

food, and wait about a minute or until the needle stops moving. One trick to using an instant-read thermometer is that the tip needs to go far enough into the food to get an accurate reading. Here's how to use it in different foods:

➤ Steaks, chops, chicken breasts: Insert the probe through the side of the meat so the tip reaches the centre.

➤ Roasts, turkey breast: Insert the thermometer so the tip is in the thickest part of the meat but not touching fat or bone. The bone conducts heat and so can provide a false reading.

➤ Whole chickens or other poultry: Insert the probe into the thickest part of the thigh, but be careful that it isn't touching the bone.

Hot Tip

If you cut a slit in poultry or meat to tell if it's done, use a white plastic knife. The juices show up better against white, and it'll be easier to tell whether they're pink or clear.

If you don't have a thermometer handy or if you don't trust what it's telling you—and food thermometers are not always 100 percent reliable, especially if you've dropped them—cut a slit in the food or pierce it with the tip of knife. The meat does lose some juices that way, so resist the temptation to poke it every other minute, and only start testing when it's been on the grill for the minimum time listed in the recipe.

The juices should run clear for any ground meat and for chicken. Pork can still have a tinge of pink. Beef and lamb (not ground) can have a fair amount of pink in the juice.

If you still can't tell, cut into the meat to see whether the centre is pink or not.

So What Are These Awful Bugs, Anyway?

So is it truly necessary to get that cautious with your food? The short answer is, yes. Here's why:

E. coli

The reason the medium-rare burger is, alas, a thing of the past. Short for *Eschericia coli*, this bacterium is found in our guts and the guts of animals, including beef cattle. In its normal form, *E. coli* helps synthesize vitamins and keep "bad" bugs at bay. However, some mutated forms, especially a variety called *E. coli* O157:H7, can be harmful. Fortunately, *E. coli* O157:H7 is fairly rare. Unfortunately, when it does hit, it can be deadly, especially to children. It has popped up in other foods, including raw milk, lettuce, and unpasteurized apple cider, but it's associated mostly with ground beef.

So why can you eat your steak, but not your hamburger, medium rare?

Ground meats always pose a greater risk than whole cuts. That's because *E. coli*, a contaminant that's often spread from the animal's intestines to its meat during slaughtering, is generally found on the surface of the meat. When the beef is ground, those surface bacteria get mixed throughout the meat.

Unlike some other bugs that have to be present in large numbers to make you sick, apparently it takes only a small amount of *E. coli* to "get" you. This is why you should ignore well-meaning food writers who advise that you lessen the risk (and presumably make rare or medium rare burgers "safer") by buying very fresh meat, keeping it cold, and grinding it yourself. No way! Besides the fact that your kitchen equipment probably isn't as clean as that in restaurants and supermarkets and your refrigerator isn't as cold, these writers are confusing *E. coli* with bugs like salmonella, which multiply rapidly in unclean or warm environments, and which must be present in large numbers to make you sick.

The good news is that the food industry has developed a simple test for *E. coli*, which is in the pilot phase. Maybe soon they'll be able to certify beef *E. coli*–free, so we can go back to enjoying juicy pink burgers. But until then, the only way to eliminate the risk of *E. coli* is to cook meat all the way through. Period.

Campylobacter jejuni

Good old "campy" is the leading cause of bacterial diarrheal illness in North America. Federal health experts blame it for 2 to 4 million cases of illness per year. Raw chicken is a common source of this bug. It tends to especially hit kids under 5 and young adults ages 15 to 29. It usually lasts a week to ten days, and while it's rarely fatal, it induces plenty of misery. To prevent poisoning, handle raw meat and poultry carefully. Wash your hands, cutting boards, and utensils in hot, soapy water, and don't let poultry juices drip onto other foods. Cook poultry all the way through.

Salmonella

This large family of bacteria causes 2 to 4 million cases of foodborne illness every year in North America. Salmonella bacteria aren't picky about where they live—you'll find them in animals, water, soil, insects, cutting boards, animal feces, raw meats, dairy products, raw poultry, raw seafood, and raw eggs. The most common sources of poisoning, though, are poultry and eggs. Salmonella poisoning is highly unpleasant, but usually goes away after a couple of days. However, it can seriously sicken and even kill infants, older people, or those who have a weakened immune system. To avoid salmonella, keep foods cold, keep your kitchen, utensils, and grilling area clean, and thoroughly cook foods, especially poultry, before eating them.

Don't Get Burned!

Don't mix anything red or dark—such as paprika, spices, spaghetti sauce, Worcestershire, or barbecue sauce—into ground beef, turkey, or other meats before grilling them. It will be very hard to see when they are no longer pink in the middle

Botulism

This one usually throws a scare into people, since the illness can often be fatal. Fortunately, this illness, caused when the spores of *Clostridium botulinum* produce potent toxins, is fairly rare. Although the spores can thrive in any nonacidic food, botulism often is associated with canned foods because it thrives in airless environments, and with vegetables such as potatoes and garlic that come into contact with the soil. From a griller's standpoint, there are two chief areas to watch out for: homemade flavoured oils (see Chapter 4), and potatoes, either baked (or grilled) in foil, or in potato salad.

Hetero What?

If you follow nutrition news at all, you've probably read about cancer-causing substances formed when meats are cooked at high temperatures. Because scientists are allergic to short words, these substances are called heterocyclic amines, or HCAs, and polycyclic aromatic hydrocarbons, or PAHs.

The bad news is that grilling, with its intense heat, definitely creates these nasty substances. The good news is that cancer researchers rank HCAs and PAHs way down on the list of things we need to worry about. Eating too much red meat, for example, is still considered a much bigger cancer risk than how you cook it. In fact, the evidence is only suggestive that HCAs might pose a cancer threat to humans. The evidence for PAHs is a bit stronger, but they're found in a lot of other places besides the food we eat, and our bodies usually excrete them within days.

Tasty Tidbit

So what did those researchers marinate the chicken in to reduce those dangerous chemicals? A tasty mixture of cider vinegar, lemon juice, olive oil, garlic, brown sugar, mustard, and salt. They pointed out, though, that there was nothing magical about the marinade they used. Soaking the chicken in any marinade showed similar results.

Still, if you eat a lot of grilled foods, you might want to know how to reduce any risks.

First, the HCAs. When you cook protein foods, but especially muscle meats (that's meat, poultry, and fish) over high heat, natural chemicals in the meat react to form these substances. Studies have shown that frequently eating well-done meats cooked at high temperatures may be linked to colorectal, pancreatic, breast, and stomach cancer.

So how can you cut the risk and still enjoy meat on the grill? There are several ways:

➤ Marinate the meat. Researchers at Lawrence Livermore National Laboratories found that soaking chicken breast even briefly in a cider vinegar–oil marinade before grilling it drastically cut the amounts of HCAs produced. It's important to note that as of this writing, they had not tested this on other meats, and could not say for sure whether the same would hold true. But marinating certainly can't hurt, and it may help.

Don't Get Burned!

When you pull up the lid of your charcoal grill during cooking, lift it to the side. When you lift it straight up, you can create a draft that draws ashes up unto the food.

➤ Microwave the meat. Partially cooking the meat first in the microwave seems to drain off HCAs in the juices. You can then finish cooking it on the grill. Don't microwave the meat until the grill is heating up and nearly ready to go. Zap it for about 2 minutes, and drain off any juices that collect. Bacteria can multiply rapidly in partially cooked meats, so you need to get it onto the grill right away.

➤ Eat meats medium-rare when it's feasible. Since foodborne bacteria pose a much bigger and more immediate threat than any slightly increased risk of cancer down the road, it would be very foolish to eat your chicken, pork, or hamburger medium-rare. But if you're eating steak or lamb chops, don't overcook them.

Now, about those PAHs. They're formed when meat juices drip onto the coals, creating that wonderfully flavourful smoke. Unfortunately, the smoke contains these cancer-causing substances, which then cling to the meat. Fortunately, your body usually excretes PAHs within days.

Probably the best way to limit exposure to PAHs is to cook lean, well-trimmed meats on the grill over medium-hot coals. This will reduce the amount of fat dripping into the coals, and thus the amount of smoke.

The Least You Need to Know

➤ Grills can be dangerous; take care in setting up and using them, and don't leave them unattended.

➤ Keep things clean to avoid cross-contamination, and keep hot foods hot and cold foods cold.

➤ Check carefully that foods are cooked through to safe temperatures.

➤ Grilling produces potentially cancer-causing chemicals in food—but the risk is nothing to get all lathered up about.

It's Your Party

Having a party outdoors is the height of the grilling experience. I find that when I have a grilling party, it gives me time not only to cook some fun food but also to enjoy my guests. It's no fun being cooped up in a kitchen on a hot day and missing the fun with friends and family. Don't let those rainy days get you down, as a large umbrella can stop that problem easily. In Canada we are sometimes blessed with the greatest weather, but sometimes no matter where you are or what event you have planned, it's going to rain or even snow. So buckle down and grill anyway.

You can party outdoors anytime, of course, whether you're celebrating Mother's Day, Victoria Day, Canada Day, Labour Day, your son's graduation, or your daughter's wedding—or nothing at all. And no matter what time of year it is, always have a backup plan in case it rains.

The advantage to outdoor cookouts is that you're right where the party is. Instead of being closeted in the kitchen while your guests nosh appetizers, you can grab a beer

Tasty Tidbit

When we throw parties, outdoor cookouts rank at the top of the list. Surveys show that when people entertain, 42 percent host an outdoor cookout, while only about 37 percent prefer dinner or cocktail parties.

or lemonade and joke with your guests while you flip the salmon steaks.

One disadvantage is that grilled foods usually have to be cooked "to order." Unless you're serving it as part of a salad or sandwich, you really can't grill that juicy steak 3 hours ahead of time and reheat it before serving.

You're also confined to one cooking method, at least in the final stages. Unlike a dinner party, where you can warm the bread in the oven while you heat the spinach on the stovetop, an outdoor cookout pretty much means cooking on the grill, period (although you may have access to a side burner on a gas grill). If you are the sort of person who buckles under pressure, or if you expect things to be particularly chaotic at the party (it's your son's sixth birthday), you can get around this limitation in several ways:

➤ Prepare a main course that takes longer to cook. Grill-roasting a chicken over indirect heat, for example, will take close to an hour, freeing up some time for last-minute preparations elsewhere.

➤ Make sure all the side dishes, desserts, and appetizers are foods that can be prepared ahead of time.

➤ Enlist a second person to help in meal preparation (always a good idea anyway).

You also can go the other way and celebrate this difference by cooking the entire meal on the grill, from the appetizers through the dessert. In fact, after you have done most of your grilling and the coals are cooling down, it is even possible to do some baking (although we wouldn't recommend, say, baking a cake from scratch on the grill). As long as you've gone to the trouble to light the grill, why not get as much cooking out of it as possible?

Hot Tip

Pressed for time or money? Make the party a potluck. Have your guests bring the salads, appetizers, bread, and desserts—all you have to do is supply beverages and throw something on the grill.

You can only cook everything on the grill, of course, if you have a large enough cooking surface to do so. If you have a hibachi, better stick with Plan A. And if you do plan to make a meal this way, you'd better be well organized.

In fact, outdoor parties always require you to have everything organized and ready before you light the coals. And by everything, we mean beverages, ice, salads, gelatin molds, bread, silverware, serving utensils, napkins—the whole enchilada.

The easiest way to do this is to make a very complete list, and check it twice. Put everything on that list: buy ice, check the cooler, start the coals, buy the flank steak, don't forget the potato salad, put out the napkins and lobster forks, husk the corn, find the barbecue tongs, soak the wood chips, warm the rolls.

A Grilling Timetable

Of course, there's no reason you can't just toss a party together. Call a few friends, pick up some ground beef on the way home, and voilà, a party. These days, though, when nearly everybody works outside the home, a little planning goes a long way.

Hot Tip

You planned a party for eight people. You bought nine steaks to be on the safe side. Then your best friend calls an hour before the party to say he's bringing his two cousins from out of town. After you throttle him, what do you do? Easy: turn the steaks (or chicken breasts, or chops) into kebabs, fajitas, or sandwiches.

While you don't have to create something quite as precise as a train timetable, you should jot down how long everything is expected to take to cook, and juggle accordingly. If you're making brisket, you'll obviously need to stick around all day to keep an eye on it. If you're making pork chops, grill-baked potatoes, and grilled apples, the potatoes need to start first. Then you add the pork chops. Finally, as the coals begin to cool, you grill the fruit.

Several Days to a Week Before

Draw up a final menu and shopping list, and shop for nonperishable foods, beverages, and paper supplies.

Make sure you're not low on charcoal or propane, and buy it if you are.

Make sure you have enough chairs and table space. If you don't, ask some of the guests if they can bring a lawn chair or two. (If you really need more chairs, you may have to rent them, which should be done sooner than this.)

Hot Tip

Just for fun, draw up a menu on your computer (or have your spouse or kids do it), and print out several copies of it. You can use them as place mats.

A Day or Two Before

Make sure the picnic furniture is clean. Scrub it down if necessary. Make sure your grilling tools are clean as well, and that the kids aren't raising toads in the ice cooler.

The day before the party, make any marinades, rubs, and sauces you'll be using. Refrigerate them if necessary.

Make a shopping list for the perishable foods, and buy them. For the amounts you'll need, consult the table. (If you're grilling shellfish, it's best to buy it the day of the party.)

Make the dessert (if it's a nongrilled one).

Table: How Much Food to Buy

These are averages, of course. If you're entertaining the twenty-something males on the softball team, they'll undoubtedly eat more than the fifty-something women from your reading club. For most parties, though, you'll find that the light eaters and heavy eaters tend to average out, and these quantities should work fine. These amounts are for main courses. For appetizer servings, cut the amounts down by one-third to one-half, depending on the type of food.

Weights are for the food as purchased, including bone and/or skin. In other words, you would buy a 3 pound (1.5 kg) chicken to feed 6 people (1/2 pound or 250 g per person). The amounts are based on "real life" servings, not necessarily the 3 ounces of lean meat or poultry recommended by nutritionists. Most people will probably eat more than that in a party setting.

When in doubt, buy a little more than you think you'll need. Eating chicken every day for a week beats running out of food.

All Red Meats (beef, pork, lamb, veal, buffalo, venison)

Boneless roasts or steaks	4 to 6 oz. (120 to 180 g)
Bone-in roasts	6 to 8 oz. (180 to 240 g)
Chops (loin or shoulder)	1 to 2 chops
Cutlets (scaloppini) or sandwich steaks	4 to 6 oz. (120 to 180 g)
Ground meats	4 to 6 oz. (120 to 180 g)
Sausages	1 med. to large link, or 3 oz. (90 g) bulk

Beef or Bison

Individual steaks (rib eye, Porterhouse, etc.)	1 steak, or 1/2 large steak
Short ribs	6 to 8 oz. (180 to 240 g)

Pork

Spareribs	3/4 to 1 lb. (375 to 500 g)
Whole pig	1 1/4 to 1 1/2 lbs. (625 to 750 g)

Lamb

Leg or shoulder (bone-in)	6 to 8 oz. (180 to 240 g)
Rack, rib or crown roast	2 ribs
Chops (rib)	2 chops

Poultry

Chicken or turkey, whole	1/2 lb. (225 g)
Chicken or turkey, boneless parts	1/4 lb. (115 g)
Turkey, parts (bone-in)	1/2 lb. (250 g)
Chicken, parts (bone-in)	1 to 2 pieces, or 6 to 8 oz. (180 to 240 g)
Duck or goose, whole	1 lb. (500 g)
Duck, boneless breast half	1/2 to 1
Cornish hens	1/2 to 1 bird
Squab, partridge	1 bird
Quail	2 birds

Fish and Shellfish

Fish, whole (gutted, with head)	3/4 lb. (375 g)
Fish, whole (headless)	1/2 lb. (250 g)
Fish, fillets	6 to 8 oz. (180 to 240 g)
Fish, steaks	1 each, or 6 to 8 oz. (180 to 240 g)
Clams, large, in shell	6 to 8
Clams, steamers	16 to 18
Mussels	8 to 10
Oysters, on the half shell	6 to 8
Oysters, shucked	6 to 8, or 1/4 pint (0.3 L)
Crab, soft shell	2 each
Crab, meat only (crab cakes)	1/4 lb. (125 g)
Shrimp, in shell	6 to 8 oz. (180 to 240 g)
Shrimp, peeled	4 to 6 oz. (120 to 180 g)
Squid, whole or in pieces	1/4 lb. (125 g)
Scallops (no shell)	1/4 lb. (125 g)
Lobster, whole	1 to 2 lbs. (500 g to 1 kg)
Lobster, cooked tail	1 each, or 5 to 6 oz. (150 to 180 g)

Side Dishes

Rolls or buns	1 or 2
Deli salads (potato or pasta salad, coleslaw, baked beans, etc.)	4 to 6 oz. (120 to 180 g)
Green salad	2 to 3 oz. (60 to 90 g)

Several Hours to a Day Before

Make any nongrilled desserts and side dishes (except, of course, for highly perishable ones like tossed salads). Refrigerate.

Trim all meats and vegetables you'll be grilling. Cover and refrigerate.

Just Before the Party

Have all the paper goods—cups, plates, forks, knives—ready to go. Spread out the tablecloth if you're using one.

Check the grilling area. Are the tools, oils, grill screen, and everything else you need handy?

Make the tossed salad if you're serving one. Cover it lightly with a damp (not wet) paper towel and refrigerate it.

Anywhere from 30 to 90 Minutes Before You Plan to Serve Food

Light the grill. How much time you allow depends, of course, on what you're cooking. Take the estimated cooking time of the food and add 30 minutes for charcoal, 15 minutes for gas. Allow some extra time if it's cold, very humid, or windy.

Hot Tip

If you have herbs in your garden, snip some sprigs, especially if they're in flower, and put them into vases of water for herb bouquets. They make casual, charming table decorations.

When the Food Is Nearly Finished Grilling

Have your spouse, kids, or some of the party guests set the table and bring out all the side dishes and condiments.

After the Party

Make sure the grill vents are closed, and the lid on, so the coals will die down.

Clean up. Remove full garbage bags and transfer them to covered trash cans so you don't get critters sniffing around your patio. Make sure the area around the grill is cleaned of meat juices, oil, and so on.

The Wine (well, beverage) List

The most popular "outdoorsy" beverages are no doubt beer, iced tea, soft drinks, and lemonade. For nonbeer alcoholic beverages, consider wine cocktails or punches, such as mimosas (champagne and orange juice) or sangria (red wine and fruit punch). Both are festive, go well with a variety of foods, and can be made low in alcohol.

If you do want to serve wine, you can either go traditional, pairing the proper wines with each course, or serve a more "picknicky," light, sipping-style wine with some fruit. For example, if the main course is a whole salmon grilled over oak, you could pair it with an oaky Chardonnay to play up the wood, or just serve a lighter wine with more fruit for the whole menu (for example, a Fume Blanc with tropical fruit undertones).

For more heavily smoked foods, a wine with a lot of fruit and a fair amount of sweetness, such as a Niagara Off Dry Riesling, is often just the ticket. If you feel out of your depth, ask your wine merchant for recommendations.

Don't Get Burned!

At a party, it's easy to get distracted and forget how long foods have been sitting out. Except for "dry" foods such as breads (plain) and cookies, cooked or raw dishes should not stand at room temperature for longer than an hour. On a really hot day, bring foods out just long enough for everyone to serve themselves. Then return the foods to the refrigerator or cooler.

Some Suggested Menus

We like the idea of cooking your entire meal—or at least, just about all of it—on the grill. Here are some menus that do just that.

Picnic in the Park

➤ Focaccia

➤ Jerk Strip Steaks

➤ Grilled Garlic Potato Skins

➤ Mixed Greens Topped with Grilled Vegetables

➤ Campfire-Style S'Mores

Backyard Family Barbecue

➤ Tortellini Vegetable Salad

➤ Carolina-Style Slow-Smoked Pulled Pork, or Chicken Pieces with Molasses Barbecue Sauce

➤ Blueberry-Apple Cobbler on the Grill

➤ Beer, iced tea, and fruit punch

Canada Day Celebration

➤ Five-Minute Mussels

➤ Cedar-Planked Salmon

➤ Grilled Tomatoes and Green Onions

➤ Apricots Topped with Raspberries and Raspberry Sherbet

Pacific Rim–Style Dinner Party

➤ Chicken Yakitori

➤ Grilled Teriyaki Salmon Steaks

➤ Asparagus and Mushrooms with Sage Brushing Sauce

➤ Wine-Brushed Pears

➤ A Riesling or a light, fruity red wine

Just Appetizers

➤ Carolina Pulled-Pork Quesadillas

➤ Seaweed Steamed Clams

➤ Focaccia

➤ Grilled Portobello Mushrooms Stuffed with Sun-Dried Tomatoes and Gorgonzola

➤ Grilled Antipasti

➤ A light red wine, such as Gamay Noir

Shore Grill Dinner 1

➤ Grilled Bacon-Wrapped Digby Scallops

➤ Coastal Shrimp in Beer

➤ Mixed Greens Topped with Grilled Vegetables

➤ Warm Apple Cinnamon Slices with Cheddar Cheese

➤ Beer, of course

Shore Grill Dinner 2

➤ Dungeness Crab–Crusted Alderwood-Planked Salmon

➤ Down By the Sea Clambake, or Whole P.E.I. Lobsters

➤ New Potatoes with Garlic and Cilantro

➤ Grilled Angel Food Cake and Pineapple

➤ A good, smooth ale

Grilling Party for Kids

➤ Buffalo Cheese and Tomato Sauce Pizza, or Cheeseburgers Deluxe

➤ Fruit Kebabs

The Least You Need to Know

➤ The key to any successful party, even a spur-of-the-moment one, is setting a timetable and following it.

➤ It's possible, and even desirable, to cook the whole dinner, from appetizers through dessert, on the grill.

➤ For outdoor parties, keep it simple. Grilling requires concentration; cleanup and preparation should require less.

Chapter 9

Chew the Fat—Not

In This Chapter

➤ The essentials of healthful eating

➤ How to trim the fat in your party without sacrificing fun or flavour

➤ Which recipes in this book are low in fat and/or vegetarian

---

Traditional etiquette holds that the guests who are on diets, have sensitive colons, are not eating meat, or are eating only foods that begin with "Y" not bother the host or hostess with their peculiarities (one exception is a genuine food allergy). A good guest should instead politely eat what's served—or at least those parts of the dinner that he or she can and will eat—and politely push the rest around the plate.

But traditional etiquette derives from the days when people didn't endlessly discuss food preferences, the best-seller lists weren't dominated by diet and vegetarian books, and people generally didn't outlive their arteries. These days, it's not unusual for a host to plan a party knowing that one guest is a vegetarian, another has diabetes, one has lost 150 pounds (68 kg) on a low-fat, high-protein diet, and still another has been put on a near-zero-fat regimen by his cardiologist. For that matter, it's not unusual for the host to be following dietary restrictions as well.

And etiquette or not, you want your guests to enjoy the party and think kindly of you as a host. Fortunately, accommodating a variety of eating styles is not at all difficult to do these days.

Pyramid Power

Of course, even without specific dietary restrictions, we should all be eating more healthfully anyway. Unless you've been stuck on an iceberg for the past decade, you've probably seen the Canada Food Guide. It emphasizes that we should be eating mostly grains, fruits, and vegetables, and small amounts of meat or poultry—3 ounces (90 g) is about the size of a deck of cards—with the fat trimmed off.

But hey, you say, it's just one cookout, and I've been craving a big ol' steak for weeks.

The good news is that it's your diet over time, not in one evening, that counts. Even better news is that with only a small amount of extra attention, it is possible to put together a menu that will satisfy just about anyone.

As just one example, you could cook up your steaks, thinly slice them, and serve them with grill-warmed tortillas, salsa, lettuce, sliced avocados, grilled onions, and sliced tomatoes. In other words, tacos al carbon, as they say in Spanish.

You can satisfy your steak craving by skipping the tortillas and everything else and just piling the meat on your plate. Your fat-watching guests can put a small amount of meat and a lot of lettuce and tomato in a tortilla. Your vegetarian guests can skip the meat altogether and stuff the tortillas with the veggies.

Hot Tip

Should you trim the fat from meats and remove the skin from poultry before or after you grill? We vote for *after*. Grilling produces dry heat, and the fat or skin helps baste the meat, keeping it moist. This method adds very little additional fat, as long as you do trim the meat or remove the poultry skin before serving.

Other Guest-Pleasing, No-Fuss Strategies

The real key to successful entertaining is variety. If you serve a lot of different foods, and make sure that at least several of them are low-fat and/or meatless, everyone should be able to find something to eat. You don't have to kill yourself to do this: You can buy all kinds of salads and other prepared foods at the supermarket or local deli. Even if you choose to cook everything yourself, what's the big deal about slapping a couple of peppers on the grill?

Here are some more tips:

➤ Trim the fat from meats and remove the skin from poultry. Serve reduced-fat—or better, fat-free—dairy products such as milk, yogurt, and sour cream.

➤ When you're choosing deli salads for side dishes, keep in mind that salads with oil-and-vinegar type dressings (or no dressing at all) tend to be lower in fat than those with creamy dressings, if only because creamy dressings are thicker and cling better to the vegetables. Some possibilities: coleslaw (with a vinaigrette-type dressing), cucumber salad, three bean salad, fruit salad, gelatin molds.

➤ If you're making your own salads, use reduced-fat or nonfat dressings. Or cut the high-fat mayonnaise or other dressing with some nonfat yogurt or sour cream.

In most cases you can also use less than the amount of dressing called for. That's especially true if you're using your mom's ancient recipe for potato salad, which probably calls for twice the dressing you actually need to moisten and flavour the salad. Oh, those devil-may-care 1950s . . .

➤ Serve high-fat sauces and condiments on the side. Pass the tartar sauce for the fish or ranch dressing for the green salad or chocolate sauce for the grilled fruit at the table so guests can help, or not help themselves, or not.

Don't Get Burned!

Watch the condiments. If you're trying to eat foods lower in fat, don't sabotage the effort by pouring on the salad dressing, mayonnaise, or other high-fat extras.

➤ One area where people seem to be especially calorie-conscious is beverages. Always make sure you have sparkling water, unsweetened ice tea, and/or diet sodas on hand.

➤ Think fruits and vegetables. If you're not grilling vegetables, put out a relish tray of raw, cut-up veggies. Vegetables in jars, such as roasted peppers and artichoke hearts, can come in handy, too. Greens in a bag make it ever so easy to serve a tossed salad. Grill some fruit for dessert—ice cream strictly optional.

➤ Think starch. Rice salad, pasta salad with a light dressing, lowfat crackers, pretzels, grilled polenta (slices of cooked corn-meal), corn tortillas, plenty of bread—all of these are filling yet low in fat.

➤ Watch the dips. If you're putting out chips or pretzels, serve fat-free bean dip and salsa in addition to or instead of the creamy dips. You can also buy lowfat creamy dips. Reduced-fat ranch dressing

Tasty Tidbit

While the number of dedicated vegetarians is still a small segment of the population, restaurateurs report a lot of interest in meatless dining. Walk into nearly any sit-down restaurant these days and you'll find several meatless selections on the menu.

Table: Lean Meat and Poultry Cuts

These numbers apply to meats trimmed of all visible fat and poultry without the skin. The servings are 3 ounces (85 g), cooked weight. All have less than 10 grams of total fat and 3 grams of saturated fat.

Meat	Saturated fat	Total fat
Turkey breast	0.2 g	0.6 g
Bison (buffalo)	0.8 g	2 g
Chicken breast	0.9 g	3 g
Turkey leg	1.3 g	3.2 g
Pork tenderloin	1.4 g	4.1 g
Beef eye of round	1.5 g	4.2 g
Beef top round	1.9 g	4.2 g
Chicken drumstick	1.3 g	4.8 g
Beef round tip	2.1 g	5.9 g
Beef top sirloin	2.4 g	6.1 g
Pork top loin	2.3 g	6.6 g
Pork centre loin	2.5 g	6.9 g
Lamb sirloin	2.8 g	7.8 g
Chicken thigh	2.6 g	9.3 g

   makes a good dip. Mix chives and other herbs into nonfat sour cream for a quick, nutritious dip.

➤ Serve two kinds of whatever it is, as long as it's not too much effort. Grill some pork brats for those who want the traditional flavour and turkey brats for those watching their fat intake. Or beef burgers for the traditionalists and veggie burgers for the vegetarians on your list. Or just grill a lower-fat cut, such as turkey breast or pork tenderloin, for everybody.

➤ Serve the lower-fat version of whatever it is: mayonnaise, crackers, chips, cheese, potato salad. It's getting hard to find a food these days that does not have a reduced-fat or even fat-free version.

➤ You often can simply eliminate the oil in a marinade, especially one made with a mellower acid such as wine or orange juice (rather than lemon juice or vinegar). You nearly always can reduce it by at least one-fourth. Or replace it with reduced-fat mayonnaise, buttermilk, or yogurt. These are also good choices for homemade salad dressings, where the fat actually matters more (most of the oil in marinades is drained off anyway).

➤ If some of your guests are vegetarians, be on the alert for animal products that are easy to overlook.

If they're just eating vegetarian for health reasons, they probably won't care if there's a trace of fish in something, but if you're entertaining a convention of animal welfare activists, better hold the Worcestershire (it's made with fish) and gelatin (beef hooves). If your guests are vegans (vegetarians who eat no animal products whatsoever), don't make cheese pizza for the main course.

Fats 101

So what's all this stuff about saturated, polyunsaturated, and monounsaturated fats? And what about trans fats?

Carbon and hydrogen chains and how they're arranged determine which kind of fatty acid predominates. (Nearly all foods have all three kinds of fat, in varying proportions.) But you don't really want to know that. So here's the short course:

Saturated fats, which are hard at room temperature, have been shown to be a risk factor for heart disease. The biggest sources in the North American diet are meats, high-fat dairy products, and chicken skin.

Polyunsaturated fats are liquid at room temperature and are generally considered OK as long as you take it easy on them. (They tend to lower both "bad" and "good" cholesterol, and in extremely high amounts could increase the risk of cancer.) The biggest sources are salad dressings, vegetable oils (such as soybean and corn), and nuts.

Monounsaturated fats have been shown to lower "bad" cholesterol while leaving "good" cholesterol alone, so some researchers theorize that these fats not only are not harmful, but may be beneficial. Two of the richest sources are olive oil and canola oil.

Trans fats occur naturally, but most of these fats in our diet come from vegetable oils that have been hydrogenated to make them hard at room temperature. Margarine, shortenings, and baked goods made with them are major sources. Researchers are discovering that trans fats act much like saturated fats in raising cholesterol.

Low-Fat and Vegetarian Recipes in the Book

Putting together a healthful menu is easy; just choose dishes from the following lists.

The following dishes are easy on the fat and saturated fat. Those followed by a "V" in parentheses are vegetarian as well.

Appetizers

Five-Minute Mussels

Focaccia

Grilled Garlic Potato Skins (V)

Grilled Antipasti (easy on the olives; V, minus the ham)

Smoked Shrimp with Chili-Orange Mopping Sauce

Main Dishes

Cantonese-Style Sweet and Sour Chicken Breasts

Grill-Roasted Turkey Breast (skin removed)

Swordfish in Buttermilk Marinade

Tarragon-Scented Striped Bass

Halibut Steaks au Poivre

Minted Sole on Lime Slices

Red Snapper Margarita

Cod with Grilled Apple Slices

Soft-Shell Crabs on the Grill (minus the butter on the side)

Whole P.E.I. Lobsters (minus the butter)

Coastal Shrimp in Beer

Prawns with Honey Brushing Sauce

Down By the Sea Clambake (minus the butter on side)

Vegetables and Grains

Asparagus and Mushrooms with Sage Brushing Sauce (V)

Mixed Grilled Vegetables in a Pita Pocket (V, main course)

New Potatoes with Garlic and Cilantro (V)

Mixed Greens Topped with Grilled Vegetables (V)

Grilled Tomatoes and Green Onions (V)

Baby Artichokes with Rosemary (V)

Baked Potato with Vidalia Onions (V; could be main course)

Desserts

Glazed Mixed Fruit Grill (V)

Apricots Topped with Raspberries and Raspberry Sherbet (V)

Grilled Angel Food Cake and Pineapple (V)

Vegetarian But Not Necessarily Low in Fat

Buffalo Cheese and Tomato Sauce Pizza (serve to 4, as main course)

Tortellini Vegetable Salad (with nonmeat-filled pasta; skip the salami)

The Least You Need to Know

➤ The key to any successful party, even a spur-of-the-moment one, is setting a timetable and following it.

➤ These days, it pays to be savvy about various dietary preferences.

➤ Serving a variety of foods is the easiest way to please everyone, including yourself.

➤ Emphasizing seafood, vegetables, fruits, and starches is an easy way to make menus more healthful.

Part 3

Ladies and Gentlemen, Start Your Grills

So now you've got the fire going . . . here's how to put it to good use. In this section, you'll learn everything you need to know about marinades, rubs, and sauces. We share the secrets of selecting, preparing, and cooking meats, poultry, seafood, and vegetables and grains for the grill. And just in case you should have some leftovers—or are smart enough to create "leftovers"—we share tips for turning grilled foods into fabulous second-day soups, salads, sandwiches, and stir-fries.

ED'S GRILL
EMPORIUM

Chapter 10

There's the Rub

In This Chapter

➤ The basics of marinades

➤ The basics of rubs

➤ The basics of finishing or table sauces

Let's face it, grilling and barbecuing techniques are pretty basic. You barbecue meat or seafood in Toronto the same way you cook it in Calgary or New Orleans or Houston or Vancouver. What sets these cities apart in how they define "barbecue" is not cooking techniques, but how they flavour the meat.

One cook uses a rub; another uses a marinade. One puts ketchup in the sauce; another blanches at the very idea. In Calgary, they like their sauce with real bite; in Toronto, they like it sweet; in New Orleans, they like it with butter; in Vancouver, they often like it with a bit of ginger, soy sauce, or juniper berries; and in Houston, they like the sauce on the side or not at all.

Historically, rubs and marinades played a large role both in tenderizing meats and in preserving them. When you're eating a very old goat, it doesn't take long to discover that marinating it in yogurt might help a little. And in the days before refrigeration, folks relied on the preservative properties of alcohol, vinegar, and spices such as garlic, rosemary, juniper, and chiles—along with smoking or drying—to keep their meats longer.

Marinades and Pastes

A marinade is a mixture that contains an acid (wine, vinegar, citrus juice) and, usually, oil and seasonings. Its purpose is to penetrate at least the outermost layers of the meat. The acid in the liquid tenderizes the meat by breaking down its proteins. The oil bathes it in moisture. And the herbs or other seasonings flavour it. Marinades are defined as liquids, though they may be pretty thick (as yogurt marinades often are). When they are thick enough to cling to the meat, we define them as pastes.

Although they can be used with any meat, poultry, or fish, or even vegetables (such as mushrooms or tofu), marinades often are used for leaner cuts such as chicken breast and skirt steak, to add both flavour and moisture.

Examples of classic dishes from around the world that are usually marinated (some grilled, some not) include German sauerbraten, Chinese cha shao (seasoned, barbecued, or roasted pork) and Peking duck, Japanese yakitori (chicken and chicken liver kebabs), Korean bulgogi (barbecued beef), Turkish shish kebab, American fajitas, and Greek souvlaki (lamb kebabs) and gyros (a mixture of lamb and beef cooked on a spit that is also found in the Middle East).

Because marinades usually contain acid, you should not marinate foods in aluminum or cast iron pans, or any other reactive metal. The acid will discolour the pan and pick up "off" flavours from the metal. Marinate foods in glass or ceramic, or stainless steel.

First, mix the marinade ingredients. Put the food in a container. Pour the marinade over it. Turn the food to make sure all parts of it are coated with the marinade. Then loosely cover the food and refrigerate it. At least once or twice during the marinating time (and three or four times if you're marinating it for several hours), turn the meat to make sure it gets coated with the liquid.

Marinades can only penetrate about the first inch of the meat's surface, so a thick cut will still need to be cooked with care so it's tender. Marinating meat for a longer period than suggested does not make it more tender, nor does it make the marinade penetrate any further. On the contrary, it can turn the surface of the meat mushy, and overpower the flavour.

Because spices and oils are at their best warm, marinades have more potency at room temperature. But you don't want to create a colony of bacteria, either. You can marinate foods up to 1 hour at cool room temperature, but for any longer than that, refrigerate them.

Any acidic foodstuff can be used in a marinade. These include yogurt, buttermilk, vinegar, wine, fruit juice, even cola soft drinks.

To make a simple marinade, mix 1/3 cup (75 mL) of wine vinegar (white or red) or lemon juice with 2/3 cup (150 mL) of olive oil, and add a couple of cloves of garlic (peel them and then smash them with the side of a knife) or some sliced onion, and whatever fresh or dried herbs and spices you like. For an Asian-style marinade, use rice vinegar or sherry instead of the wine vinegar, a couple of pieces of ginger, a tablespoon of soy sauce, and peanut or canola oil.

You also can skip the vinegar and use equal parts of wine and oil. Or use orange juice and oil. Do not add salt to a marinade or use cooking wine, which contains a lot of salt. Salt can toughen foods if added prematurely—and besides, your guests will want to salt their food to taste at the table.

Don't Get Burned!

It's tempting to make flavoured oils at home. The problem is that garlic and other herbs or vegetables can contain traces of the spore that causes botulism. And smothering them in oil creates the airless environment that botulism loves. Commercial processors add acid or other preservatives to their oil. It's safest not to mess with homemade flavoured oils, but if you must, refrigerate the oil and use it within two weeks.

An hour or two in a marinade is a long enough bath for most foods. Fish marinates for less time; if you overmarinate it, the fish will "cook" in the acid. However, large cuts of meat that are to be slow-cooked may call for several hours of marinating, even as long as overnight.

Pastes are a cross between marinades and rubs. They are wet, like marinades, but chunkier and thicker, either because they contain less liquid or because the liquid ingredient is thick (examples: sour cream and yogurt). Classic pastes include the various fiery Thai chile pastes; the equally fiery north African berbere (made with chiles and spices); the Italian basil pesto (which means—surprise—"paste"); the blend of lemongrass, sugar, shallots, and fish sauce used to season grilled meats in Vietnam; the curried sauce that flavours and tenderizes Indonesian satay; the yogurt/spice mixture

Hot Tip

A mini–food chopper can make chopping herbs, garlic, and other ingredients, as well as making pastes, a snap. Regular food processors are too big to handle these small jobs, and few cooks own a mortar and pestle.

used to marinate tandoor-grilled chicken in India; and the mustard/spice blend slathered on pork in the Carolinas.

Because they're thick, pastes have to be worked into the meat. They work very well for foods with a lot of crevices, such as whole poultry. The only effective way to apply a paste is to dip your hands in the mixture and rub it over the meat, making sure you get every nook and cranny. Put the meat in a glass, ceramic, or stainless steel container, loosely cover it, and let it marinate for the recommended amount of time. Because paste adheres to the surface, you don't need to turn the meat.

If the paste is very thick, you'll want to scrape some of it off and pat the meat dry before grilling it.

Rubs

When you marinate meat, you drain it before cooking, leaving traces of the marinade behind. Rubs, on the other hand, stay on the meat as it cooks, lending their bold, toasted-spice, crusty personalities to the finished dish.

Think of Jamaican jerk chicken, Montreal spice rubbed steak, Western barbecued beef, Cajun blackened redfish (OK, so it's not cooked on a grill), and French steak au poivre. Their fame lies in the rub.

What's What

Jerk refers to a seasoning mixture traditionally used to flavour slow-cooked pork in Jamaica. Its ingredients vary, but it always contains Jamaican pimento, or allspice. Other common ingredients include chiles, ginger, thyme, and garlic. Jerk is used either dry as a rub or in a marinade. It's most commonly used on pork and chicken, but is also excellent with beef or fish.

Although it may have a few moist ingredients (such as fresh garlic or a dab of oil), a rub is basically a dry mixture of spices. A typical rub will contain at least four or five different seasonings, usually something hot and something sweet. Besides flavouring the meat and, depending on the spices, tenderizing it a little, the rub forms an oily crust on the surface of the meat when it cooks, which helps seal in juices. Unlike marinades, rubs often contain salt and sometimes contain sugar as well.

You can easily make your own rubs, or buy a nice spice mixture for an instant rub. Lemon pepper, chili powder, curry powder, Chinese five spice—all can be used as rubs. Just crack up a bunch of peppercorns, press them into your steak and voilà, steak au poivre. Or go the Cajun route by combining garlic, onion, thyme, red pepper, celery salt, and a bit of basil. Dried or finely grated fresh citrus peel is also very nice in rubs.

Because rubs are dry, they don't always cling well to the meat. Coarser rubs, such as cracked peppercorns, can be pressed firmly into the meat. For finer rubs, you may want to lightly brush the food with a bit of olive oil first. Use your fingers to press the rub into the meat. Put the meat on a plate, cover it loosely with plastic wrap, and refrigerate it for the recommended length of time.

Rubbed meats are either served plain, as in Montreal spiced rib steak, or with a finishing sauce, as in baby back ribs or Carolina pulled pork.

What's What

In normal cooking terminology, *dust* is a verb meaning to very lightly coat a food with flour or any other fine powder. We've borrowed the term to mean a very fine, powdery rub.

Basting and Finishing Sauces, and Condiments

If you've ever eaten Carolina pulled pork or New Orleans barbecued shrimp, you know the importance of a great finishing sauce. In fact, you could argue pretty convincingly that the New Orleans shrimp sauce, a rich mix of butter and spices, could easily finish you.

Marinades and rubs are nothing to basting and finishing sauces. Rib joints guard their barbecue sauce recipes under lock and key. The finishing sauces and condiments offer the real culinary road map of the continent: the shot of bourbon in Kentucky, the yellow mustard that defines a ballpark hot dog anywhere in the North America, that sprinkling of cinnamon and cumin in New Mexico, the malt vinegar in eastern Canada, the tartar sauce on Great Lakes smoked whitefish, the whisper of maple syrup in Quebec, the dash of soy or sprinkling of lemongrass in Vancouver.

Finishing sauces often are added to the food after grilling and before serving. That's the case with the Carolina sauce, in which a mixture of vinegar, salt, and red chiles is tossed lightly with the shredded pork. It's also the case with New Orleans' famous shrimp, which are tossed with melted butter, hot pepper, and herbs. Sometimes the sauces are served as a dip on the side, which is generally true with ribs anywhere and beef in the West. The ribs usually are basted with the sauce during cooking as well.

"Barbecue" sauce, as most of the country knows it, is usually a blend of ketchup, vinegar, sugar in one form or another, and whatever else the creator feels like putting in it. Worcestershire sauce is a pretty standard ingredient. Barbecue sauce contains the ingredients you want in a basting sauce: acid for a bit of tenderness, spices for flavour, and sugar, which caramelizes on the grill to give foods that irresistible smoky sweetness.

Don't Get Burned!

To prevent cross-contamination of foods, never reuse a marinade or barbecue sauce in which you've soaked raw meat, poultry, or fish without first reheating it to a full boil. Once it has been boiled, it's safe to use as a basting or table sauce. Also, throw out any sauce you've used to brush raw meat on the grill.

Sugar burns easily, so you should baste foods with barbecue sauce only during the last 5 to 10 minutes of the cooking time. It's usually best not to marinate foods in barbecue sauce, but if you have, you should turn the food very often as you cook it.

If your supermarket has a limited selection of barbecue sauces, don't despair. You can always get some interesting sauces, many with distinctive regional flair, by mail order or over the Web. You don't really have to make your own sauce, but it is a good way to get a sauce that's truly to your taste. (And who knows, it may make you famous as well.)

Start with about 1 cup (250 mL) of ketchup, 1/4 cup (50 mL) of vinegar, and 1/4 cup (50 mL) of brown sugar or molasses. Heat the mixture till the sugar melts, then add seasonings until you get the flavour you like. Possibilities include Worcestershire, whiskey, smoke flavouring, soy sauce, mustard, cayenne, cumin, chili powder—well, your imagination is the only limit here.

Barbecue sauces keep very well. Pour the sauce into a sterilized glass jar (you can sterilize it in boiling water or just run it through the dishwasher), cover it tightly, and refrigerate for up to a month.

The Least You Need to Know

➤ Marinades and pastes are liquids that are used to tenderize, moisten, and flavour foods.

➤ Rubs are dry spice rubs that are used to flavour foods and help seal in their juices on the grill.

➤ Basting and finishing sauces are used mostly for flavour and to caramelize foods, and vary widely by the region and the cook's whim.

➤ Remember to add barbecue sauce to grilled foods during the last quarter of cooking time as not to burn.

Chapter 11

The Meat of the Matter

In This Chapter

➤ Selecting the right cuts of meat for grilling

➤ Grilling steaks and burgers

➤ Slow–cooking ribs or brisket

➤ Pork, lamb, and veal on the grill

➤ Flavours that go well with red meats

When it comes to choosing the best red meats to grill, the rules are simple. If you can broil it, you can grill it. If you can roast it or pan-fry it, you can grill it over indirect heat or, possibly, direct heat if you marinate it first. If you'd normally cook it in liquid, it's too tough for regular grilling, but with some care, you may be able to slow-cook it in a smoker.

Steaks and Burgers

No matter how much you may try to eat healthfully, we'd wager that when we say "beef on the grill," your mind probably jumps to steak. Not one of those lean 3 ounce (90 g) nutritionist-approved steaks, either, but a thick, well-marbled prime rib-eye or

Porterhouse, crusty on the outside and still oozing juices on the inside.

Or maybe your imagination runs more to a thick, juicy hamburger, with all the fixings, on a grill-toasted bun.

As for which red meats North Americans love to grill, there's really no contest. Every survey shows that it's steaks and burgers.

Well, we're here to help you broaden your horizons, at least when it comes to cooking red meat on the grill. At the same time, we have no intention of ignoring steaks and burgers. After all, they're favourites for a reason.

A Juicy Steak

Just about everybody would agree that when it comes to beef, nobody knows how to grow it or cook it better in Canada than an Albertan. Canadians love their beef and the best comes from Alberta. Triple A Alberta beef is rated the best homegrown beef in the Country. Now many would argue that our friends south of the boarder have better beef. Well, I have a friend in the beef business in Calgary and he would disagree. He also can grill a mean steak. Here's how he describes the process:

"Cooking it right is a matter of knowing your grill. You need to find the hot spot. Every grill—indoor, outdoor, gas, coal, campfire—has one. The trick is to sear the steak for 45 seconds a side on the hot spot; the theory being that searing the steak seals in the juice. Anything that will caramelize—barbecue sauce, marinade, whatever—will also help.

"Once the meat is seared, move it to the medium heat spot of the grill and cook it 90 seconds a side. One rotation is rare; two rotations, medium rare; three rotations is generally considered burnt. Anything beyond that doesn't bear thinking about. With a really good piece of meat, you can knock the first rotation down to 45 to 60 seconds on a side and serve it up what I call very rare, and what the French, in an interesting display of colourblindness, call *bleu*.

What's What

Rare (130 to 135°F, or 55 to 57°C) refers to meat that is still mostly red inside and feels soft. *Medium-rare* meat (145°F or 63°C) is still quite pink in the centre, but warm. *Medium* (155°F or 68.5°C) is pinkish in the centre. *Medium well* (160°F or 71°C) is brown throughout, with perhaps a trace of pink. *Well done* (165°F or 74°C) is completely brown throughout.

"Unfortunately, nowadays, the only way to order a steak in a restaurant is to ask for it 'as rare as your lawyers will allow you to cook it.'"

Alas, we need to point out here that our lawyers would no doubt insist that we tell you to follow the Agriculture Canada meat safety guidelines and cook steak to at least 145°F (63°C). So we offer the above primarily as a historical curiosity.

Here's a roundup of beef steaks that are great for the grill. We have to admit we were surprised to learn that a cut from the chuck—that's the pot roast part of the steer—ranks right under the filet mignon in tenderness. As a bonus, it's usually a lot cheaper than T-bones and strip steaks.

Table 1: The Most Tender Steaks

Tenderloin (also known as filet mignon)

Top blade steak (boneless chuck or charbroil steak)

T-bone

Strip steak (top loin, New York strip, Kansas City)

Rib-eye steak (Delmonico, Spencer)

Top sirloin steak

Source: Texas A&M University

Others would describe a somewhat different method for steaks. Sear them over hot charcoal for 2 minutes per side, then finish cooking over medium heat.

To sear meats on a gas grill, turn all the burners to high and preheat the grill to 500 to 550°F (260 to 288°C). Place the meat on the cooking grate. Close the lid and sear the steak for 2 minutes per side if it's 1 inch (2.5 cm) thick and 4 minutes if it's 1 1/2 to 2 inches (4 to 5 cm) thick. Then turn the steak and grill it over medium heat, turning it halfway during the cooking time.

The Perfect (and safe) Hamburger

Alas, the threat of *E. coli* has banished the juicy, medium-rare hamburger. To be safe, ground beef (and any other ground meat) should be cooked to 160°F (71°C), or until there's no longer any pink in the middle. Here are some tips to help make these well-cooked hamburgers both safe and edible:

Don't Get Burned!

Get that spatula away from that burger! Flattening a burger with the spatula just presses out juices, drying out the meat.

Hot Tip

For a juicy, flavourful burger, add a little ground pork to the beef. In some parts, they call this a "sooo-ee" burger.

➤ If fat content is not a major concern, use ground chuck rather than ground round or sirloin. It has a higher fat content, and will stay moister when cooked to medium-well.

➤ Completely defrost ground beef before shaping it into patties. Otherwise, it may cook on the outside and still be underdone on the inside.

➤ Thoroughly wash your hands and any surfaces or utensils the raw meat has touched with hot, soapy water.

➤ Grill the burgers over medium-hot coals. If the coals are too hot, the meat will cook quickly on the outside and be burnt and dry by the time the inside is cooked through.

➤ Make the patties about 1/2 inch (1 cm) thick. Any thicker and they will burn on the outside before the inside is cooked.

➤ Grill 1/2 inch (1 cm) patties 11 to 13 minutes, or until there is no longer any pink in the centre (160°F or 71°C). Turn them once during cooking.

➤ Do not mix red or dark-coloured spices or liquids (ketchup, paprika, barbecue sauce, soy or teriyaki sauce, etc.) into the meat before cooking, since it can mask pink meat. However, it's not a bad idea to baste the burgers with sauce during the last 5 minutes of cooking; it can help keep them moist.

➤ Do not put the cooked burgers on the same platter that held the raw burgers, unless you have washed it thoroughly first.

Table 2: To Marinate or Not to Marinate: Meats on the Grill

Beef

Marinate, season, or just grill as is

Sirloin or top sirloin steak

T-bone steak

Top loin steak

Porterhouse steak

Beef tenderloin (filet mignon)

Rib steak

Rib-eye steak

Marinate first

Flank steak

Skirt steak

Top round steak

Tip steak

Marinate or rub and slow-cook (either over indirect heat or in a smoker)

Short ribs

Back ribs

Brisket (must use a smoker)

Bison, Veal, Pork, and Lamb

Marinate, season, or just grill as is

Bison rib-eye, New York, or strip steaks

Veal cutlets (scaloppine)

Lamb rib chops

Lamb riblets

Pork or lamb loin chops

Pork tenderloin

Marinate or rub and slow-cook

Veal leg

Veal breast

Veal shoulder

Leg of lamb or leg of lamb roast

Fajitas

Skirt steak is a stringy cut, but it has a lot of flavour. It's the preferred cut for fajitas, although a lot of folks use flank steak these days. Traditionally soaked in lime and chiles, it's marinated in just about anything these days. Cook flank steak quickly over direct heat; medium rare is best. It should be sliced very thinly and served in warmed tortillas, accompanied by pico de gallo (fresh tomato salsa) and guacamole.

Tasty Tidbit

Fajita is the diminutive form of *faja*, which is Spanish for "girdle." On a steer, the girdle (just behind the front legs) is where skirt steak comes from. So "chicken fajitas" is a contradiction in terms. Fajitas probably were invented by Mexican and African-American cowboys on the King Ranch, a massive spread that eats up a good portion of southwestern Texas. The ranch owners got the best cuts of meat; the hired hands got the tough stuff, which they turned into a great dish by marinating it, grilling it, and slicing it real thin.

Ribs and Brisket: Take Your Time

When you say "barbecue," a high percentage of people think "ribs." All ribs should be marinated and grilled over indirect heat, or cooked even more slowly in a smoker. Both beef and pork ribs are done when the thickest portion reaches an internal temperature of 160 to 165°F (71 to 74°C), or when you can easily tear the meat from the bone.

Spareribs

This very popular cut comes from the pig's underbelly or side. Spareribs have a high percentage of fat, which helps keep them moist on the grill, and a rich flavour. They have the least meat of the rib cuts, though. They can be grilled over indirect heat, and usually are marinated or rubbed.

Baby Back Ribs (loin ribs)

Baby back ribs, which can be either pork or beef, come from the blade and centre section of the loin. They have less meat than spareribs but are very flavourful.

Country-style "ribs," which come in both pork and beef varieties, also come from the loin. They're very meaty and are usually eaten with a fork and knife. You can get them with or without the bones. Our suggestion is to go for the bones—they add flavour.

Short ribs, flanken ribs, or cross-cut ribs come from the beef chuck. These are not particularly tender, so they are best marinated and slow-cooked.

Lamb riblets are less popular, but delicious. They're small and don't have much meat, but are very tender. Unlike most ribs, they can be marinated and grilled over direct heat.

A Beautiful Brisket

The brisket is about the toughest cut of beef you can find. Normally, it's not edible unless it's cooked for hours in liquid—and some might argue it's not edible even then. However, Texans are famous for barbecuing it to perfection. You cannot rush brisket. It requires long hours of cooking in a smoker to get tender—figure on a good hour or more a pound (over 2 hours a kilogram). Barbecue it fat-side up. About halfway through the cooking time, wrap the brisket in foil to keep it from drying out too much. It's done when the inside reaches 160°F (71°C).

Pork Chops, Tenderloin, and Roast

We love pork tenderloin on the grill. As meats go, it's actually a very virtuous cut, rating just below chicken breast in saturated fat and total fat. And as long as you don't overcook it, it's also quite a delicious piece of meat.

The tenderloin, a strip from the centre of the loin, usually weighs about 3/4 to 1 pound (375 to 500 g); tenderloins often come two to a package. They're very good rubbed with a mixture of finely minced garlic, black pepper, and rosemary or sage. Or, give them an Asian touch with hoisin sauce, ginger, and garlic.

To keep it from toughening, cook the tenderloin over direct heat for a fairly short amount of time, usually about 18 to 25 minutes. It should get nicely crusted on the outside and be cooked through in the centere but still very juicy.

Pork chops are delicious on the grill, and should be cooked like steaks, without the searing. Unlike steaks, they should not be served medium rare; cook them to 160°F (71°C).

Boneless rolled pork loin roasts also are excellent on the grill. Cook them over indirect heat.

Carolina pulled pork is made with pork butt, a roast that can be hard to find sometimes, at least outside of the Carolinas. Some folks cook the pork shoulder. This is another smoke-it-all-day affair (for a recipe, see page 246.)

Lamb

Lamb chops are superb on the grill, over direct heat. It's OK to cook them to medium-rare (145°F or 63°C).

Lamb sirloin roast or a leg half can be cooked over indirect heat. So can a whole leg, although slow-cooking in a smoker is probably the better way to go.

Veal

Although we mention it in the list above, veal is not a favourite for grilling. It's very lean and dries out quickly. Veal cutlets can be cooked quickly over direct heat. Roasting cuts can be cooked over indirect heat, but marinate them and serve them with some sort of sauce.

Flavours That Go Well with Meats

Vibrant, strong flavours go wonderfully with red meats, especially beef and lamb. Try orange or tangerine, onion, garlic, rosemary, cumin, cinnamon, red wine, beer, tomatoes, soy sauce, chiles, or black pepper—just for starters. Red wine or red wine vinegar marinades are a natural.

For smoking woods, hickory, pecan, oak, and mesquite all go very nicely with beef or lamb. Mesquite is really too heavy for pork, though, so try pecan, corn cobs, or a fruit wood such as apple.

The Least You Need to Know

➤ Steaks, burgers, chops, and pork tenderloin should be cooked quickly over direct heat.

➤ Roasts and ribs should be marinated and cooked over indirect heat.

➤ Match red meats with deep, vibrant flavours.

Chapter 12

Birds of a Feather

In This Chapter

➤ Basic poultry preparation and grilling techniques

➤ Types of poultry, and how best to cook them

➤ Flavours that go well with poultry

Next to steaks and burgers, chicken is the most popular food item to grill. From the wonderfully simple chicken to Cornish hen, turkey, quail, and most any other game bird, poultry is superb on the grill.

Poultry on the Grill

Chicken breast is one of the most popular cuts for grilling. It's lean, not too expensive, and cooks quickly. Its leanness also works against it, though. If you're not careful, chicken breast can turn to shoe leather on the grill. Here's how to keep it moist (the same tips apply to turkey breast, by the way):

➤ Grill it in its skin. The fat will help baste the meat. You can still get rid of nearly all the fat by removing the skin before serving.

➤ Marinate skinless, boneless breasts in a liquid that contains oil, or simply brush lightly with olive oil before grilling.

➤ Don't overcook it. Chicken breast is done when it reaches 170°F (77°C). It will feel firm, and when you pierce it the juices will run clear.

Check poultry for doneness by wiggling a drumstick (it should move freely), by piercing the skin (the juices should run clear), or by inserting an instant-read thermometer in the thickest part of the bird but not touching bone. The thermometer should read 170°F (77°C) for the breast, 180°F (82°C) for dark meat.

Don't worry if the meat near the bone looks bloody, if the chicken is otherwise cooked through. This is caused by the red hemoglobin seeping out of the bones, and is especially common in young chickens. It's harmless.

Poultry generally does not need long marinating: 1 to 2 hours should be enough in most cases.

When you cook poultry with the skin over direct heat, set it a bit off centre on the grid, rather than directly over the hot coals, so the fat dripping from the skin does not cause flare-ups.

Hot Tip

When you grill whole poultry or the wings by themselves, cut off the tips of the wings. They burn easily. Store them in freezer bags and use them to make chicken stock. (To do that, just cover with water, toss in some pieces of carrot, celery, and onion, and simmer for 1 to 2 hours.)

If you smoke poultry for longer than 2 hours, the skin will be tough. Remove it before serving.

Should you wash poultry before using it? This gets rid of surface bacteria on the bird, but also tends to splatter said bacteria around the sink area. If you do rinse poultry, be sure to carefully clean up the sink and surrounding area with hot, soapy water.

Slip herbs under the skin for more flavour. Place the whole chicken or turkey breast side up on a clean surface, with the cavity facing you. Gently ease up the skin on one side of the breastbone, trying not to tear the skin, to form a pocket. Using your fingers, carefully enlarge the pocket until your fingers are inside (or your whole hand, depending on the size of the bird). Don't force the skin away where it's attached to the breastbone or bottom of the drumstick. Repeat on the other side of the breastbone. Rub spices, garlic, and/or herbs between the chicken meat and the loosened skin. As the bird grills, fat from the skin will combine with the flavourings to baste the bird and produce a delicious dish.

Don't salt poultry before cooking; that draws out its juices.

Cutting slits into chicken or turkey legs will help the marinade or paste penetrate deeper in the meat. If you're not marinating the bird, never pierce or cut slits in it before grilling; the chicken will lose juices and dry out.

To butterfly poultry, use poultry shears or a boning knife to remove the backbone. Then press on the bird to flatten it. You'll hear a few joints crack (hopefully they're the bird's, not yours). Butterflied poultry cooks more quickly and evenly. You'll only need to butterfly poultry when there's no one else around who can do it—after all, that's what butchers are for. Don't be afraid to ask your butcher to cut an order to your liking.

Ditto for boning chicken breast. If you have a recipe for grilling boneless breasts and all you have in the fridge is bone-in breasts, just make the recipe with the bone-in breasts and extend the cooking time a bit. Life really is too short to bone a chicken breast unless you're getting paid to do it.

Never thaw poultry, especially whole birds, at room temperature. Instead, remove it from the freezer to the refrigerator. In a pinch, you also can thaw poultry, still wrapped, in a sinkful of cold water, replenishing the water frequently. Smaller chicken pieces, such as boneless breasts and thighs, can be thawed in the microwave as long as you cook them immediately. Never defrost whole poultry in the microwave.

Hot Tip

When you grill or rotisserie a whole chicken or turkey, tuck or tie the legs and wings close to the body. This helps keep them from burning before the interior of the bird is done.

So, What About That Thanksgiving Turkey?

Won't your friends and family be impressed when you've cooked your holiday turkey on the grill? Can a brisket be far behind?

Of course, what you don't have to reveal to your friends is that cooking large pieces of poultry on the grill requires more time and patience than skill. Besides yielding a totally luscious bird, cooking turkey on the grill frees up your oven for the side dishes. And as anyone who's juggled a holiday menu knows, that's no minor consideration.

Here's how to do grill a 12 to 14 pound (5.5 to 6.3 kg) turkey (enough to feed 8 to 10 people, with leftovers), step by step:

1. The No. 1 important step: Make sure your grill is large enough to hold the turkey you have in mind! A tabletop

Don't Get Burned!

Food safety experts recommend not stuffing turkey or other whole poultry, but instead cooking the stuffing on the side. The raw poultry juices drip into the stuffing, which may not get hot enough to kill salmonella and other bacteria by the time the meat is cooked through.

model won't cut it here. The average grill has a large enough cooking grid to accommodate a 12 to 14 pound (5.5 to 6.3 kg) turkey, but you also need to make sure the lid is deep enough to cover the grill with no gaps. If in doubt, take a measuring tape to the store. (If nothing else, it will amuse your fellow shoppers.)

2. If the turkey is frozen, you'll have to thaw it first. Remove it from the freezer to the refrigerator a good 2 1/2 days before you plan to cook it. A 12 to 14 pound (5.5 to 6.3 kg) turkey shouldn't take more than 2 days to thaw, but the extra half day is "insurance" in case your refrigerator runs a bit colder than normal.

3. If you like, you can marinate the turkey for a couple of hours in a mixture of white wine, a little olive oil, and herbs of your choice. This is just for flavour, and not necessary for tenderness; the fat from the skin will baste the turkey nicely.

4. Remove the neck and giblets from the body cavities (usually there will be two bags, one in the neck cavity and one in the tail end). Rinse the turkey inside and out, and pat it dry.

5. Place the turkey on a roasting rack in a heavy-duty foil roasting pan. Tuck the legs and wings in to streamline the turkey's shape as much as possible. For best results, fold down the flap of neck skin to cover the cavity, and tie the legs together with cotton string or twine. If the turkey has a metal piece holding the legs in place, leave it in place (that is, if you can get the giblets out without removing it). If you like, you can stick a couple of garlic cloves, some lemon or orange slices, or bay leaves in the cavity. Brush the outside of the bird with a little melted butter or olive oil.

6. Prepare your charcoal or gas grill for indirect heat. Refrigerate the turkey while the coals heat.

7. Place the turkey, in its roasting pan, on the center of the cooking grid over the drip pan (or in a gas grill, the burner(s) that's off). Grill for 11 to 13 minutes per pound (24 to 28.5 per kilogram), or until a thermometer inserted into the thickest part of the thigh reads 180°F (82°C). The drumsticks should move easily when wiggled. The total cooking time will be about 2 1/4 to 3 hours. Adjust the time upward if you're grilling in a snowstorm.

8. If you are using a charcoal grill, you will have to replenish the charcoal every now and then. Check the coals every 45 minutes, and add more lit coals as necessary.

9. Let the turkey stand for 15 minutes, then carve it.

You can cook a turkey breast or breast roast the same way. Grill it to an internal temperature of 170°F (77°C). You also can cook turkey legs over indirect heat, to a temperature of 180°F (82°C).

Types of Poultry, and How to Prepare and Grill Them

Regardless of type, most whole birds should be cooked over indirect heat, and should stand for 15 minutes before carving, so the juices have a chance to settle.

Broiler/fryer

Young chickens weighing about 2 to 3 1/2 pounds (1 to 1.75 kg), these are mildly flavoured, tender, and a bit fatty. Whole broiler/fryers and large pieces are cooked indirectly. Figure on 45 minutes to an hour for a whole bird. Cut-up pieces (drumsticks, thighs, breast halves) can be cooked over direct heat.

Free-Range Chicken

A broiler-fryer that's been raised in the yard, rather than in cages. Most free-range birds also are raised without the use of feed additives, hormones, and so on. Aficionados (who include us) say they have a slightly richer flavour than conventionally raised chicken. They tend to be smaller, averaging 1 1/2 to 3 1/2 pounds (0.75 to 1.75 kg). Unless they're butterflied or cut into serving pieces, they should be cooked over indirect heat.

Chicken Wings

Brush them lightly with sauce and cook briefly over direct heat. Because you cannot really remove the skin without removing much of the meat, wings do tend to be high in fat—which is probably why they're so popular. Snip off the wing tips before grilling so they won't burn.

What's What

The most famous chicken wing dish is undoubtedly Buffalo wings, named for the city in New York where they originated at the Anchor Bar Restaurant. To make them, you snip the wings in two (making a mini-"drumstick" and a wing portion), marinate them in a spicy red pepper rub, and grill. If your calorie and fat allotment allow, you can drizzle them with a mixture of butter, lemon juice, and hot sauce before serving. Buffalo wings are traditionally served with celery sticks and a blue cheese dip.

Capon

The traditional roasting chicken, a capon is a male bird that has been castrated to make it fatter. An average bird weighs in at about 6 to 8 pounds (2.7 to 3.5 kg). It has a bit more fat than a broiler/fryer. You should grill-roast capon whole, over indirect heat.

Cornish Hen

These small (16 to 20 oz., or 450 to 550 g), fairly lean birds have a mild flavour. If they're butterflied, they can be cooked over direct heat; otherwise, cook them by the indirect method.

Duck and Goose

These birds are so fatty that it's best not to cook them over direct heat; you'll have nothing but one flare-up after another. However, they're both great cooked over indirect heat or, even better, slow-cooked in a smoker.

Boneless duck breast is great on the grill. Unfortunately, it's also rather hard to find outside of gourmet markets and some meat markets. You can buy it mail order (see Appendix C: Resources). Duck breast is a rich, full-bodied meat that needs little dressing up. Cook it with the skin on direct heat, but off to the side a bit so it's not right over the coals. It will cause flare-ups.

Because of different processing methods, duck is less subject to salmonella than chicken is. Thus, duck breast often is served with some pink in the middle.

Both duck and goose are dark meat poultry, and often are served with red wine.

Quail

Tiny birds that usually weigh in at about 3 to 6 ounces (90 to 180 g). Plan on two per serving. They are small enough to be cooked over direct heat. Quail have lean, dark meat that's a bit on the chewy side, and benefit from being marinated for an hour or two. You'll find fresh or frozen quail in some Asian markets (they're popular in Vietnamese cooking), gourmet food stores, and some larger supermarkets.

Squab

Somewhat larger than quail but rarely bigger than Cornish hens, squab are actually . . . well, pigeons. We hasten to add that these are not the cooing intruders that poop all over your windowsill, but young, domesticated pigeons that have never flown, making them nice and plump and tender. Squab usually weigh under a pound (500 g), and can be grilled like Cornish hens. They're available frozen, and occasionally fresh, in some gourmet markets.

Ground Turkey or Chicken

Depending on whether it's just the breast meat or has the skin ground in as well, ground turkey can be very lean, or as fatty as ground beef. Grill it the same way you grill lean ground beef, being very careful not to overcook it. Brushing turkey breast burgers with a little olive oil helps keep them moist.

Turkey or Chicken Sausages

Generally lower in saturated fat, and usually total fat, than their all-beef or pork cousins, turkey and chicken sausages come in all sorts of flavours these days, from Italian to bratwurst to California-style with garlic and sun-dried tomatoes. Grill them as you would any sausage, but be extra careful not to overcook them since they can be leaner than their porky counterparts.

Actually, regardless of the type of sausage, we find it often works best to simmer the sausages first, then just heat them through on the grill.

Flavours That Go Well with Poultry

Both rich and delicate, poultry is a good foil for nearly any flavour you match it with. That's why the "poultry herbs" include just about all of them: basil, rosemary, dill, oregano, garlic, marjoram, lavender, cilantro, sage, and tarragon. Citrus, especially lemon, is also a good friend to chicken and turkey, as is nearly any white wine. Among the sweet spices, ginger, nutmeg, and allspice are great paired with poultry.

Duck, goose, and dark-meat chicken are rich and hearty enough to go with a "deeper" range of flavours, such as sherry, soy, Chinese fermented black beans, thyme, or red wine.

Fruit is fabulous with all poultry. Try Cornish hens or duck with grilled plums for a memorable feast. Cranberry sauce, of course, is a natural with turkey.

Smoke chicken over pecan or fruit woods. Duck or goose is assertive enough to stand up to hickory and possibly even mesquite.

Hot Tip

Chinese-style tea-smoked duck or chicken is delicious. Mix 1/2 cup (125 mL) loose black tea with 1 cup (250 mL) brown sugar, and place it in the centre of a double thickness of aluminum foil. Fold up the edges of the foil slightly. Place the tea packet right on the coals in your smoker. Or, put it on the coals or heat diffusers in a regular grill, cooking the poultry by the indirect method.

The Least You Need to Know

➤ Chicken breasts and other small or thin pieces should be cooked directly over the coals.

➤ Whole poultry is best cooked over indirect heat.

➤ There are very few seasonings that don't go with poultry.

Chapter 13

The Angle on Fish

In This Chapter

➤ The basics of fish preparation and grilling

➤ The basics of shellfish preparation and grilling

➤ Flavours that go well with fish and shellfish

You may never have enjoyed the memorable pleasure of catching a rainbow trout, or walleye, or salmon, and cooking it over a fire that very same afternoon. Or of digging up clams and roasting them in a pit in the bracing salt air. But even if you don't fish, you have access to very fresh fish and shellfish, thanks to the wonders of modern transportation. A snapper that was merrily swimming around the Gulf Coast a couple of days ago can be jetted into Toronto in time for today's fish delivery, and be on your plate tonight.

Farm raising of fish has made a difference as well. It has its drawbacks (as anyone who's tasted farm-raised salmon side by side with its wild cousin can attest), but it has made really fresh salmon, trout, mussels, and other delicacies readily available across the country.

Surveys show that North Americans still don't grill fish much. We think that's a real shame: there's no better way to cook a good piece of fish or shellfish. Grilling allows seafood to keep its native flavours, while acquiring an intriguing hint of char. And don't even get us started on the wonders of smoked salmon, or mussels, or shrimp, or trout . . .

Freshness Is Everything

Because fish and shellfish are highly perishable and begin to deteriorate soon after they're caught, it's essential to make sure you get the freshest piece of seafood possible.

Choosing a good fish market is the first step. First, the place should smell briny but clean. While occasional smells are unavoidable, you definitely want to avoid anyplace that makes you want to hold your nose when you walk in. If there are strong fishy smells, it means the market's storage and/or cleanup practices aren't up to par. And that probably extends to the fish as well.

Second, the market should have a high turnover. If the shrimp and salmon look like they've been sitting in the case for a while, they have.

What's What

When a whole fish is *dressed*, that doesn't mean it's wearing clothes. It does mean that the fish has been scaled and gutted and is ready to cook.

Third, the folks behind the counter should exhibit some knowledge. If you ask where the shrimp is from and whether it's been frozen before, they should know. If you ask them for a good substitute for halibut on the grill, they should know that too.

Fourth, but not necessarily last, the cooked fish and shellfish should be segregated from the raw stuff. And, signs should clearly label fish as fresh, or as previously frozen (or as supermarkets like to say, "thawed for your convenience").

Buying It

So, you've found a good market. How do you judge the freshness of an individual piece of fish? Let us tell you the ways:

➤ With rare exceptions (walleye being the most notable), whole fish should have clear, not cloudy eyes. It should look pink or faintly red, not brown, around the gills.

➤ Fish fillets and steaks, as well as scallops and shrimp, should look moist and shiny, not dull or milky. If you're on friendly terms with the fishmonger, ask to touch and smell the fish. It should smell faintly briny or somewhat nutty and sweet, never like ammonia. When you touch a fish fillet or steak, the flesh should be elastic enough to spring back.

➤ The tail on a live lobster should curl under its body, and it should wave its antenna and look fairly interested.

➤ Crabs should move when you poke them.

➤ Mollusks such as oysters, clams, and mussels should have tightly closed shells. Occasionally mussels will open their shells slightly, but should snap them smartly shut when you tap the shell with a fingernail or rap it lightly on the counter. Discard any shellfish whose shells won't close. They're dead, and deteriorating rapidly.

Hot Tip

Maybe the No. 1 rule when buying fish is, be flexible. Freshness is essential with fish. If you want salmon, but the salmon doesn't look as fresh as the trout, get the trout instead.

If you buy frozen fish, be absolutely certain that it is frozen solid. Ideally, frozen fish should be in an undamaged, moisture and vapour proof wrapping. It should have no odor. If you detect any aroma, or notice any drying, white spots, deterioration, or spotting—or even suspect that the fish has been thawed and refrozen—do not buy it.

Fish Forms

Whole fish can be small, such as trout, or large, such as salmon. Small fish can be cooked over direct heat; large fish can be cooked over direct or indirect heat, depending on how thick it is and whether it's stuffed.

Fillets are cut lengthwise from the side of the fish and are usually boneless. They should go skin side down on the grill, and are not turned unless they're at least an inch thick.

Steaks are cut crosswise. Salmon, swordfish, mahi mahi, and other fairly firm fish are sold this way. It's safe to assume that any fish sold as steaks can be grilled.

Kebabs. These are 1 to 1 1/2 inch (2.5 to 4 cm) cubes cut from the steaks. You can cut kebabs from the fillets, but they'll be thinner pieces that may need to be threaded in 2 or 3 places on the skewers.

Storing and Thawing It

Fresh fish is very perishable; use it within 2 days of buying it. Use shellfish within one day. Frozen, raw fish will keep for 1 to 6 months. Plan to use frozen fish with a high fat content, such as salmon, within a month or two.

Never refreeze fish. It ruins the texture. You can store cooked fish in the refrigerator and use it within 2 days.

If you cannot cook the fish within a day or two, you'll have to freeze it. (This is assuming that it was fresh, not frozen, to begin with.) Plenty of fish markets and experienced anglers suggest placing fish fillets and steaks or live or cooked shellfish in a self-sealing freezer bag. Fill the bag with water, zip it shut, and put it in the freezer. (You can also pack the fillets in rinsed out milk cartons filled with water.) For whole fish or crab, they recommend that you freeze it for 48 hours, remove it from the freezer, dip it in water to form a glaze, then put it in a plastic bag and return it to the freezer. Both the water-in-the-bag method and the glazing method help prevent freezer burn.

Thaw fish in its wrapper in the refrigerator for 5 to 24 hours. Never thaw fish at room temperature. If necessary, you can thaw the fish quickly by placing it, still tightly wrapped, in cold water. It will take about 1 hour per pound to thaw it by this method; refresh the water every 30 minutes. Frozen fish can also be thawed in the microwave on 10 percent power for 10 to 15 seconds. Repeat the cycles until the fish is nearly thawed. Let it stand for another minute or two, then cook it immediately.

Great Catches on the Grill

Hot Tip

Have a second pair of tweezers (you know, the type you use to pluck your eyebrows) reserved for kitchen use. They're indispensable for picking those bones out of fillets that the fish market missed.

As long as it's been cleaned, fish needs little preparation before cooking. Just rinse it under cold running water and pat it dry. If you're cooking fillets, remove any bones you find with tweezers. (For steaks, it's easier to remove the bones after cooking. You can marinate it if you like; white wine and olive oil marinades are good with fish.)

If the fish is not marinated, brush it very lightly with olive oil or canola oil before cooking it. Keep it refrigerated until the coals are ready.

Except for large, whole fish, nearly all fish and shellfish cook quickly, over direct heat. Another exception is smoked fish, which, of course, you slow-cook in a smoker. You can cook thin fillets of fish that are still frozen, as long as you allow a little extra time.

Besides the fact that fish skin is much easier to remove after the fish is cooked than when the fish is raw, it adds flavour, so leave it on during grilling. It does tend to stick to the cooking grid, though, so make sure both the skin and the grid are well-oiled.

Keep fish refrigerated until it's time to put it on the grill. This not only helps keep it safe, but slows the cooking time so the fish will absorb more flavour from the smoke and aromatics. Don't salt fish or shellfish before cooking, as this will toughen it.

Fishy Flavours

Because you really should buy the freshest fish (and hopefully, one that also happens to be on sale), here's a chart showing how fish can be substituted for each other. The fish in each column can be substituted for one another. Note that this chart is based on flavour only; you may have to adjust cooking methods or times when you substitute fish.

Mild, sweet: sea bass, striped bass, grouper, snapper, halibut, mahi mahi, ocean perch, freshwater perch, catfish (farm-raised), cod, scrod, flounder, haddock, pollack, orange roughy, ono, sole

Medium-mild, distinct: tuna (all kinds), pompano, salmon (farm-raised), shark, swordfish, rainbow and brook trout, walleye, whitefish

Oily, distinctive flavour: Bluefish, mackerel, lake trout, salmon (wild)

Firm-textured fish are great on the grill; they don't fall apart, and can be used for kebabs. They include such favourites as catfish, grouper, ono, shark, swordfish, and tuna.

Thin, delicate fillets, such as sole, whitefish, or cod, can be cooked on the grill. Rather than laying them directly on the grid, lay some orange, lemon, or lime slices, sliced peppers or onions, or sprigs of tarragon or other herbs on the grid, then lay the fish atop them (oil it first). Cover the grill, and do not turn the fish during cooking. Delicate fish can also be cooked in an oiled grill basket, on a nonstick grill screen, or on a double-thickness of oiled aluminum foil into which you've poked a bunch of holes.

Fish also is an excellent choice for smoking. Whitefish, trout, salmon, shrimp, and mussels are very good smoked.

The classic cooking rule for fish is 10 minutes per inch (2.5 cm) of thickness, regardless of the type of fish or cooking method. About 90 percent of the time, it works like a charm. Fish is done when it turns opaque (but not dry) and flakes when prodded with a fork. Or use a thermometer; fish must cook to an internal temperature of at least 145°F (63°C).

What's What

What, exactly, do we mean by *flake*? If you look at a fish fillet, you'll see that it's in sections, marked by faint lines in the flesh. When you prod cooked fish gently with a fork, these sections will begin to separate into pieces that look like large flakes. The same test works for most fish steaks, although they'll flake lengthwise instead of horizontally. However, the fish should not fall into pieces when you prod it; if it does, it's overcooked.

123

Marvellous Mollusks

If you like oysters raw on the half-shell, you'd better learn to shuck them, or order them out in restaurants. But if you want to cook your mollusks—whether you're talking mussels, oysters, or clams—on the grill, the good news is that there's no reason to pry open the shells and risk losing a thumb. Just put them on the grill, and when they get hot enough, the shells will pop open. Nothing could be easier.

What's What

Just so this doesn't come as a shock, shellfish is called that because it has shells. Shellfish are divided into *mollusks* such as clams and mussels, which live inside hard shells, and *crustaceans*, which include shrimp, lobster, crayfish, and similar critters who wear their skeletons on the outside.

Mollusks and small crustaceans such as shrimp should be cooked on a grill screen so that they don't fall between the wires of the cooking grid. And unlike most foods, they're cooked over red-hot (glowing) coals. This heats them through quickly without turning them to rubber. Be very careful not to overcook shellfish; you want them to stay plump and juicy.

Mussels: These days, nearly all mussels are farm-raised and very clean. Just lightly scrub them, snip any "beards" (seaweed) hanging from the shells, and they're ready.

Clams: When they're harvested, most clams clamp their shells shut, trapping sand and other stuff inside. This can make them gritty. To purge them of sand and other impurities, put the clams in salt water (1/3 cup or 75 mL of salt to 1 gallon or 3.8 L of water) to which you've added a handful of cornmeal. Leave them for an hour. Drain off the water and debris, scrub the clams under cold water, and they're all set for the grill.

Scallops: Fortunately, these mollusks are nearly always shelled before they come to market. They require no preparation before cooking, other than an optional marinade. You can grill bay scallops, but they are so small they have to be grilled quickly and on a grill screen. Sea scallops (about the size of a jumbo marshmallow) work best on the grill. If fresh ones are not available, frozen scallops are acceptable.

Oysters: You can thread shucked oysters on skewers (they're really good alternated with pieces of soft-cooked bacon) and cook them, kebab style, over direct heat.

Crispy Crustaceans

Crustaceans do need a certain amount of preparation before cooking, but if you're smart,

Hot Tip

Although any kind of clams will cook on the grill, we suggest using the smaller varieties, such as cherry-stones, for grilling. They're generally more tender than the larger clams. Clams are available on both the West Coast and the East Coast.

you'll have the fishmonger do it. Note that crustaceans sold live, such as lobsters and crabs, must be cooked within hours of being killed and cleaned. So if you have the fishmonger clean them, buy them the same day you plan to grill them.

Lobsters: For quicker cooking, ask the fishmonger to butterfly the lobsters for you. If you cannot buy them the same day you'll be cooking them, you will have to buy them whole (that is, live) and refrigerate them. You can try butterflying them yourself: Put the lobster on its back, and with a very sharp knife, make a deep slit from thorax to tail. Then cut the lobster in half lengthwise without cutting through the topshell. Open and press the lobster flat, and remove and discard the stomach and the white intestinal vein. The green tomalley (liver) and roe can be left in place.

If all this is too much for you, serve lobster tails or grill them whole after killing them (plunge a knife through the lobster right below the head). You can buy them frozen.

More to the point is how you eat a whole lobster. Pick the cooked lobster up in one hand and with the other hand, twist off the claws, one at a time. Pick up the lobster cracker (a tool that resembles a nutcracker) in your right hand, insert one of the lobster claws into it, and press down hard until the shell breaks. Break the lobster claw-shell in several places. Remove as much of the shell as possible with your fingers and eat the meat from both claws.

Next, pick up the whole lobster, holding the tail in one hand and the body/head section in the other, and bend the lobster up in the middle so it cracks in half; you'll have one section in each hand. Lay the tail section down and hold the body/head section belly side up. Stick your thumb between the meat and the shell and lift, using your fingers to pull the meat out of the shell. Break off the tiny claw-legs connected to the meat you've removed and reserve them for a moment. Then remove the second, softer undershell, called the belly shell.

Next, discard the black vein that runs the length of the body meat. You should also discard the small sac at the base of the lobster's head called the sand sac. Everything else—including the tomalley (green-coloured liver)—is safe to eat. You may even find some coral-coloured roe (eggs), if your lobster is female. Both the tomalley and the roe are delicious.

Finally, pick up the tail section. Bend the tail back and break the flippers off the end. Insert a lobster fork into the hole you've made and gently push the tail meat out the other end. Remove the black vein that runs the length of the tail and discard. To eat the small claw legs, put the open end of each into your mouth, and suck out the meat as if using a straw.

Or with a sharp knife or scissors, cut away the translucent membrane from the tail meat, then use the knife to pry the lobster meat from the shell.

Shrimp: They can be shelled before or after cooking. To shell shrimp, tear open the shell on the inside of the curve (where the legs are), then peel off the rest of the shell. Although it is perfectly safe to eat the shrimp without removing the black sand vein located along the curved back, it is usually preferable to remove it for aesthetic purposes. Make a shallow cut down the back of the peeled shrimp and wash the black vein out under cold running tap water. Or slip the tip of a small knife underneath it and pull it out. If you wish to cook the shrimp in their shells, split the shell down the back and remove the vein without removing the shell.

Soft-Shell Crabs

Although they look pretty passive in the fish case, crabs are sold live (unless they're already cooked). Have the friendly fishmonger clean them for you, and plan to grill them the same day you buy them. Soft-shell crabs are superb on the grill; just brush them with butter, and cook. You eat the shell right along with the meat.

If you grill hard-shell crabs, you follow basically the same procedure, with variations of course, that you do for getting the meat out of a lobster: crack, pick, and pry.

Flavours That Go Well with Fish and Shellfish

Citrus (lemon, lime, orange, tangerine, and sometimes grapefruit) was born to go with fish of any kind. The same holds true for dill and tarragon. Cilantro, fennel, and basil also are "fish-friendly."

Woods and aromatics: Try looking around your garden. Dried lilac twigs, soaked for 30 minutes, drained and scattered on the hot coals, delicately flavour fish. Alder is a time-honoured smoking wood for fish, especially Northwest salmon. Be careful of hickory, mesquite, or other strong-flavoured woods, which can overpower delicate fish. However, stronger fish such as mackerel or salmon can stand up to bold flavours.

The Least You Need to Know

➤ The fresher the fish or shellfish, the better.

➤ Handle and cook fish gently.

➤ Never refreeze fish.

➤ Never cook mussels, clams, or oysters whose shells stay open before cooking, or serve those that aren't open after cooking.

➤ "Ten minutes per inch [2.5 cm]" is a good cooking rule for fish.

Chapter 14

Fruits, Vegetables, and Grains

In This Chapter

➤ Grilling methods that work well with vegetables and fruits

➤ Which fruits and vegetables grill well, and how to prepare them

➤ Grain foods that can be grilled, and how to prepare them

➤ Flavours that go well with vegetables and grains

Grilling is usually associated with meat. That's probably a natural side effect of culinary evolution. Our forebears needed to build pits for cooking animals. They did roast the occasional root vegetable as well, but tended to eat a lot of their veggies raw and their fruits raw or dried.

With the modern grill, it's silly not to cook vegetables and fruits this way. Many of them taste downright luscious on the grill, and it's simply a matter of putting your equipment and fuel to good use. While you're grilling six hamburgers, why not brown some potato skins as well?

Most vegetables and fruits need to be cut or sliced before they go on the grill. That also means they have to be cooked on a grill screen, or threaded on skewers.

If you're cooking a roast or whole chicken over indirect heat, toss some vegetables on the grill as well, during the last 15 to 20 minutes of the meat's cooking time. Simply put them on a double-thickness of foil, add a tablespoon or two of water, and seal up the foil into a loose package. The vegetables should get tender-crisp in 15 to 30 minutes, depending on the type of vegetable.

Vegetables

These vegetables are especially suited for grilling.

Artichokes

You'll need to use either fresh baby artichokes—the kind that can be eaten whole, with just a little trimming—frozen artichoke hearts, or marinated artichokes from a jar. Drain them well before grilling. They're great seasoned with rosemary, parsley, and/or basil; or with garlic and a squeeze of lemon.

Asparagus

This one's easy. Just trim the woody bottoms from the stalks, brush the stalks lightly with oil, and grill until they begin to brown.

Beets

Because they're so dense, beets can be tricky. You can wrap them in foil and cook them right in the embers, like potatoes. But it's probably easier to boil them until they're fork-tender but still firm. Drain them, peel them, cut them in half, brush them lightly with oil, and char on the grill. If you like, soak them in an orange juice-based marinade for an hour first. They have a high sugar content and can burn easily, so keep an eye on them.

Don't Get Burned!

Because they're high in sugar, fruits—and some vegetables—burn very easily. Grill them over the charcoal after it's started to cool down (or on a gas grill at 250 to 300°F, or 120 to 148°C). And keep an eye on them, removing them from the grill as soon as they begin to lightly brown.

Hot Tip

To trim asparagus, just hold the stalk toward the bottom and bend gently until the paler, woody bottom snaps off. Discard the bottom.

Carrots

They're very good grilled, but really need to boiled briefly first, or cooked by the foil-packet method. Brush them lightly with butter or oil, and sprinkle with mint or tarragon.

Corn

The classic way to grill corn is as whole ears. Old-time recipes will tell you to first use roasting ears—whatever that means. You're likely to have one or two varieties of sweet corn to choose from—whatever your store or farmers market is selling that day. Just about all the sweet corn sold these days is the sugar-enhanced stuff that can burn easily on the grill.

The most common method is to pull down the husks of each ear, but without pulling them off. Remove as much of the silk as possible. Replace the husks, and tie the top. Soak the ears of corn in a tub of cold water for at least 30 minutes, and preferably an hour or so. Then put on the grill over medium-hot coals. Cover, and grill for at least a half-hour.

However, for the sake of convenience and excellent flavour, we find it works a bit better to husk the ears, cut them into three pieces each, and just grill directly for about 6 minutes, turning them 2 or 3 times, until slightly charred. You don't need to soak the corn when you use this method, though you should lightly brush it with butter or oil.

Eggplant

Small eggplants just need to be trimmed.

Trim off the cap of the eggplant and cut it lengthwise into 1/4 to 1/2 inch (0.5 to 1 cm) slices. Grill directly over the coals, turning at least 2 or 3 times, until lightly charred and tender. This can take a good 20 minutes.

Garlic

Grill-roasted garlic is a real treat. Peel off the outermost papery skin, but leave the inner skin intact. Leave the head of garlic whole; don't separate the cloves. Brush it lightly with olive oil, then wrap it loosely in foil. (This keeps it from charring and turning acrid.) Cook over direct heat for about 30 minutes, or indirect heat for about 45 minutes, or until the garlic softens enough that you can squeeze it out of its skin, like toothpaste.

Hot Tip

Some eggplants, especially the larger, seedier ones, tend to be bitter. To avoid this, slice the eggplant, salt the slices on both sides, and let the eggplant drain in a colander for 20 to 30 minutes. Rinse, then pat dry. This draws out the bitter juices.

Mushrooms

These are great on the grill. An especially good grilling mushroom is the Portobello. Brush the whole or sliced caps with oil, sprinkle with marjoram or rosemary, and grill until browned and tender, about 4 minutes for smaller caps, 10 minutes for very large ones. Smaller mushrooms can be grilled the same way.

What's What

Its fancy name aside, the *Portobello* (also called *Portabella*) is essentially just a large *Cremino*, or brown domesticated mushroom. You can buy whole mushrooms or the sliced caps in the produce department. Portobellos have a very chewy (some might say meaty) texture and deep flavour that make them a good meat alternative. They're good on pizzas and in sandwiches, or as an appetizer, grilled and sprinkled lightly with herbs.

Onions

It's best to cut these into thick rings or wedges. Brush lightly with olive oil and cook over direct heat (but not the hottest part of the grill) for about 10 minutes, or until lightly charred and tender. Green onions (scallions) are really good grilled; just trim, brush with oil, and grill for about 5 minutes.

Peas

For obvious reasons, you can't grill regular old round peas on the grill, even with a screen. Snow peas and snap peas, though, can be lightly grilled, either directly for a minute or two, or in foil packets for a few minutes. Cook them just until they turn bright green.

Peppers

To roast peppers, leave them whole. Place them on the grill over medium-hot or glowing-hot coals. When the pepper is charred and blistered, rotate it a quarter turn (or turn it over if it's a fairly flat pepper) and roast that side. Continue until the pepper is charred all over. While it's still hot, place it in a heavy-duty self-sealing plastic bag for 5 minutes to steam. Then remove them from bag, and pull and scrape the skin off under cold running water. Cut off the stem, cut the pepper in half lengthwise, and remove the core and seeds. Serve immediately, refrigerate for up a week, or put the peppers in freezer bags, seal tightly, and freeze.

Potatoes

Potatoes can be wrapped in foil, pierced in several places, and cooked either on the grid over indirect heat or right in the coals (charcoal grill only). They'll take anywhere from 45 to 90 minutes to cook. Serve immediately, or refrigerate.

Summer Squash

Zucchini and yellow squash are very good on the grill. Just slice them lengthwise, brush them with some olive oil, sprinkle with a few herbs, and grill for a couple of minutes on each side.

Sweet Potatoes

Sweet potatoes can be wrapped in foil and cooked in the embers, like regular potatoes, for about 60 to 90 minutes, depending on their size. Or, boil or microwave the sweet potatoes until tender but still firm, cut them in half lengthwise, brush with a bit of butter or oil, and grill, cut side down, until charred. Sprinkle them with candied ginger.

Tomatoes

Cherry tomatoes are a longtime standard on kebabs. Or cut larger tomatoes in half lengthwise, salt lightly if desired, brush with oil, and grill cut side down. Tomatoes should be grilled only briefly so they don't get too soft.

Winter Squash

Winter squash can be cooked over indirect heat, just like you would bake it in the oven. Pierce it in several places, and cook until fork-tender.

Vegetables You Can't Grill

Lettuce, spinach, cabbage, cucumbers, radishes, celery. They'll either shrivel, or grilling will bring out their bitterness. Save them for the salad. Oh, and olives. Theoretically you could probably grill them, but why would you? And forget avocados; they'd turn to mush.

Fruits

One of the simplest, best-tasting desserts of all is grilled fruit, plain or sprinkled with a bit of sugar. A hint of smokiness beautifully enhances the sweetness of bananas, kiwifruit, melon, oranges—you name it. For a taste-tempting selection of fruit-based desserts, see Chapter 23.

Do remember that because of its sugar content, fruit burns easily. Be sure to keep an eye on it while it cooks.

Apples

These are very nice on the grill, either as a dessert or as a side to savoury foods such as fish or pork. Core and slice them, brush lightly with butter, and grill just until tender and beginning to brown.

Bananas

These were born for the grill. They discolour, so they should be peeled and sliced lengthwise shortly before grilling. Sprinkling them with a little lemon or lime juice will help keep them from turning too brown. Brush them with a bit of melted butter, sprinkle lightly with cinnamon, nutmeg, or allspice, and grill, cut side down, until they just begin to caramelize. Grilled bananas are out of this world with vanilla ice cream or frozen yogurt.

Cantaloupe

Remove the peel and seeds and cut it into wedges or slices. Brush with a little oil, sprinkle lightly with brown sugar, and grill just until warmed through.

Citrus Fruits

These make a great foil for fish, pork, and poultry. Lemons and limes can be sliced and put under fish, or used as a flavouring agent in the drip pan. Grapefruit makes a tangy relish for fish. Directly grilling lemons and limes could make them acrid, but orange sections or slices are great sprinkled with sugar and briefly warmed on the grill.

Kiwifruit

This one's easy. Cut it in half crosswise, brush lightly with oil or butter, and grill, cut side down, just until toasted a bit. Your guests can scoop the fruit out with spoons to eat it.

Tasty Tidbit

Did you know that a medium kiwifruit has more vitamin C than an orange? In fact, the jewel-green fruits also are excellent sources of fibre, potassium, and vitamin E. All this, and they're good-looking, too. Don't put them in a gelatin mold, though; a substance in the kiwi inhibits jelling.

Mangoes

Marvellous. Cut lengthwise through the fruit on all four sides, cutting as close to the pit as possible. You'll want large, lengthwise slices. It may be easiest to leave the skin on until after they're cooked. Brush the mango slices lightly with butter and grill, cut side down, just until they begin to lightly brown.

Papayas

Perfect. Prepare them like cantaloupe.

Peaches or Nectarines

Fabulous when brushed with a bit of melted butter and/or melted peach jam. Peaches should be peeled first. You'll have to cut up the fruit just before grilling it, since it can discolour.

Pears

They're great. Prepare them like apples.

Pineapple

Here's another fruit that was born to be grilled. Grill thick pineapple rings (preferably fresh) just until lightly browned. Sprinkle with a bit of rum and/or brown sugar if you prefer.

Legumes and Grains on the Grill

No, you probably don't want to cook beans on the grill—although placing a pan of already baked beans over charcoal can infuse them with a pleasing smokiness. But tofu grills beautifully. So do breads and polenta (cooked cornmeal). You can even brown cake on the grill. Pair it with grilled fruit for a superb finish to your meal.

Hot Tip

Polenta, or cooked cornmeal, is instant gratification on the grill. Buy a log of prepared polenta, slice off pieces, brush them lightly with olive oil, and grill. Top them with just about anything you like: salsa, spaghetti sauce, chopped fresh tomatoes and pesto, grilled onions.

Breads

The heat on a grill is a bit too variable to successfully bake most breads from scratch. You can bake a pizza crust, though (see page 220), and warm up tortillas and other breads of every description.

Cake

No, you can't bake it on the grill, of course. But you can slice a dense cake such as pound cake, brush it lightly with butter, and lightly toast it on the grill. Superb! For more information and for recipes incorporating grilled cake, see Chapter 23.

Tasty Tidbit

Once found only in health food stores, vegetarian burgers have a pretty good slot in the freezer case these days. They're made of various ingredients, including tofu, soy protein, cracked wheat, mushrooms, cheese, grated vegetables, and seasonings. They vary widely in flavour; experiment with brands to see which one you like. All are far lower in saturated fat than beef burgers. Because they are so lean, you should brush the vegetarian burgers lightly with olive oil before grilling them

Tofu

Also known as soybean curd, this is actually more of a protein food than a vegetable. Firm tofu, with the liquid squeezed out of it, is very good on the grill. Squeeze out the liquid by cutting the tofu into 1/2 inch (1 cm) thick slices; place between paper towels, and gently but firmly press on the tofu.

Tofu takes well to any marinade, and will absorb flavours like a sponge. Just marinate it in your favourite barbecue sauce (or in a mixture of soy sauce and molasses), pat dry, and grill on an oiled grill screen until golden and crusty.

Flavours That Go Well with Vegetables and Grains

You normally don't have to marinate fruits and vegetables, although you can if you want to add some flavour. In general, sweet herbs and spices go with sweet vegetables, and salty or sweet-salty sauces are nice with more bitter vegetables. Try ginger, hoisin sauce, or barbecue sauce. Rosemary goes with an incredible array of vegetables and fruits. So does basil.

For smoking, pick fruit woods for sweet vegetables: apple or pear for sweet potatoes, and so on. Pecan goes beautifully with all vegetables. Be careful about using strong flavours such as hickory or mesquite with starchy foods such as potatoes, or with tofu; they can absorb quite a bit of smoke, becoming unpleasantly bitter.

The Least You Need to Know

➤ Vegetables and fruits can be cooked or warmed very successfully on the grill.

➤ Fruits burn easily on the grill, so keep an eye on them.

➤ You can't bake breads, other than pizza crust, from scratch on the grill, but you can warm them.

Chapter 15

A Second Life

In This Chapter

➤ Properly storing grilled leftovers

➤ Heating them up

➤ Soups, sandwiches, salads, and other dishes to use up grilled favourites

---

You will, of course, have no leftovers from your grilling parties. Everyone will gobble down every last bit of food and praise you for cooking it so beautifully. On the off chance, however, that you do have a scrap of tuna, chicken, or potato left, we want to point out that grilled foods taste wonderful in a vast variety of "recycled" soups, salads, and sandwiches.

We've put together a list of ideas for using up grilled leftovers. These are not recipes, but merely ideas. How you use them depends entirely on what you've grilled, how much you have left, and whatever ingredients you can scrounge up.

Storing Leftovers

Foods must be refrigerated promptly. If the barbecued chicken has been sitting out on your patio for 4 hours, toss it. Foods should be refrigerated, in shallow containers,

Hot Tip

Whenever you grill, try to cook more than you'll need. "Planned leftovers" make future meals much easier. This also means thinking ahead when you're thawing meats; take out not only the steaks for tonight's meal, but the chicken breasts you'll grill for tomorrow's dinner.

Don't Get Burned!

The microwave can turn meats into rubber if you overcook them. Start off at 80 percent power and short cycles (a minute or two), and repeat until the food is heated through. If your microwave does not have a rotating surface inside, turn the plate a quarter-turn between cycles.

within 1 hour of when they finished cooking. Cover them with plastic wrap so they don't dry out.

Grilled foods should be used within a few days. They may be frozen, although not for as long as raw foods. See Chapter 4 for specifics on storing foods.

Heating Them Up

The cardinal food safety rule—keep hot foods hot and cold foods cold—applies to cooked leftovers as much as it does to raw foods. You can slice that grilled steak cold from the refrigerator for a nice sandwich, but if you're going to heat it, heat it all the way through. While cooking does kill bacteria, foods pick up bacteria from the air, your knife, and even the plate you put them on. Bacteria thrive in that zone between 40 and 140°F (4.5 to 60°C).

One of the easiest ways to reheat leftovers is in the microwave. But it also poses a danger, because the microwave tends to cook foods from the outside in, meaning that chicken breast can look steaming hot on the outside and still be cool or warm in the centre. The most efficient way to reheat in the microwave is to cut food into slices or other small pieces, arrange it on a plate with the thickest portions facing out, and cover the plate loosely with waxed paper.

If you're using meats in soups or stir-fries, just add them to the dish and stir until they're heated through.

Creative "Recycling"

So, here are some ideas for fabulous soups, casseroles, salads, and sandwiches made with various grilled foods.

How you use leftovers depends on how they're seasoned. You don't really want to add chicken flavoured with basil and rosemary to a Chinese-style dish.

Poultry

➤ *Chicken noodle soup.* Heat up a large can of chicken broth. Toss in some grilled, diced chicken, some cooked spaghetti, and some sliced scallions and/or herbs. To make an even richer soup, toss any wing tips (raw) that you've saved into the boiling broth.

➤ *Chicken salad.* Cut the chicken into small cubes. Toss it with some chopped raw celery and onion, and cubed apples or pears, or halved grapes. Moisten with mayonnaise, French dressing, or another dressing of your choice. Serve in sandwiches or on a bed of lettuce.

➤ *Chicken Caesar.* Chop up some Romaine lettuce (or buy a bag or two already chopped). Cut the cooked chicken into strips. Mix the lettuce with some Caesar salad dressing. Add the chicken and a generous handful of grated fresh Parmesan cheese. Toss well. Top with seasoned croutons. If you like, you can finely chop a drained anchovy fillet or two and add it to the salad, or just wipe it around the bowl for subtle flavouring.

➤ *Chicken slaw.* Shredded, cold grilled poultry of any kind can be added to broccoli slaw or cabbage slaw. Add a handful of raisins and some coleslaw dressing, and toss.

➤ *Poultry-grain salad.* Chop the chicken or turkey and add it to stuffing (made from scratch or a mix), a grain salad, or tabbouleh (a bulgur salad of Middle Eastern origin—delicious).

Don't Get Burned!

Chicken should not be overcooked on the grill as it will get dry and tasteless. When the chicken begins to look done, cut into one piece and check the centre. The chicken is done when all traces of pink are gone but the juices still flow freely.

Tasty Tidbit

Caesar salad is not named for the man of "Et tu, Brute" fame—at least not directly. This Romaine lettuce salad, dressed with a garlic vinaigrette and tossed with grated Parmesan, is named after Italian chef Caesar Cardini, who supposedly created it in 1924 at his restaurant in Tijuana, Mexico.

➤ *Turkey deli sandwich.* Thinly slice grilled turkey, chicken, or duck. Put on toasted egg bread (such as challah) that has been spread with cream cheese and cranberry sauce.

➤ *Instant burritos.* Thinly slice the chicken and roll it up in warmed tortillas with refried beans and a light sprinkling of cheese. Serve with salsa.

Beef

➤ *Philly-style sandwich.* Thinly slice grilled steak. Reheat it and pile it on a length of French bread, with grilled onions and melted American cheese.

➤ *Beef and peppers.* An awesome combo. Thinly slice the beef and grilled red or green peppers, and pile between slices of French or Italian bread. Season with a bit of Italian dressing.

➤ *Tacos al carbon.* Spread guacamole thinly over a flour tortilla. Thinly slice grilled beef and roasted chiles, and arrange them evenly on the tortilla. Wrap up tightly, and cut crosswise in half.

➤ *Roast beef sandwich, deli style.* Put thinly sliced grilled beef on dark rye rolls with good pickles and a generous smear of grated horseradish.

➤ Chop up the meat and put it in chili.

➤ Cut the beef into cubes and add it to beef or vegetable stew (homemade or canned).

Pork

➤ *Pork and fruit salad.* Cold, seasoned pork is good sliced and served with apple wedges, sliced pears, or pineapple chunks.

➤ *Midwest-style sandwich.* Slice pork thinly and put between slices of whole-grain bread, with grainy brown mustard and thinly sliced red onions.

➤ *Quick stir-fry.* Cut pork into slices and add to a stir-fry with broccoli and hoisin or oyster sauce (to keep from overcooking the meat, add it to the stir-fry during the last minute or two, just to warm through).

➤ *Asian-inspired salad.* Cut cold pork into slices. Make a salad by arranging the pork on a plate with canned, drained mandarin oranges (or fresh orange or tangerine segments) and canned, drained water chestnuts. Drizzle with an orange, poppyseed, or sesame dressing, and sprinkle with chopped green onions.

➤ *Pork 'n beans.* Cut it into small cubes, and add to baked beans, either homemade or out of a can.

➤ *Pork fried rice.* Cut it into small cubes, and add it to fried rice or lo mein. (No need to make them yourself, either—just add the pork to your Chinese takeout favourites.)

Sausage or Ground Meats (any kind)

➤ *Skillet casserole.* Cut one or two baking potatoes into small cubes (you can peel or not, as you like) and cook in a bit of oil until nicely browned. Crumble the meat and add it to the potatoes, along with some chopped onion and whatever seasonings you like. Cook until the onion is tender and the meat is heated through. For an even quicker version of this dish, use frozen hash browns instead of fresh potatoes.

➤ Or, crumble the meat and add it to chili or spaghetti sauce.

➤ Sausage is good with beans of any kind.

Lamb

➤ *Lamb and bean salad.* Dice up lamb and add it to a can or two of drained cannelini or other white beans, along with chopped tomatoes (preferably grilled), chopped fresh sage, olive oil, and salt and pepper. This dish is good cold or hot.

➤ *Lamb tacos.* Roll the meat up in tortillas with grilled onions, tomatoes, and a bit of salsa.

➤ *Mediterranean rice salad.* Add lamb to cooked rice and some chopped artichokes (if you have them), and dress with a mixture of wine vinegar, olive oil, and mint.

➤ *Gyros-style sandwich.* Place slices of grilled lamb and grilled onions or roasted garlic in pita pockets. Add a dab of yogurt.

Fish and Shellfish

➤ *Tuna salad niçoise.* Arrange grilled cold tuna, separated into chunks, with green beans and potatoes on a plate. Drizzle with a white wine vinaigrette and a sprinkling of tarragon.

➤ *Scandinavian-inspired sandwiches.* Separate grilled fish (any kind, but salmon or tuna is especially good) into chunks, and put into pita bread pockets with cucumber salad, some mayonnaise or yogurt, and a sprinkling of dill.

➤ *Seafood pasta.* To angel hair pasta with Alfredo sauce, add scallops, cut in half; or fish (any kind), separated into chunks; or chopped crab.

➤ *Bagel spread.* Flake grilled salmon and mix with softened cream cheese and a sprinkling of chopped chives or dill to make a great topping for bagels.

Hot Tip

A nice marinara sauce (bottled or homemade) makes a great base for leftover grilled foods. Chop up grilled clams or mussels and toss them in. Or add grilled, crumbled beef, turkey, or sausage to the sauce. For a meatless sauce, toss in grilled, chopped artichokes or tomatoes.

➤ *Fish cakes.* Leftover crab, salmon, or tuna can be made into patties. To avoid making the already-cooked fish dry and mealy, mix it with mashed potatoes and some olive oil to moisten, and cook it gently, just until heated through.

➤ *Tropical shrimp salad.* Chop up grilled shrimp, moisten with a mayonnaise-style salad dressing, and serve in a sandwich or on a bed of lettuce. This is great with papaya or mango slices.

➤ *Greek-style shrimp.* Heat chopped onions in a little olive oil. Stir in chopped fresh or canned tomatoes (grilled tomatoes are great if you have them), a little red wine, some chopped fresh parsley, and a sprinkling of dried oregano. Cook over medium-high heat until the tomato sauce thickens slightly. Add chopped grilled shrimp and cook just until heated through. Sprinkle with crumbled feta cheese, and serve with plenty of Greek or Italian bread. This is also good with any white fish.

Hot Tip

Salad dressings aren't just for salads. Spread your favourite dressing thinly on bread, or drizzle it over the meat or other ingredients, when making sandwiches.

Vegetables

➤ *Mushroom sandwich.* Grilled Portobello mushrooms can be sliced and put in a sandwich with roasted peppers, grilled or thinly sliced raw onions, and a little mayonnaise or extra-virgin olive oil.

➤ *Almost beef Stroganoff.* Cook onions in a little oil, add grilled beef and grilled mushrooms, a little mustard, and a touch of nonfat sour cream. If the mixture is too dry, add a little beef broth. Serve with noodles. For a vegetarian version, just skip the beef.

➤ *Veggies Parmesan.* Season grilled summer squash or eggplant, tomatoes, and onions with fresh rosemary, basil, or oregano, some olive oil, and salt and pepper. Sprinkle with Parmesan cheese and bake in an oven at 350°F (175°C) until heated through, about 10 to 15 minutes. The same vegetables make a great topping for a pizza crust; top them with mozzarella and Parmesan. Or, chop all the vegetables up and use as a sauce for pasta.

➤ *Asian-style sweet potatoes.* Grilled sweet potatoes are great reheated and splashed with a bit of soy sauce, sesame oil, and sesame seeds. Top with chopped green onions if you like.

➤ *Grilled tomato sauce.* Just mash grilled tomatoes with some minced garlic (or roasted garlic), chopped fresh basil, and salt and pepper. This sauce is good hot or cold on pasta or polenta.

➤ *Sweet potato purée.* Peel and mash grilled sweet potatoes, put in an airtight container, and freeze. Thaw, and use as an ingredient in sweet potato pie or quickbreads.

➤ *Post-holiday sandwich.* Slice grilled sweet potatoes and layer them with sliced turkey and cranberry chutney between slices of white or millet bread.

➤ *Cold asparagus.* Grilled asparagus is great in a pasta salad. Or serve as is (cold), drizzled with a mixture of mayonnaise and orange juice.

➤ *Vegetarian gravy.* Heat grilled onions and/or mushrooms in a skillet with a little butter or oil. Sprinkle lightly with flour, then stir in a bit of vegetable broth. Cook until thickened. Use as a topping for noodles, toast, rice, or baked potatoes.

➤ *Nouveau mashed potatoes.* Grill-baked potatoes can be mashed with a bit of light sour cream or yogurt, and salt and pepper, and reheated in a microwave.

The Least You Need to Know

➤ Store cooked leftovers promptly.

➤ Cooked foods should either be served still cold, or reheated completely through.

➤ Grilled leftovers can be used in all kinds of dishes, from chili to sandwiches.

141

Part 4
Hot Stuff: The Recipes

Now that you know every last thing about grilling, it's time to dig in.

We've rated recipes as easy, intermediate, and advanced. Easy recipes require little more than mixing ingredients, marinating a meat, and grilling it. Intermediate recipes require some basic cooking skills in addition to grilling, or require a bit more grilling effort, such as cooking over indirect heat. Advanced recipes require more than basic skills, such as kneading bread.

Each recipe also includes an "At the Ready" notation. This tells you what you will need to have on hand near the grill either just before, during, or after cooking. You'll of course need to have serving plates, salads, beverages, silverware, and other obvious items ready. "At the Ready" includes only those tools or ingredients used in the actual recipe.

All recipes are based on these assumptions:

➤ *You'll be preparing a charcoal grill by piling up the coals, igniting them, spreading them out as they glow, then letting them burn to ash (medium-hot), unless otherwise instructed.*

➤ *If you have a gas grill, you'll be preheating it to high, then cooking over medium heat. (What constitutes "medium" may vary from grill to grill. On some grills, you'll set all the burners to medium, or 350 to 375°F (175 to 190°C); on others, you may need to turn one or more burners off to get the grill down to that temperature.)*

➤ *Unless otherwise stated, you will be cooking the food 4 to 6 inches (10 to 15 cm) above the coals. (Nonadjustable cooking grids are always at that height, so you're all set.)*

➤ *For smoked recipes, you are using a water smoker, rather than a wood smoker or a regular grill.*

Here's the Rub

It's the rub, marinade, or sauce that lifts a plain old hunk of grilled meat out of the ordinary. Although we've included suggested uses for these marinades and seasonings, feel free to experiment with different foods.

These rubs will spice up a variety of meats, poultry, fish, or vegetables. Use your hands to work them thoroughly into every nook and cranny of the food. If the rub mixture doesn't want to stick, lightly brush or rub the food with oil before rubbing in the spice mixture.

Prairie Dust All-Purpose Barbecue Spice Rub

Yield: About 1 1/4 cups (300 mL)

Level: Easy

Prep: 5 minutes

At the Ready: Mixing bowl, a self-sealing plastic bag or small covered container

This barbecue spice rub is especially good with beef, pork, and poultry, but can also perk up seafood and vegetables.

4 tablespoons (60 mL) paprika
2 tablespoons (25 mL) cayenne pepper
2 tablespoons (25 mL) salt
1 tablespoon (15 mL) garlic powder
1 tablespoon (15 mL) onion powder
1 tablespoon (15 mL) sugar

1 tablespoon (15 mL) mustard powder
1 tablespoon (15 mL) celery salt
1 tablespoon (15 mL) ground cumin
1 tablespoon (15 mL) ground black pepper
1 tablespoon (15 mL) chili powder

Stir paprika, cayenne, salt, garlic powder, onion powder, sugar, mustard powder, celery salt, cumin, black pepper, and chili together in a small bowl. Spoon the spice mixture into a container and seal tightly. Store it in the refrigerator or in the freezer. It will keep for several weeks, but it's best to use it as soon as possible.

What's What

Coarse kosher salt can be found in most grocery stores in the kosher food section. If not, you may find it in specialty food shops. If you cannot find coarse kosher salt, use coarse sea salt instead. But do not use pickling salt.

Montreal Steak Spice

Yield: About 1 1/2 cups (375 mL)   **Prep**: 5 minutes

Level: Easy   **At the Ready**: Mixing bowl, self-sealing plastic bag or small covered container

Montreal steak spice is a wonderful coarse spice blend that when used as a crust adds great flavour to steaks. It is also good on veal and pork

1/2 cup (125 mL) coarse kosher salt
1/4 cup (50 mL) cracked black pepper
2 tablespoons (25 mL) cracked coriander seeds
2 tablespoons (25 mL) dehydrated granulated garlic
2 tablespoons (25 mL) dehydrated granulated onion flakes
1 tablespoon (15 mL) mustard seeds
1 tablespoon (15 mL) cracked dill seeds

Stir kosher salt, black pepper, coriander, garlic, onion, mustard seeds, and dill seeds together in a small mixing bowl. Spoon the spice mixture into a container and seal tightly. Store it in the refrigerator or in the freezer. It will keep for several weeks, but it's best to use it as soon as possible.

Great Lakes Fish and Seafood Seasoning

Yield: About 1 1/2 cups   **Prep**: 5 minutes

Level: Easy   **At the Ready**: Mixing bowl , self sealing plastic bag or small covered container

This fish and seafood seasoning rub is delicious on grilled lake fish like pickerel, lake trout and bass, but is also good on salmon, halibut and shrimp

3 tablespoons (50 mL) lemon pepper seasoning
2 tablespoons (25 mL) sea salt
2 tablespoons (25 mL) dry rubbed thyme
2 tablespoons (25 mL) dry rubbed dill weed
1 tablespoon (15 mL) mustard powder
1 tablespoon (15 mL) dehydrated onion flakes
1 tablespoon (15 mL) dehydrated garlic

Stir the lemon pepper seasoning, sea salt, thyme, dill, mustard, onion, and garlic together in a small mixing bowl. Spoon the spice mixture into a container and seal tightly. Store it in the refrigerator or in the freezer. It will keep for several weeks, but it's best to use it as soon as possible.

Canadian Whiskey Barbecue Sauce

Yield: About 3 cups (750 mL)

Level: Intermediate

Cooking Time: 20 minutes

At the Ready: Saucepan, wooden spoon, covered container

This sauce (and all similar sauces) should be brushed on the food late in the cooking process, and/or served on the side. If you like your food a bit more charred, though, you can "break the rules" and brush the meat before grilling. Just be sure to watch the food carefully and turn it frequently, since the sugar in the sauce burns easily.

3 tablespoons (50 mL) vegetable oil
4 cloves garlic, minced
1 medium onion, minced
3/4 cup (175 mL) ketchup
2 ripe tomatoes, minced
1/4 cup (50 mL) cider or red vinegar
1/4 cup (50 mL) brown sugar

2 to 3 tablespoons (25 to 50 mL) Canadian whiskey, or to taste
1/2 cup (125 mL) water
Dash of Tabasco sauce, or to taste
1 tablespoon (15 mL) chili powder
2 teaspoons (10 mL) ground cumin

Heat the oil in a saucepan over medium heat. Add the garlic and onion and cook about 5 minutes, until tender, stirring occasionally. Stir in the ketchup, tomatoes, vinegar, brown sugar, whiskey, water, Tabasco, chili powder, and cumin. Reduce the heat to a simmer and continue cooking, uncovered, for 15 minutes, stirring occasionally. The sauce will thicken.

Remove the sauce from the heat and let it cool. Taste and adjust the seasonings. Pour the sauce into a container, cover tightly, and refrigerate until needed. The sauce will keep for up to a week.

Hot Tip

Use a marinade when you want to add a bit of zest to a food without overpowering its natural flavours. These acidic mixtures keep well, and can be made as long as a week in advance.

Herb Marinade for Fish

Yield: About 1 2/3 cups (400 mL)

Level: Easy

Prep: 15 minutes

At the Ready: Bowl, whisk, plastic self-sealing bag or covered container

1 cup (250 mL) vegetable oil or olive oil
1 teaspoon (5 mL) crumbled dry thyme
2/3 cup (150 mL) lime juice
1 teaspoon (5 mL) crumbled dry dill

2 cloves garlic, smashed
1/4 teaspoon (1 mL) freshly ground black pepper

Whisk the olive oil together with the juice in a glass bowl. Whisk in the garlic, herbs, and pepper. Taste and adjust the seasonings if necessary. Pour into a covered container or self-sealing plastic bag and refrigerate for up to a week.

Hot Tip

For the best flavour, use freshly squeezed citrus juices. Pasteurized or frozen juices are acceptable; use bottled juices only as a last resort. You can substitute lemon or orange juice in this marinade.

Orange or Tangerine Marinade for Poultry or Pork

Yield: 1 3/4 cups (425 mL)

Level: Easy

Prep: 15 minutes

At the Ready: Mixing bowl, whisk, self-sealing bag or covered container

1 cup (250 mL) cider vinegar
1 tablespoon (15 mL) dark-brown sugar
1/2 cup (125 mL) orange or tangerine juice

1 teaspoon (5 mL) paprika
1/4 cup (50 mL) vegetable oil
1 clove garlic, smashed

In a small bowl, mix together the cider vinegar, orange juice, oil, brown sugar, paprika, and garlic. Pour the marinade into a self-sealing plastic bag or a container, seal or cover tightly, and store in the refrigerator for up to a week.

Don't Get Burned!

If you want to use the remaining marinade as a brushing sauce, it must be brought to a boil first.

Ginger Marinade for Chicken or Pork

Yield: 1 scant cup (250 mL)

Level: Easy

Prep: 5 minutes

1/2 cup (125 mL) rice vinegar
2 cloves garlic, peeled and smashed
1/4 cup (50 mL) vegetable oil
2 tablespoons (25 mL) soy sauce

At the Ready: Mixing bowl, whisk, self-sealing plastic bag or covered container, ginger grater or paring knife

1 tablespoon (15 mL) grated or finely minced fresh ginger
1/2 teaspoon (2 mL) five-spice powder
Finely minced fresh ginger

In a small mixing bowl, whisk together the vinegar, oil, ginger, garlic, soy sauce, and five-spice powder. Place the marinade in a self-sealing bag or a container. Seal or cover tightly, and refrigerate it until you're ready to use it. Use it within a day or two. This recipe can easily be doubled.

Hot Tip

Five-spice, a mixture of cinnamon, cloves, fennel, star anise, and Sichuan peppercorns, is available in many supermarkets and Asian food stores.

Red Wine Marinade for Meat

Yield: About 1 1/2 cups (375 mL)

Level: Easy

Cooking Time: 5 minutes

At the Ready: Small saucepan, bowl, whisk, plastic self-sealing bag

1 cup (250 mL) dry red wine
1/4 cup (50 mL) red wine vinegar
2 tablespoons (25 mL) grainy mustard
1/4 cup (50 mL) vegetable oil, canola
   blend oil, or olive oil
3 cloves garlic, peeled and smashed

2 tablespoons (25 mL) sugar
2 tablespoons (25 mL) chopped fresh
   basil, or 1 tablespoon (15 mL) dried
   basil
1/4 teaspoon (1 mL) black pepper or
   crushed red pepper

In a small saucepan, whisk together the wine, vinegar, mustard, oil, garlic, sugar, basil, and pepper. Bring the marinade to a boil over medium heat. Reduce the heat to a simmer and continue cooking for 2 minutes, stirring occasionally. Let cool.

Do not use the marinade until it has cooled completely, as the warmth may encourage bacterial growth in uncooked meat. Store the marinade in a covered container or in a self-sealing plastic bag until ready to use. The marinade will keep in the refrigerator for several days, but it is best to use it soon.

Rosemary Brushing Marinade for Lamb

Yield: About 3/4 cup (175 mL)

Level: Easy

Prep: 10 minutes

At the Ready: Food processor or blender, mixing bowl, whisk, self-sealing plastic bag or small covered container

4 cloves garlic, peeled
1 small red onion, peeled, cut in half
1/4 cup (50 mL) olive oil
1/4 cup (50 mL) red wine
3 tablespoons (50 mL) fresh lemon juice
1 tablespoon (15 mL) fresh rosemary,

chopped, or 1 1/2 teaspoons (7 mL)
   dried rosemary
2 tablespoons (25 mL) fresh oregano,
   chopped, or 11/2 teaspoons (7 mL)
   dried oregano
1/4 teaspoon (1 mL) fresh ground black
   pepper

Using a food processor fitted with a steel blade, process the garlic and onion a few seconds until slushy. Add the oil, wine, lemon juice, rosemary, oregano, and pepper, and combine.

Pour the marinade into a self-sealing bag or a container. Seal or cover tightly, and refrigerate. Use within a couple of days.

151

Cranberry Raisin Ketchup

Yield: 1 1/2 cups (375 mL)

Level: Intermediate

Cooking Time: 15 to 20 minutes

At the Ready: Medium saucepan, wooden spoon, fine-meshed sieve, covered container

This ketchup makes an excellent condiment for chicken, turkey, and pork.

2 pounds (1 kg) fresh cranberries, washed and picked over, and with shrivelled ones discarded
3/4 cup (175 mL) red wine vinegar
1 cup (250 mL) packed dark brown sugar

1/2 cup (125 mL) dark raisins
1 tablespoon (15 mL) ground cinnamon
1/2 (5 mL) teaspoon salt
1/4 teaspoon (1 mL) ground allspice
1/4 teaspoon (1 mL) ground cloves

In a heavy, medium-size saucepan, cook the cranberries over medium heat until they pop, about 4 to 6 minutes. Remove from the heat. Press the cranberries through a sieve. Then return the pulp to a clean pan. Mix in the vinegar, brown sugar, raisins, cinnamon, salt, allspice, and cloves.

Simmer the mixture on medium-low heat for about 15 minutes, stirring often, until the sauce thickens. Taste, and adjust the seasonings. Cool.

Pour the ketchup into a container, cover tightly, and refrigerate until ready to serve, or up to 1 week. Stir the ketchup before serving.

Hot Tip

Buy cranberries when they are in season and freeze them for later use. For an easier recipe, substitute 2 cans of jellied cranberries (16 oz. or 500 g each) for the fresh cranberries, and reduce the amount of brown sugar to 1/4 cup (50 mL). If using canned berries, you do not have to pass the mixture through a sieve.

Hot Tip

Thick and piquant, ketchup, salsas, and tartar sauce add flair to grilled meats, poultry, or fish. They go best with foods that have not been heavily spiced.

Pineapple Salsa

Yield: 1 1/2 cups (375 mL)   **Prep**: 15 to 20 minutes

Level: Easy   **At the Ready**: Glass bowl

This is great with pork, chicken or turkey, or mildly flavoured fish.

1 cup (250 mL) chopped fresh pineapple   1/2 teaspoon (2 mL) salt
1/4 cup (50 mL) lime juice   1/2 cup (125 mL) chopped fresh cilantro
1 small red onion, peeled and chopped

In a glass bowl, toss the pineapple with the onion, cilantro, lime juice, and salt. Taste the salsa and adjust the seasonings as you like.

Cover the salsa lightly and refrigerate until ready to serve, or up to 3 days. Toss the ingredients again before serving.

Tartar Sauce

Yield: About 1 1/2 cups (375 mL)   **Prep**: 10 minutes

Level: Easy   **At the Ready**: Glass serving bowl

2 cups (500 mL) mayonnaise (regular or   2 tablespoons (25 mL) capers, drained
   reduced-fat)   2 cloves garlic, peeled and minced
1 small onion, minced   Salt and pepper to taste
3 tablespoons (50 mL) fresh lemon juice   1/3 cup (75 mL) minced dill pickle

Put the mayonnaise in a mixing bowl. Blend in the lemon juice, garlic, minced pickle, onion, and capers. Season with salt and pepper.

Spoon the sauce into a serving bowl, cover, and refrigerate until ready to serve. Stir the sauce again before serving it. The tartar sauce will keep for 4 to 5 days in the refrigerator.

The Least You Need to Know

➤ Marinades work best when you want the natural flavours of the food to shine through.

➤ Sweet barbecue sauces normally are brushed on foods near the end of the grilling time.

➤ Condiments such as ketchup and salsas go best with grilled foods that are not heavily spiced.

Appetizers

Making appetizers on the grill means you can stay outside with your guests. It also means your guests will have something to nibble as they smell the enticing aromas of the main course wafting around your yard.

If you want to serve a hot appetizer, you certainly should plan on grilling it. Otherwise, you'll wind up running back and forth between the stove or oven and your grill. Most of the following dishes can be cooked quickly on the grill and served to guests to keep them occupied while you go on to grill the main course. The coals will stay medium-hot for quite a while.

Of course, there's also no reason you can't just serve a variety of these delicious morsels for a party—and forget the main course. Just round out the menu with a good salad and some wonderful bread.

Five-Minute Mussels

Yield: 6 servings

Level: Easy

Grill: 5 minutes

At the Ready: Grill screen

Note that these should be cooked over hot, not medium-hot, coals.

3 cups (750 mL) chopped fresh
  tomatoes
2 tablespoons (25 mL) capers, drained
1/2 teaspoon (2 mL) salt
1/4 teaspoon (1 mL) pepper

2 tablespoons (25 mL) red wine vinegar
3 dozen mussels, scrubbed and
  debearded (see Chapter 13 for
  instructions on cleaning mussels)

Toss the tomatoes, capers, salt, pepper, and vinegar in a bowl. Cover and refrigerate until ready to serve.

Prepare the grill for direct heat. Oil or spray the grill screen. When the coals are glowing hot, set the mussels on the grid, 4 to 6 inches (10 to 15 cm) from the heat. Grill the mussels, covered, for 5 minutes. When you uncover the grill, the mussels should be opened. If not, cover and grill a few minutes longer until the shells open. Discard any mussels that don't open even after additional cooking.

Put the mussels on individual plates and spoon the chopped tomato mixture on top. Serve hot.

Grilled Forest Mushroom Soup

Yield: About 8 servings

Level: Intermediate

Grill: 10 to 12 minutes

Cook: 20 to 30 minutes

At the Ready: Vegetable grilling basket, soup pot

Grilling the mushrooms prior to preparing the soup adds a smoky flavour to the soup.

Grilled Mushroom Ingredients
4 large Portobello mushrooms
2 cups (500 mL) shiitake mushrooms
2 cups (500 mL) cremini brown
   mushrooms
1 cup (250 mL) oyster mushrooms
1 medium Spanish onion
6 cloves garlic, chopped
1/4 cup (50 mL) olive oil
1/4 cup (50 mL) cup balsamic vinegar

2 tablespoons (25 mL) chopped fresh
   thyme
Salt and pepper to taste

Soup Ingredients
2 tablespoons (25 mL) olive oil
1/2 cup (125 mL) red wine
4 cups (1 L) chicken stock
2 tablespoons (25 mL) chopped fresh
   thyme
Salt and pepper to taste

Brush the mushrooms of all excess dirt. Slice Portobello mushrooms into 1/2 inch (1 cm) slices. Quarter the shiitake and cremini mushrooms and tear the oyster mushrooms into 1/2 inch (1 cm) strips.

Slice the onion into 1/2 inch (1 cm) slices. In a large bowl, mix together the mushrooms, onion, garlic, olive oil, balsamic vinegar, and thyme. Season to taste with salt and pepper and place in a barbecue grill basket.

On a preheated grill over medium-high heat, grill the mushroom and onion mixture for 10 to 12 minutes, turning the basket a couple of times until the mushrooms and onions are slightly charred and tender. Carefully remove from the grill basket and set aside to cool. When the mixture is cool, cut the mushrooms and onions into bite-size pieces.

To prepare the soup, heat the oil over medium-high heat in a large soup pot. Add the grilled mushroom and onion mixture and sauté for 3 to 4 minutes. Add the red wine and reduce the liquid by half. Add the chicken stock and bring the mixture to a rolling boil. Reduce heat to medium-low and let simmer to 20 to 30 minutes. Finish with fresh thyme and season with salt and pepper to taste.

Serve immediately with grilled garlic bread and freshly grated Parmesan cheese.

Greek Cheese with Garlic Pita Chips

Yield: 8 servings

Level: Easy

Grill: 2 to 5 minutes

At the Ready: Oil or nonstick cooking spray, long-handled spatula, grill screen, brush

1 cup (250 mL) milk
1 egg, lightly beaten
1 1/2 cups (375 mL) fine bread crumbs
1 pound (500 g) Greek saganaki cheese,
cut into eight 1/2 inch (1 cm) pieces
3 tablespoons (50 mL) brandy, preferably Metaxa
Garlic pita chips (recipe follows)

In a shallow bowl, mix together the milk and egg. Set the bread crumbs on a plate. Roll the cheese slices in the milk mixture and then in the bread crumbs. Place the cheese on a dish and refrigerate, covered, for at least 1 hour.

Prepare the grill for direct heat. Oil or spray a grill screen. When the coals are medium-hot, set the cheese pieces on the grill screen, and set that on the cooking grid, about 4 to 6 inches (10 to 15 cm) from the heat. Grill the cheese, uncovered, about 2 minutes on each side, turning the pieces over with a long-handled spatula. The cheese should be lightly browned on the outside, and runny but not completely melted on the inside.

Set the cheese on individual plates and sprinkle with the brandy. Serve immediately with garlic pita chips (recipe follows).

Garlic Pita Chips

Yield: 6 to 8 servings

Level: Easy

Grill: 2 to 4 minutes

At the Ready: Melted butter for brushing, brush, long-handled spatula, kitchen scissors

1/3 cup (75 mL) melted butter or margarine
4 pita breads
1 tablespoon (15 mL) minced garlic

Using a serrated knife, carefully cut crosswise through each pita to make 2 rounds. In a small bowl, mix the melted, cooled butter with the garlic. Brush the pita rounds with the butter mixture.

Prepare the grill for direct heat. Oil or spray a grill screen. When the coals are medium-hot, set the pita bread rounds on the grill screen, and set that on the cooking grid, about 4 to 6 inches (10 to 15 cm) from the heat. Grill, uncovered, about 1 to 2 minutes on each side. The bread will begin to colour slightly. Do not overcook. Remove the pita rounds to a work area and, using a pair of kitchen scissors, cut each round into 6 pieces. Serve the chips hot.

Don't Get Burned!

The pita chips heat quickly, so pay attention and do not leave to do something else while they grill.

Glazed Polish Sausage

Yield: 8 servings

Level: Easy

Grill: 12 minutes

At the Ready: Small sharp knife, oil for brushing, grill screen

1 cup (250 mL) orange marmalade
2 tablespoons (25 mL) Dijon mustard

1 tablespoon (15 mL) water
2 pounds (1 kg) smoked Polish sausage

Combine the orange marmalade and water in a small saucepan. Heat the mixture over medium for a few minutes, stirring often until the marmalade thins and is hot. Remove the marmalade from the heat and stir in the mustard.

Prick the sausages with a fork and brush them with the sauce. Prepare the grill for direct heat. Lightly oil or spray the cooking grid. When the coals are medium-hot, set the sausages on the grid. Grill them, uncovered, for about 12 minutes, turning them every 3 minutes, until they're nicely browned and cooked through.

Remove the sausages from the grill to a wooden board and cut on the diagonal into serving-size pieces. Serve hot.

Grilled Lamb Ribs with Roasted Garlic Barbecue Sauce

Yield: 8 servings

Level: Intermediate

Prep: Oven 1 hour, Grill 10 to 12 minutes

At the Ready: Oven proof dish 9 x 14 (2 L), small sauce pot, aluminum foil, barbecue tongs, basting brush

These ribs are good either as an appetizer or as a main course for 4 to 6 people. This recipe requires a fair amount of time to make the ribs tender and succulent. But the time spent is well worth the wait.

8 racks (about 4 pounds or 2 kg) lamb ribs
2 tablespoons (15 mL) barbecue seasoning (page 146)
1 medium onion, thinly sliced
12 cloves garlic, peeled
2 Jalapeño peppers, cut in half and seeded

1 bottle dark beer

Roasted Garlic Barbecue Sauce
1 cup dark beer
2 cups (500 mL) hickory smoke–flavoured barbecue sauce
Salt and pepper to taste

Preheat oven to 375°F (190°C). Using a sharp knife, score the lamb ribs in a diamond pattern on the bone side of the racks of ribs about a 1/4 inch (0.5 cm) deep. Season the ribs with the barbecue seasoning, making sure to rub the spices into the flesh of the ribs.

Mix the onions and garlic together and place evenly in the ovenproof dish. Lay the seasoned lamb ribs evenly onto the onion garlic mixture. Pour the dark beer over the ribs and cover tightly with a piece of aluminum foil.

Place in the oven and cook the ribs for 60 to 75 minutes until the meat is tender and is coming away from the bone. Remove from the oven and let cool slightly. Transfer the ribs to a platter and set aside.

On the stove or side burner of your grill, place the cooked onion and garlic mixture in the sauce pot. Add the beer and bring the mixture to a boil over medium-high heat. Add the barbecue sauce and return to a boil. Remove from the heat and season to taste with salt and pepper. If you wish, you may purée the sauce mixture, but we like it chunky.

On a preheated grill over medium-high heat, grill the cooked lamb ribs for 5 to 6 minutes per side, basting liberally with the roasted garlic barbecue sauce until the ribs are heated through and slightly charred.

Cut the ribs between every other bone and serve.

BBQ Carolina Pulled Pork Quesadillas

Yield: 8 servings

Level: Easy

Grill: 5 to 6 minutes

At the Ready: Nonstick cooking spray, grill screen

If and when you ever have any left over BBQ Carolina pulled pork, this is a simple recipe to use it up as an appetizer.

2 cups (500 mL) leftover BBQ Carolina pulled pork
8 tablespoons (100 mL) barbecue sauce
1 small red onion, thinly slice
2 green onions, finely chopped
1 medium red pepper, seeded and thinly sliced

1 tablespoon (15 mL) chopped fresh cilantro
1 tablespoon (15 mL) wine vinegar
Salt and pepper to taste
Eight 10 inch (25 cm) flour tortillas
2 cups (500 mL) shredded aged Canadian Cheddar cheese

In a medium bowl, mix together the leftover barbecue pork, barbecue sauce, red onion, green onion, red pepper, cilantro, and wine vinegar. Season to taste with salt and pepper.

Lay one flour tortilla on a flat work surface. Place 1/4 of the barbecue pork mixture in the centre of the flour tortilla and spread evenly over the surface to within 1/2 inch (1 cm) of the edge. Sprinkle with 1/4 of the cheddar cheese.

Using cold water, brush the edge of the flour tortilla. Place another tortilla on top of the cheese and barbecued pork mixture and press down the edges firmly. Repeat 3 more times with the remaining ingredients.

Note: While preparing the remaining quesadillas, place a moist paper towel over the prepared appetizers to keep them from drying out.

Preheat grill to medium-high. Spray grill screen with nonstick cooking spray and place on grill. Lightly spray both sides of the quesadillas and place them two at a time on the grill. Grill for 2 to 3 minutes per side until golden brown and crisp. At this time the cheese should be melted and the barbecued pork hot.

Remove from the grill and let rest for 2 minutes. Cut into 6 or 8 wedges and serve with salsa, sour cream, and guacamole.

Focaccia

Yield: 8 servings

Level: Easy

Grill: About 6 to 7 minutes

At the Ready: 3 baking tiles suitable for the grill, cookie sheet or grill screen, long-handled spatula, oil for brushing, basting brush

Focaccia is a pizza-style bread heated and served right from the grill. The toppings can be changed to your taste.

1 large onion, sliced thin
2 tablespoons (25 mL) butter
1 plain, store-bought focaccia (already-baked pizza crust or Italian flatbread)

Olive oil
1 large tomato, sliced thin
1/4 cup (50 mL) sliced, pitted black olives

Cook the onion in the butter over medium heat for about 7 to 8 minutes, until soft and translucent but not browned. Remove from the heat and let cool slightly.

Brush the top of the focaccia lightly with oil. Arrange the tomato slices decoratively on top. Arrange the sautéed onion and olives over the tomatoes.

Prepare the grill for direct heat. When the coals are medium-hot, set a cookie sheet or grill screen on the grill about 4 to 6 inches (10 to 15 cm) from the heat source, then set the tiles atop that. (Using a cookie sheet or grill screen makes it easier to remove the tiles from the grill, and also lowers the heat slightly so that the focaccia is less likely to burn.) Preheat for at least 5 minutes. Put the focaccia on a pizza pan and then set it on the tiles. Cover. Grill for about 3 minutes, then turn the bread halfway around. Cover and continue cooking for 3 minutes, or until the focaccia is hot. Watch that it doesn't char.

Set the focaccia on a serving table and cut it into serving-size pieces. This is good hot or warm.

Hot Tip

Portobello mushrooms, like most mushrooms, have a large percentage of water. When you are grilling them, that moisture quickly evaporates because of the dry heat. To compensate, soak mushrooms in hot tap water for 10 to 15 minutes. Then marinate and grill.

Stuffed Portobello Mushrooms with Sun-Dried Tomatoes and Gorgonzola

Yield: 8 servings

Level: Intermediate

Grill: 14 to 15 minutes

At the Ready: 2 to 3 large to medium bowls for mixing, oil or nonstick cooking spray, grill screen, long-handled spatula

8 large Portobello mushroom caps, stems removed
4 cups (1 L) hot water
1/4 cup (50 mL) olive oil
1/4 cup (50 mL) balsamic vinegar
Salt and pepper to taste
2 cloves minced garlic
1 small red onion, finely diced
1/2 cup (125 mL) sun-dried tomatoes, chopped

1 teaspoon (5 mL) chopped fresh thyme
1 tablespoon (15 mL) chopped fresh basil
1 tablespoon (15 mL) balsamic vinegar
1/2 cup (125 mL) softened cream cheese
1 cup (250 mL) Gorgonzola cheese
Salt and pepper to taste
1 cup (250 mL) bread crumbs
1/2 cup (125 mL) grated Parmesan cheese

Brush Portobello mushrooms of any excess dirt. Remove stems and place in a large bowl. Cover with 4 cups (1 L) of hot water and let stand for 10 to 15 minutes. Drain on paper towels and pat dry. Mix olive oil and balsamic vinegar together and season with salt and pepper. Set aside to marinate while making the stuffing mixture.

In a bowl, mix together the garlic, onion, sun-dried tomatoes, thyme, basil, vinegar, cream cheese, and Gorgonzola cheese. Season to taste with salt and freshly ground black pepper. Divide the mixture into 8 equal portions and flatten to the similar shape of the Portobello mushroom caps.

In a separate bowl, mix together the bread crumbs and Parmesan cheese.

Preheat grill to medium-high. Spray the grill screen with nonstick cooking spray. Place on the grill and preheat for 5 minutes. Place the marinating Portobello mushrooms gill side down and grill for 4 to 5 minutes until slightly charred and just tender.

Turn mushrooms over and place the cheese stuffing mixture onto each cap. Top with a liberal dusting of the breadcrumb mixture. Close the grill lid and continue to cook for 7 to 8 more minutes, until the cheese is hot and bubbling and the bread crumbs are golden-brown. Remove from grill and serve with mixed greens and a simple salad dressing.

163

Grilled Garlic Potato Skins

Yield: 8 servings

Level: Easy

Grill: About 4 to 6 minutes, plus 1 hour

for baking or grilling potatoes

At the Ready: Aluminum foil; small, sharp kitchen knife

6 large baking potatoes, skin on, scrubbed

1 teaspoon (5 mL) ground cumin

Vegetable oil for brushing

1/2 teaspoon (2 mL) black pepper

2 teaspoons (10 mL) garlic powder

Scrub the potatoes under cold running water. Prick them several times with the tip of a sharp knife. Wrap the potatoes in aluminum foil. Prepare the grill. When the coals are medium-hot, carefully set the potatoes directly on the coals if you're using a charcoal grill, or on the rack if you're using gas. Cover the grill and cook the potatoes about 1 hour, or until they can be pierced easily with a fork, turning them 2 or 3 times during grilling. Or bake the potatoes, minus the foil, in a preheated 425°F (220°C) oven for about 1 hour. The potatoes are done when you can pierce them easily with a fork. Let cool. The potatoes can be grilled or baked the day before. Refrigerate them.

When the potatoes are cool enough to handle, cut in half lengthwise. Scoop out the potato, leaving 1/4 inch (0.5 cm) of potato lining the skins. Refrigerate the potato meat and reserve it for another recipe. Cut the potato skins again in half lengthwise. Brush the skins with oil and sprinkle with the garlic powder, cumin, and pepper.

Prepare the grill for direct heat. Oil or spray a grill screen. When the coals are medium-hot, set the potato strips, skin side down, on the grill screen and then set that on the grid, about 4 to 6 inches (10 to 15 cm) from the heat. Cover and grill for about 3 to 4 minutes. Turn the potato skins over and continue grilling until they are hot and beginning to brown.

Using a long-handled spatula, remove the potato skins to a serving plate. Serve hot. These are good sprinkled lightly with cheese or served with dabs of sour cream.

Don't Get Burned!

When you wrap potatoes in foil to cook them, be sure to serve them while they're still hot. If you don't plan to serve them until later, refrigerate them. This will reduce the risk of botulism.

Crostini

Yield: 8 servings

Level: Easy

Grill: About 3 to 4 minutes

At the Ready: Oil for brushing, grill screen, brush, long-handled spatula

This is an adaptation of a classic Italian dish. Here we use thin slices of Provolone cheese and anchovy slices on Italian bread.

8 slices of fresh Italian or French bread, 1/2 inch (1 cm) thick
Olive oil for brushing

1/2 pound (500 g) Provolone cheese, sliced thin
1 can (2 oz. or 55 g) anchovies, drained

Prepare the grill for direct heat. Oil or spray a grill screen. Brush the bread slices lightly with olive oil on both sides. When the coals are medium-hot, put the grill screen on the grid about 4 to 6 inches (10 to 15 cm) from the heat. Put the bread on the grill screen and grill, uncovered, for only a minute or until lightly toasted. Working quickly, remove the bread from the screen. Turn the bread over and place 2 slices of cheese on top of each piece of bread, then set an anchovy atop that. Return the bread to the screen and grill a minute or until the bread is just lightly toasted on the bottom. The bread burns quickly, so watch it closely and do not leave the grill. In fact, you might want to make the crostini in two batches so you can watch it carefully. Serve hot.

What's What

Elephant garlic isn't actually garlic, but a relative of the leek. It looks like giant garlic, though. Its extra-large, white-skinned bulbs have a milder flavour than regular garlic.

Grilled Antipasti

Yield: 8 servings

Level: Intermediate

Grill: 5 to 12 minutes

At the Ready: Basting brush, oil for brushing, grill screen, long-handled spatula

Substitute seasonal vegetables of your choice for any of the vegetables in this recipe. You can prepare the vegetables ahead of time and refrigerate them until grilling time.

8 cloves elephant garlic, unpeeled, brushed with olive oil

8 brown Italian or white mushrooms, cleaned, stems removed

2 large yellow or red peppers, seeded and cut in 1/2 inch (1 cm) circles

3 medium-small zucchini, cut lengthwise into thin slices

1 jar (6 1/2 oz. or 185 g) marinated

artichoke hearts, drained

Olive oil

Lemon juice

Salt and pepper to taste

6 ounces (185 g) thinly sliced deli-style ham

1 small ripe cantaloupe, seeded, cut in 1 inch (2.5 cm) slices

1/2 pound (250 g) black olives

Wrap the oiled garlic cloves in aluminum foil and set aside. Prepare the mushrooms, peppers, zucchini, and artichokes. Brush the vegetables lightly with oil and sprinkle with lemon juice, salt, and pepper. Wrap a half-slice of ham around each cantaloupe piece, leave cut side down, and brush the ham with oil.

Prepare the grill for direct heat. Oil or spray a grill screen. When the coals are medium-hot, set the grill screen on the cooking grid about 4 to 6 inches (10 to 15 cm) from the heat. Set the garlic on the screen first, cover the grill, adjust the vents, and let the garlic cook about 10 minutes, turning once. Remove the cover and add the remaining vegetables and the wrapped cantaloupe to the grill screen. Grill the wrapped cantaloupe 1 or 2 minutes on each side, then remove to a platter. Grill the remaining vegetables 5 to 10 minutes, turning as necessary, until tender and beginning to brown. Remove the vegetables as they cook. The garlic will take about 20 minutes to become tender. Remove one clove with a spatula, remove the foil, and squeeze to see if it is tender, being careful not to burn your fingers as it will be very hot.

Put all the vegetables, the ham-wrapped cantaloupe, and the garlic cloves decoratively on a platter, along with the olives. Sprinkle with more olive oil and lemon juice. Serve hot with Italian bread.

Vine-Skewered Jumbo Shrimps with Lime and Honey Marinade

Yield: 6 servings

Level: Easy

Grill: 5 to 6 minutes

At the Ready: Grape vine skewers or bamboo skewers or metal skewers

Using grape vines as skewers for these shrimp adds a little bit of flavour but is mostly for the wonderful presentation created.

18 jumbo shrimp, peeled and deveined approximately 1 lb. or 500 g)
18 grape vine skewers (see *What's What*)
1 teaspoon (5 mL) sesame oil
1/4 cup (50 mL) rice wine vinegar
2 limes, juiced
4 tablespoons (60 mL) honey

1 jalapeño pepper, seeded and finely chopped
1 tablespoon (15 mL) chopped fresh mint
3 cloves garlic, chopped
1 tablespoon (15 mL) Great Lakes seafood seasoning
Salt and pepper to taste

Soak the grape vine skewers in warm water for 1 hour. Skewer one shrimp onto one end of skewer lengthwise, tail to head.

In a small bowl, whisk together the sesame oil, rice vinegar, lime juice, honey, jalapeño, mint, and garlic. Season to taste with salt and pepper.

Season shrimp skewers with the Great Lakes seafood seasoning (page 147), then place in a shallow glass dish. Pour marinade over shrimp skewers and let marinate for 15 minutes.

Preheat grill to medium-high. Remove shrimp from marinade (reserving marinade for basting). Grill shrimp for 2 to 3 minutes per side, basting frequently with reserved marinade until they are opaque and tender.

Serve immediately with pineapple salsa (page 153)

What's What

If you happen to live in a wine region, it is quite easy to obtain grape vines to make skewers. If you do not, you may find them at a specialty food shop. If all else fails, use bamboo skewers, which are easily obtained at your local grocery store.

The Least You Need to Know

➤ Cooking the appetizers on the grill allows you to stay outside with the guests.

➤ You can create a whole party menu of nothing but "appetizers."

Meats

Beef, pork, and lamb—these are the foods the grill was invented for. Here's a collection of recipes that showcase red meats at their best. They run the gamut of flavours and traditions from Canada's multicultural background, from tender ribs, to Montreal spiced steaks, to Greek Town shish kebab, to jerk steak.

It's important to watch meats carefully, especially the leaner cuts. Overcooking will make them tough and stringy. On the other hand, undercooking meats—especially ground meats—can be unsafe. Steaks and chops benefit from searing: quickly browning the outside of the meat over hot coals to seal in the juices. Finish cooking them over medium-hot coals.

Skirt Steak with Grilled Peppers and Shallot Marinade Sauce

Yield: 6 servings

Level: Easy

Grill: About 7 to 9 minutes

At the Ready: Oil for brushing, brush, grill screen, long-handled spatula

This acidic marinade helps tenderize the beef skirt, a fairly tough but very flavourful cut.

1/4 cup (50 mL) light (reduced-sodium) soy sauce
3 shallots, peeled and minced
2 tablespoons (25 mL) light brown sugar
1/4 cup (50 mL) pineapple juice

1/4 cup (50 mL) cider vinegar
2 pounds (1 kg) beef skirt steak, trimmed and cut into 6 serving pieces
3 large green or red bell peppers, seeded and cut in rings

In a small saucepan, combine the soy sauce, shallots, brown sugar, pineapple juice, and vinegar. Bring the mixture to a boil over medium heat, stirring often. Remove the pan from the heat and cool.

Set the meat in a glass bowl and cover with the marinade. Cover lightly and marinate for 1 hour in the refrigerator, turning once. Drain.

Prepare the grill for direct heat. Oil or spray the cooking grid. When the coals are medium-hot, set the steak on the oiled grid. Cover the grill and adjust the vents. Grill the steak for 4 minutes. Turn the steak over and put the peppers on the grill. Grill the peppers about 2 to 3 minutes on each side, until they begin to char and are tender. Continue grilling the steak for another 4 to 5 minutes, or until just cooked through. The time depends on the thickness of the steak; do not overcook. Serve the meat and peppers hot, with guacamole on the side.

Baby Back Ribs with Orange Mustard Barbecue Sauce

Yield: 6 to 8 servings

Level: Advanced

Prep: 1 1/2 hours

Grill: 12 to 15 minutes

At the Ready: Roasting pan, aluminum foil, barbecue tongs, basting brush

There is nothing better than tender, succulent baby back ribs. If you do not have the many hours required to slowly smoke the ribs over low heat on your barbecue or smoker, this method of cooking ribs in the oven first and then finishing the ribs on the grill makes for an easier method.

The cooking of ribs is an art form. I love ribs, and to me the meat should fall off the bone.

6 racks pork baby back ribs (around 1 1/2 pounds each), fully trimmed
1/2 cup (125 mL) barbecue seasoning (recipe page 146)
2 oranges, thinly sliced
2 cups (500 mL) orange juice
1cup (250 mL) water

Orange Mustard Barbecue Sauce
2 tablespoons (25 mL) vegetable oil
2 cloves garlic, chopped

1 medium onion, chopped
1 teaspoon (5 mL) ground cumin
1 tablespoon (15 mL) mustard seeds
2 jalapeño peppers, seeded and chopped
1 cup (250 mL) orange marmalade
1/2 cup (125 mL) honey
1 cup (250 mL) prepared mustard
1 cup (250 mL) orange juice
1 tablespoon (15 mL) chopped fresh thyme
Salt and pepper to taste

Preheat oven to 375˚F (190˚C). Season the back ribs with the barbecue seasoning. Place the ribs in a deep roasting pan, meat side down. You may need to layer the racks to get them to fit in the pan. Place 4 slices of orange on each rack. Add orange juice and water to the pan and cover tightly with aluminum foil. Bake in the oven for 1 1/2 hours until tender. Remove from oven and let cool.

While the ribs are cooking, prepare the orange mustard barbecue sauce. In a medium saucepot, heat the oil over medium-high heat. Add the garlic and onions and sauté for 2 to 3 minutes until tender. Add the cumin, mustard seeds, and jalapeño peppers and continue to cook for another 2 to 3 minutes. Add the marmalade, honey, mustard, orange juice, and thyme. Bring to a boil; reduce heat to medium and let simmer, stirring occasionally, for 15 minutes. Season to taste with salt and pepper. If you wish, you may purée this sauce to make it smooth, but chunky also fine. Set aside to cool.

Preheat the grill to medium-high. Grill the ribs for 6 to 7 minutes per side, basting liberally with the barbecue sauce. Serve hot with coleslaw.

Jerk Strip Steaks

Yield: 6 servings

Level: Easy

Grill: About 10 minutes

At the Ready: Food processor, blender or mortar and pestle, brushing sauce, brush, long-handled fork

We call for jalapeño peppers in this marinade because they're easier to find in most supermarkets. To be more authentic, you can use one or two habanero peppers, the fruity, super-hot, bonnet-shaped beauties.

1 large onion, peeled and roughly chopped

3 jalapeño peppers, seeded and minced

3/4 cup (175 mL) light (reduced-sodium) soy sauce

1/4 cup (50 mL) vegetable oil

1/4 cup (50 mL) dark brown sugar

1 teaspoon (5 mL) dried crumbled thyme

1/2 teaspoon (2 mL) black pepper

1/2 teaspoon (2 mL) ground allspice

1/2 teaspoon (2 mL) ground cinnamon

6 beef strip steaks, about 8 ounces (250 g) each, trimmed of all fat

Put the onion, peppers, soy sauce, oil, sugar, thyme, pepper, allspice, and cinnamon in the container of a food processor fitted with a steel blade. Process for about 15 seconds to make a paste. Spoon the paste into a small bowl. Cover and set aside.

Rub the steaks with the jerk paste and place them on a glass plate. Cover lightly and refrigerate for 3 to 4 hours.

Prepare the grill for direct heat. When the coals are medium-hot, set the steaks directly on the cooking grid. Cover the grill and adjust the vents. Grill the steaks 4 to 6 minutes on each side, or until they reach desired doneness. Serve the steaks hot on individual plates with grilled vegetables.

Montreal Steak Spiced Rib-Eye Steak with Blue Cheese Butter

Yield: 8 servings

Level: Easy

Grill: About 10 to 12 minutes

At the Ready: Food processor, barbecue tongs

This is a simple and delicious recipe. Use lots of the Montreal steak spice when seasoning the rib-eye steaks. In this case, more is better.

Eight 10 ounce (300 g) boneless rib-eye steaks cut about 1 inch (2.5 cm) thick

3/4 cup (175 mL) Montreal steak spice (page 147)

Blue Cheese Butter
1/2 pound (250 g) butter, softened

1/2 pound (250 g) blue cheese (Stilton, Canadian Eremite, or Danish blue)

1 teaspoon (5 mL) ground black pepper

1 tablespoon (15 mL) chopped fresh thyme

2 tablespoons (25 mL) sherry

Get your local butcher to cut you some rib-eye steaks about 1 inch (2.5 cm) thick. Divide the Montreal steak spice evenly over the rib-eye steaks and push the spice rub into the flesh of the steaks. Make a heavy crust. It adds great flavour. Set aside and let marinate for 15 minutes while making the butter.

In a food processor, blend the butter until smooth. Add the blue cheese, black pepper, thyme, and sherry. Using the pulse button on the food processor, blend until all is just incorporated. The idea here is to maintain a visual of blue cheese. Remove from the food processor and transfer to a plastic container. This may be stored in the refrigerator for 2 to 3 weeks or in the freezer for up to 2 months.

Preheat the grill to medium-high. Grill the Montreal steaks for 5 to 6 minutes per side for medium doneness—a little less time for rare and more for well done. Serve the steaks with a tablespoon of the blue cheese butter.

Peameal Bacon Steaks, Eh!

Yield: 6 servings

Level: Easy

Grill: 8 to 10 minutes

At the Ready: barbecue tongs, basting brush, nonstick cooking spray

Canadian back bacon was made famous by those two hosers Bob and Doug Mackenzie. Back bacon or peameal bacon is a sweet-brined cured pork loin with a cornmeal crust. Sometimes it may even be smoked. Our friends south of the border prefer the smoked pork loin back bacon; Canadians embrace peameal bacon.

Six 6 ounce (180 g) portions Canadian peameal bacon steaks
1/4 cup (50 mL) maple syrup

1/4 cup (50 mL) barbecue sauce
1/4 cup (50 mL) orange juice
Salt and pepper to taste

Preheat the grill to medium-high. Spray the peameal steaks with the nonstick cooking spray. In a bowl, whisk together the maple syrup, barbecue sauce, and orange juice. Season with salt and pepper. Grill the peameal steaks for 4 to 5 minutes per side, basting liberally with the maple barbecue sauce.

Serve on grilled thick sliced toast with mayonnaise and crushed chilis. Delicious, eh!

Cheeseburger Deluxe

Yield: 6 servings

Level: Easy

Grill: About 10 minutes

At the Ready: Grill screen, oil for brushing, brush, long-handled spatula

2 pounds (1 kg) ground beef sirloin
1 small onion, peeled and minced
3 tablespoons (50 mL) barbecue sauce
1/2 pound (250 g) blue cheese or aged Canadian cheddar, crumbled (for children or less adventurous appetites, use a slice of mild cheese)

6 hamburger buns, split and brushed with melted butter
Lettuce leaves
Sliced tomatoes
Thinly sliced red onions
Grainy mustard and ketchup

In a large bowl, mix the ground beef with the onion. Shape the meat mixture into 6 equal patties. Brush lightly with the barbecue sauce. Set the patties on a plate and refrigerate them until ready to grill.

Prepare the grill for direct heat. Oil or spray the cooking grid. When the coals are medium-hot, set the hamburgers on the grid. Cover the grill and adjust the vents. Grill the hamburgers about 5 to 6 minutes on each side, or until they are completely cooked through, with no pink in the middle. While they cook, brush once on each side with barbecue sauce. If you are using Cheddar cheese, place it atop the burgers a minute or so before they're done.

Toast the open rolls on the grill (not directly over the coals) about 1 to 2 minutes, watching carefully as they burn easily.

Arrange a lettuce leaf and tomato slice on each bun. Set a burger on top and sprinkle with the blue cheese if using. Pass the sliced onions, mustard, and ketchup at the table. Serve hot.

Beer-Basted Short Ribs

Yield: 6 servings

Level: Intermediate

Grill: 50 to 60 minutes

At the Ready: Long-handled fork, basting sauce

4 pounds (2 kg) beef short ribs, cut 1 inch (2.5 cm) thick and trimmed of fat

Beer Basting Sauce
1 can (12 oz. or 340 mL) dark beer
2 teaspoons (10 mL) chili powder

1/2 cup (125 mL) packed, dark-brown sugar
1 teaspoon (5 mL) cumin
1/2 cup (125 mL) cider vinegar
1/4 teaspoon (1 mL) cayenne
1/2 cup (125 mL) chili sauce

In a saucepan, combine the beer, brown sugar, vinegar, chili sauce, chili powder, cumin, and cayenne. Bring the sauce to a boil over medium heat, stirring often. Reduce the heat to a simmer and continue cooking for about 4 to 5 minutes. Let cool.

Remove 1 cup (250 mL) of the sauce for brushing the ribs at the grill. Brush the ribs with the remaining sauce and put them in a glass bowl. Cover and refrigerate for 2 hours.

Prepare the grill for indirect heat. When the coals are covered with a thick layer of ash, place the ribs on the grill. Cover the grill and adjust the vents. Grill the ribs 50 to 60 minutes or until cooked through, turning occasionally. You will probably need to add a few coals now and then, just enough to keep the heat going. (If you're using a gas grill, you want the temperature at between 225 and 250°F, or 107 to 121°C.) Brush the ribs with sauce as you turn them. Serve hot. These are good with grilled corn, red chili beans, and coleslaw.

Don't Get Burned!

The recipe for beer-basted short ribs requires indirect heat and low heat. If you're using a charcoal grill, keep the heat low by using fewer coals, waiting until they are ashen, and adding only enough lit coals periodically to keep the fire going. These ribs are worth the effort.

Barbecue Capocollo Pork Butt Steaks with Lemon and Onions

Yield: 6

Level: Intermediate

Grill: 12 to 15 minutes

At the Ready: Large glass dish, barbecue tongs, your favourite barbecue sauce, basting brush

Pork steaks cut from the shoulder of the pig are succulent and inexpensive. Using lots of onions and lemons makes this a delicious recipe.

Six 8 ounce (180 g) pork butt steaks
2 large onions, thinly sliced
6 cloves garlic, chopped
2 lemons, thinly sliced

1 tablespoon (15 mL) cracked black pepper
1 tablespoon (15 mL) chopped fresh oregano
Salt to taste

In a mixing bowl, toss together the onions, garlic, lemons, pepper, and oregano. In a large glass dish, cover the bottom with half of the onion/lemon mixture. Place the pork steaks on the onions. Cover with remaining onion/lemon mixture. Cover and refrigerate for 24 hours.

Preheat the grill to medium-high. Remove the pork steaks from the onion/lemon mixture and discard the onion/lemon mix. Season the pork with salt and grill for 6 to 8 minutes per side for medium doneness. While the steaks are grilling, baste with your favourite barbecue sauce.

Grilled Double Thick Cut Pork Chops with Newfie Screech BBQ Sauce

Yield: 6 servings

Level: Intermediate

Grill: 18 to 24 minutes

At the Ready: Saucepot, basting brush, barbecue tongs

For this recipe you may use a bone-in pork rib chop or a boneless chop. For the best results, have your butcher cut these chops nice and thick—say, 1 1/2 to 2 inches (4 to 5 cm) thick and weighing about 12 ounces (350 g). Chops this thick take a while to cook, but are worth the wait.

Six 12 ounce (350 g) thick cut pork chops
3 tablespoons (50 mL) barbecue spice (page 146)
3 tablespoons (50 mL) vegetable oil
1/4 cup (50 mL) Newfoundland Screech rum
4 cloves garlic, chopped
1 tablespoon (15 mL) chopped fresh sage

Newfie Screech Barbecue Sauce
2 tablespoons (25 mL) vegetable oil
1 medium onion, finely chopped
4 cloves garlic, chopped
1 cup (250 mL) Newfoundland Screech rum (or a rum of your choice)
1/4 cup (50 mL) cider vinegar
1 cup (250 mL) barbecue sauce
1/2 cup (125 mL) cup molasses
1 tablespoon (15 mL) chopped fresh sage
Salt and pepper to taste

Rub the pork chops liberally with the barbecue spice and place in a large glass dish. In a bowl, whisk together the vegetable oil, rum, garlic, and sage. Pour this over the pork chops. Turn the chops over to evenly coat them in the rum mixture. Cover and refrigerate to marinate for 4 to 6 hours.

While the pork chops are marinating, heat the oil over medium-high heat in a small saucepot. Add the onion and garlic and sauté for 3 to 4 minutes until tender. Add the rum, vinegar, barbecue sauce, and molasses and bring to a boil. Reduce heat to medium-low and let simmer for ten minutes, stirring occasionally. Add the sage, and season to taste with salt and pepper. Remove from heat and set aside to cool.

Preheat grill to high. Remove the pork chops from the marinade and discard remaining marinade. Grill the pork chops over direct heat for 3 to 4 minutes per side to sear. Transfer the chops to the side of the grill with little or no fire and let them cook slowly for another 8 to 10 minutes per side. While they are cooking, baste the chops with the barbecue sauce.

Just before serving, place the chops over the direct heat for another minute and baste one more time liberally with the barbecue sauce.

Serve immediately with extra heated sauce.

Greek Town Shish Kebabs

Yield: 8 servings

Level: Intermediate

Grill: 9 to 12 minutes

At the Ready: 16 long, oiled metal skewers; barbecue tongs

You can prepare these kebabs hours a head of time and keep them covered and refrigerated until ready to grill. Lots of garlic makes these just outstanding.

3 pounds (1.5 kg) lean leg of lamb or shoulder, trimmed of fat and cut into 1 1/2 inch (4 cm) cubes
3 tablespoons (50 mL) barbecue spice (page 146)
1/2 cup (125 mL) olive oil
1/2 cup (125 mL) balsamic vinegar
12 cloves garlic, minced
1 tablespoon (15 mL) chopped fresh rosemary
1/2 teaspoon (2 mL) ground coriander

2 tablespoons (25 mL) Dijon Mustard
1 tablespoon (15 mL) cracked black pepper
2 medium zucchini
2 green bell peppers, halved and seeded
2 red bell peppers, halved and seeded
2 medium red onions, peeled
24 large white mushrooms, wiped of excess dirt
Salt and pepper to taste

In a large bowl, combine the lamb cubes and barbecue spice. Mix thoroughly, making sure the meat is well seasoned with the spice. Add the olive oil, balsamic vinegar, garlic, rosemary, coriander, mustard, and black pepper. Thread lamb onto eight skewers, cover, and refrigerate to marinate for 4 hours.

Cut zucchini, peppers, and onions into large pieces. Skewer onto remaining eight skewers, alternating with jumbo mushrooms. Season with olive oil, balsamic vinegar, salt, and pepper.

Prepare the grill for direct heat. Grill lamb skewers for 2 to 3 minutes per side (8 to 10 minutes total cooking time for medium-rare). When the lamb has been cooking for 3 minutes, place the vegetable skewers on the grill and cook them for 6 to 8 minutes. Remove from the grill and serve.

Hot Tip

When skewering the meat and vegetables, use two skewers, one for the meat and one for the vegetables. Meat and vegetables cook at different times, so using two skewers makes grilling easier.

Greek-Style Lamb Chops

Yield: 6 servings

Level: Easy

Grill: About 8 to 10 minutes

At the Ready: Long-handled spatula, oil or nonstick cooking spray, grill screen, brush

If you like, you can use oregano rather than rosemary in this recipe.

12 lamb loin chops, about 4 1/2 to 5 ounces (130 to 150 g) each, trimmed of fat
4 cloves garlic, peeled and minced
3 tablespoons (50 mL) minced fresh

rosemary, or 1 tablespoon (15 mL) chopped dried rosemary
1/4 cup (50 mL) olive oil
1/2 teaspoon (2 mL) black pepper
2 lemons, cut in half

Arrange the lamb chops in a flat glass dish. In a small bowl, mix the garlic, rosemary, olive oil, and pepper together. Brush the chops on both sides with the mixture, and squeeze the lemon halves over them.

Prepare the grill for direct heat. Oil or spray the cooking grid. When the coals are medium-hot, set the lamb chops on the grid. Cover the grill and adjust the vents. Grill the chops for 5 minutes. Turn them and continue grilling for 5 minutes, or until they are done to taste. Do not overcook. Remove the chops to individual plates and serve hot. These are good with potato skins or potatoes baked on the grill.

Lamb Burgers

Yield: 6 servings

Level: Intermediate

Grill: About 8 to 10 minutes

At the Ready: Oil or nonstick cooking spray, grill screen, basting brush, long-handled spatula, 3 to 4 handfuls of dried grape vine twigs soaked in water 30 minutes and drained (optional)

Serve these in warmed pita bread with yogurt or crumbled feta cheese, and olives.

1 3/4 to 2 pounds (875 g to 1 kg) ground lamb
1 tablespoon dried oregano
4 cloves garlic, peeled and minced

1 teaspoon (5 mL) ground coriander
1 small onion, peeled and minced
1/2 teaspoon (2 mL) salt
1 egg white

Put the ground lamb in a mixing bowl. Mix in the garlic, onion, egg white, oregano, coriander, and salt.

continues

continued

Using clean hands, shape the lamb mixture into 6 equal patties. Place them on a platter. Cover and refrigerate until ready to grill.

Prepare the grill for direct heat. Oil or spray a grill screen. When the coals are medium- hot, scatter the drained grapevines over the coals if desired. Set the burgers on the grill screen, then set it on the grid, about 4 to 6 inches (10 to 15 cm) from the heat. Cover and adjust the vents. Grill the burgers for 4 minutes. Turn them over and continue grilling until cooked through, about 4 to 5 minutes, depending on the thickness of the burger. All pink should be gone from the centre, but do not overcook them or they'll dry out.

Remove the burgers from the grill, place on individual plates, and serve hot.

The Least You Need to Know

➤ Meats take well to grilling.

➤ It's important to watch meats carefully so they're not overcooked or undercooked.

➤ Searing can help seal in the juices in steaks and chops.

Poultry

"Poultry is for the cook what a canvas is for the painter," wrote the famous nineteenth-century food authority Jean Anthelme Brillat-Savarin. We couldn't agree more. The naturally delicate flavours of chicken, turkey, and quail allow you to use sauces, flavoured woods, and herbs in creative ways to tempt the tastebuds.

In this assortment of recipes, we "paint" the birds with a variety of colourful flavours:

the pungency of cinnamon sticks, the sweetness of maple syrup, the tart-sweet flavour of apricots, the tang of sweet-and-sour sauce and the kick of chili.

As a bonus, the white meat of turkey or chicken is naturally low in fat (when you remove the skin). If you're watching your fat or cholesterol, you'll be delighted with the Cantonese-style sweet and sour chicken breasts, grill-roasted turkey breast, and turkey burgers with dried cranberries (use lean, all-white-meat ground turkey).

Don't forget, large pieces of poultry such as whole chicken, turkey, or Cornish hens, boneless turkey breasts, and turkey legs must be cooked over indirect heat so the centre cooks through before the outside burns.

Cantonese–Style Sweet and Sour Chicken Breasts

Yield: 6 servings

Level: Intermediate

Grill: About 10 minutes

At the Ready: Long-handled spatula or tongs, vegetable oil, basting brush, the cooked sauce

This Cantonese sauce also works well on grilled pork, turkey, or fish.

6 boneless, skinless chicken breast halves
Lemon juice to cover chicken
1 tablespoon (15 mL) peanut oil or canola blend oil
1/4 cup (50 mL) red wine vinegar
1/4 cup (50 mL) light-brown sugar

1/2 cup (125 mL) ketchup
1 cup (250 mL) pineapple juice
2 tablespoons (25 mL) cornstarch mixed with 3 tablespoons (50 mL) water
1 large tomato, cut into thin wedges
1 large green bell pepper, seeded and cut into strips

Place the chicken breasts in a glass bowl. Cover the chicken with lemon juice and marinate, covered, in the refrigerator for 3 to 4 hours, turning once or twice. Drain.

While the chicken is marinating, heat the oil in a small saucepan over medium heat. Stir in the vinegar, brown sugar, ketchup, and pineapple juice. Mix the cornstarch with water and blend it into the sauce. Continue cooking until the sauce turns clear and thickens slightly, and remove from the heat. Remember to reheat the hot sauce before serving.

Prepare the tomato and green pepper, cover, and refrigerate until ready to serve.

Prepare the grill for direct heat. Oil or spray the cooking grid. When the coals are medium-hot, brush the chicken breasts lightly with oil and place them on the grid, 4 to 6 inches (10 to 15 cm) from the heat. Grill, uncovered, about 5 minutes. Turn, again brush with oil, and continue cooking about 7 to 9 minutes, or until the chicken is fork tender and the juices run clear. Do not overcook. Cut the chicken into slices, then set on individual plates. Add the tomato and green pepper to the reheated sauce and pour it over the chicken. Serve immediately. This is good with cooked white or brown rice.

Whole Grilled Chicken with Apricot Sauce

Yield: 4 to 6 servings

Level: Intermediate

Grill: About 1 hour, or until thermometer inserted in thickest part of thigh registers 180°F (82°C)

At the Ready: 3 to 4 cups (750 mL to 1 L) hickory chips, soaked in water 30 minutes and drained, cutting board, long-handled tongs or spatula, pot holders, meat or instant thermometer

1 whole chicken, about 3 1/4 to 3 1/2 pounds (1.5 to 1.6 kg), washed and patted dry
2 tablespoons (25 mL) vegetable oil
3/4 cup (175 mL) dry white wine
3 cloves garlic, peeled and minced
1/4 teaspoon (1 mL) black pepper
1/3 cup (75 mL) chopped fresh parsley

Apricot Sauce
1 cup (250 mL) dried apricot halves
1 teaspoon (5 mL) ground cinnamon
1 cup (250 mL) orange juice
2 tablespoons (25 mL) light brown sugar
1/4 cup (50 mL) chicken broth
1/2 cup (125 mL) canned cranberry sauce
3 tablespoons (50 mL) orange liqueur, or 3 additional tablespoons (50 mL) orange juice

Remove any visible fat from the chicken. Put the chicken in a large, self-sealing plastic bag. In a bowl, mix together the oil, wine, garlic, pepper, and parsley. Pour the marinade over the chicken. Seal the bag securely. Turn the bag several times, coating the chicken with marinade. Place the bag in a large bowl and refrigerate for 3 hours. Drain the chicken.

Prepare the grill for indirect heat. When the coals are medium-hot, sprinkle the soaked hickory chips over them. Place the chicken, breast side up, on the grid directly over the drip pan (or over the unlit burner on a gas grill). Cover the grill and adjust the vents. Grill the chicken for about 1 hour. If you're using a charcoal grill, check the coals after 30 minutes and replenish with lit coals as necessary.

To test for doneness, insert a thermometer into the thickest part of the thigh; it should read 180°F (82°C). Or insert a knife into the deepest part of the thigh. If the juices run clear and the joints move easily, the chicken is done. Let stand for 10 minutes before serving.

While the chicken is grilling, prepare the sauce. Put the apricots in a pot and add enough water to cover them. Bring to a boil, reduce the heat to a simmer, and continue cooking over medium heat until the apricots are tender, about 10 minutes. Transfer them with any remaining cooking liquid to a food processor or blender, and purée. Stir in the remaining ingredients.

Serve the hot chicken cut into serving pieces, with the sauce.

Hot Tip

The sauce can be prepared early in the day, and the vegetables cut and refrigerated. When the chicken is cooked, working quickly, reheat the sauce and mix in the vegetables.

Chicken Yakitori

Yield: 6 servings

Level: Intermediate

Grill: 10 to 12 minutes

At the Ready: 12 short bamboo skewers, soaked in water at least 20 minutes and drained, vegetable oil or nonstick cooking spray, grill screen, basting brush

4 boneless, skinless chicken breast halves, washed and patted dry, and cut into 1 to 1 1/2 inch (2.5 to 4 cm) slices

12 chicken livers, cut in half

3/4 cup (175 mL) light (reduced-sodium) soy sauce

1/2 cup (125 mL) dry white wine

2 tablespoons (50 mL) sugar

1 clove garlic, smashed

1 teaspoon (5 mL) grated ginger, or a 1 inch (2.5 cm) piece of fresh ginger, smashed

1/4 teaspoon (1 mL) cayenne pepper

1 can (6 1/2 oz. or 170 g) whole water chestnuts, drained

4 small green bell peppers, cut into 1 inch (2.5 cm) pieces

Put the chicken and liver pieces in a large, self-sealing plastic bag.

Mix the soy sauce, wine, sugar, garlic, ginger, and cayenne together. Pour the marinade over the chicken and liver. Turn the bag several times to coat the meats with the marinade. Set the bag in a large bowl. Marinate in the refrigerator for 2 hours. Drain.

Thread the skewers, alternating the chicken, livers, water chestnuts, and peppers.

Prepare the grill for direct heat. Oil or spray a grill screen. When the coals are medium-hot, place the skewers on the grill screen, then set it on the cooking grid. Grill the kebabs, uncovered, for 10 to 12 minutes, turning about every 3 minutes. Serve with hot brown rice or fried rice.

Cinnamon–Skewered Honey Garlic Orange Chicken Thighs

Yield: 4 servings

Level: Intermediate

Grill: 10 to 15 minutes

At the Ready: Cinnamon sticks, about 5 inches (12 cm long and fairly thin), barbecue tongs, basting brush

Using cinnamon sticks as skewers adds not only to the presentation of the dish but also to the overall flavour of the chicken thighs. Cinnamon sticks can also be used in the fire as smoking chips to add another dimension of flavour to grilling foods.

16 cinnamon sticks, the thinner the stick the better
8 boneless, skin-on chicken thighs
2 teaspoons (10 mL) ground cinnamon
1 tablespoon (15 mL) cracked black pepper
6 cloves garlic, chopped
1 tablespoon (15 mL) chopped fresh ginger
1/4 cup (50 mL) olive oil
1/4 cup (50 mL) honey

1 cup (250 mL) hoisin sauce (hoisin sauce can be found in most grocery stores in the ethnic food section)
1/2 cup (125 mL) orange juice
1 tablespoon (15 mL) sesame seeds
1 teaspoon (5 mL) sesame oil
2 tablespoons (25 mL) rice wine vinegar
1 tablespoon (15 mL) chopped fresh cilantro
Salt and pepper to taste

Skewer the chicken thighs with two cinnamon sticks. Place the sticks about 1 inch (2.5 cm) apart. This will give the chicken thighs some stability and add flavour.

In a small bowl, whisk together the ground cinnamon, black pepper, garlic, ginger, and olive oil. Rub this mixture all over the chicken thighs and let marinate for 4 to 6 hours.

In a separate bowl, whisk together the honey, hoisin sauce, orange juice, sesame seeds, sesame oil, rice vinegar, and cilantro. Season to taste with salt and pepper.

Preheat the grill to medium-high. Grill the cinnamon-skewered chicken thighs starting with the skin side down for 6 to 7 minutes per side, until the chicken is fully cooked. While the chicken is grilling be sure to baste generously with the honey hoisin orange sauce.

Paella

Yield: 6 servings

Level: Advanced

Grill: 25 minutes

At the Ready: Olive oil for brushing, grill screen, tongs, basting brush, the cooked rice, the cooked peas

2 cups (500 mL) long-grain or converted rice

3 3/4 cups (925 mL) water or reduced-sodium chicken broth

2 pinches saffron, or 3/4 (4 mL) teaspoon turmeric

2 cups (500 mL) frozen green peas, cooked according to package directions

1 chicken, about 3 to 3 1/2 pounds (1.5 to 1.75 kg), cut into serving pieces

Paprika to taste

Salt and pepper to taste

1 pound (500 g) spicy sausage, pricked with a fork in several places

1 large onion, cut into 1/2 inch (1 cm) slices

3 tomatoes, sliced

24 mussels, cleaned

12 large, unshelled shrimp, washed

Prepare the rice according to the package directions, but substituting the chicken broth for the cooking water. Omit salt and add the saffron or turmeric to the chicken broth.

Meanwhile, cook the peas and set aside.

While the rice is cooking, brush the chicken with oil and sprinkle with paprika, salt, and pepper.

Prepare the grill for direct heat. Oil or spray the cooking grid, and a cooking screen. When the coals are medium-hot, put the chicken on the grid.

Cover the grill and adjust the vents. Grill the chicken pieces about 15 to 25 minutes, turning them occasionally. The wings should cook in about 10 to 15 minutes; the legs and breast will take at least 5 to 10 minutes longer. While the chicken is cooking, set the sausages on the grill rack and cook them about 10 to 15 minutes, turning occasionally. Remove the sausages when they are cooked and browned. Cut into pieces and set aside.

Near the end of the chicken's cooking time, place the grill screen on the grid, and place the onion slices, tomatoes, mussels, and shrimp on it. Grill the vegetables and seafood about 5 minutes, turning once, until the mussels are open, the shrimp is opaque, and the vegetables are tender. Discard any mussels that do not open during grilling.

Toss the sausage pieces and the vegetables with the hot cooked rice. Arrange the shrimp, mussels, and chicken on the rice. Serve hot.

What's What

Paella is a Spanish dish that has numerous variations, depending on the cook. There are many recipes for paella, some including both seafood and meat, others using only seafood, and still others using only vegetables. For example, you can add more chicken and not use the shrimp, or use a pinch of turmeric in the rice in place of the saffron, or eliminate the sausage and maybe add some grilled shrimp. Make it your own recipe by using the foods that you prefer.

Sweet and Spicy Grilled Chicken Wings

Yield: 4 servings

Level: Intermediate

Grill: 15 to 20 minutes

At the Ready: Barbecue grill basket, barbecue tongs, large bowl, self-sealing plastic bag

Grilling wouldn't be complete without grilled chicken wings. This great appetizer or main course can easily be done on the grill with the use of a barbecue grill basket.

4 pounds of chicken wings (tips removed and cut into winglets and drumettes)
1/4 cup (50 mL) barbecue seasoning, (page 146)
1/4 cup (50 mL) cider vinegar
1/4 cup (50 mL) hot sauce

Marinade
1/2 cup (125 mL) maple syrup
1/2 cup (125 mL) barbecue sauce
1/2 cup (125 mL) hot sauce
1/4 cup (50 mL) butter, melted
2 tablespoons cider vinegar
Salt to taste

Place the chicken wing pieces in a large, self-sealing plastic bag. Add the barbecue seasoning, cider vinegar, and hot sauce. Close the bag and shake vigorously. Refrigerate for 4 to 6 hours.

Preheat the grill to medium-high. Remove the chicken from the bag and discard the marinade. Place the chicken wings in a barbecue grill basket. Grill for 8 to 10 minutes per side until the chicken is fully cooked and crispy. Carefully remove the chicken wings from the grill basket and place in a large bowl. Add the maple syrup, barbecue sauce, hot sauce, melted butter, and vinegar. Season to taste and serve immediately with celery sticks and chunky blue cheese dip.

Grilled Sea Chickens

Yield: 6 portions

Level: Advanced

Grill: 12 to 16 minutes

At the Ready: Sharp boning knife, plastic wrap, kitchen mallet, barbecue tongs, vegetable oil

This is truly a decadent barbecue dish. The stuffing mixture of Brie cheese and P.E.I. lobster meat is a wonderful addition to everyday chicken.

Six 6 ounce (175 g) boneless, skin-on chicken breasts
3 tablespoons (50 mL) Great Lakes seafood seasoning (page 147)
1/2 cup (125 mL) Brie cheese, coarsely chopped
1 cup (250 mL) lobster meat (frozen tinned lobster meat works best for this recipe)
2 green onions, finely chopped
1 tablespoon (15 mL) lemon juice
1 tablespoon (15 mL) chopped fresh dill
Salt and pepper to taste

Place a sheet or two of plastic wrap on a flat work surface. Place the chicken breast skin side down on top of the plastic wrap.

Remove the chicken tenderloin and set aside. Using a sharp boning knife, make an incision from the top of the breast to the bottom about 1/2 inch (1 cm) deep. Carefully using the tip of the knife, make a butterfly incision on either side of your initial cut. You are making a large pocket. Using your finger, push the meat aside to make a large pocket. Place a sheet of plastic over the chicken breasts and, with a meat mallet, gently pound the chicken breasts to slightly flatten them. Slightly flatten the reserved chicken tenderloins as well. Remove and discard the top sheet of plastic. Season the chicken breasts inside and out with the seafood seasoning.

In a bowl, mix together the Brie, lobster, green onions, lemon juice, and dill. Season to taste with salt and pepper. Divide the mixture into 6 equal portions and form into an oval shape, firmly packed.

Place one lobster stuffing oval in each cavity of the chicken. Cover with the flattened chicken tenderloin and tuck the edges into the cavity. Fold the edges over and press firmly to make a tight seal. Cover and refrigerate for 1 hour to allow the meat to rest and the stuffing to set.

Preheat the grill to medium-high. Lightly brush the chicken breasts with olive or vegetable oil.

Grill sea chickens skin side down to start for 12 to 16 minutes until the chicken is fully cooked and the stuffing hot.

Remove from the grill. Slice each chicken breast in half on the bias, and serve with grilled asparagus.

Grill-Roasted Turkey Breast

Yield: 6 to 8 servings

Level: Easy

Grill: About 1 1/4 hours

Tangerine Marinade
1 cup (250 mL) red wine
1/2 cup (125 mL) tangerine juice or
  orange juice
1/4 cup (50 mL) chopped fresh basil or
2 tablespoons (25 mL) dried basil

At the Ready: Aluminum foil, water
  pan, pecan pieces or aromatic wood of
  choice, soaked 30 minutes and
  drained (optional)

1/2 teaspoon (2 mL) black pepper
One 3 to 3 1/2 pound (1.5 to 1.75 kg)
  boneless turkey breast
3/4 cup (175 mL) barbecue sauce
3/4 cup (175 mL) grape jelly

In a small bowl, mix together the wine, juice, basil, and pepper. Set the turkey in a glass bowl or large, self-sealing plastic bag.

Pour the marinade over the turkey. Seal the bag and turn it several times so that all areas of the turkey are coated with the marinade. Set the turkey in a glass dish. Refrigerate for 4 to 6 hours. Drain.

Prepare the grill for indirect heat. In a bowl blend together the barbecue sauce and jelly. Brush the turkey breast with the sauce. When the coals are medium-hot, sprinkle pecan pieces over them. Set the turkey on a sheet of aluminum foil, and place it on the grill over the water pan. Cover the grill, adjust the vents, and grill the turkey breast for 1 to 1 1/4 hours, or until the juices run clear when you pierce the turkey with the tip of a knife. If you're using a charcoal grill, replenish the grill with lit coals as necessary. Rotate the turkey several times during grilling.

Remove the turkey breast to a cutting board, cover with foil, and let rest for 10 to 12 minutes. Slice and serve. This is good with chutney or cranberry sauce and garlic mashed potatoes.

Turkey Burgers with Dried Cranberries

Yield: 6 servings

Level: Easy

Grill: 10 to 12 minutes

At the Ready: Long-handled spatula, grill screen, oil for brushing, a brush

These are great with grilled sweet potato wedges on the side.

2 pounds (1 kg) ground turkey
1 teaspoon (5 mL) ground sage
1 large onion, minced
Salt and pepper to taste

1 egg
6 onion hard rolls, split
3/4 cup (175 mL) dried cranberries

In a large mixing bowl, blend together the ground turkey, onion, egg, dried cranberries, sage, salt, and pepper. Shape into 6 equal patties. Put the patties on a plate, cover with plastic wrap, and refrigerate until ready to grill.

Prepare the grill for direct heat. Oil or spray a grill screen. When the coals are medium-hot, set the burgers on the grill screen, and set that on the cooking grid. Cover the grill and adjust the vents. Grill about 10 to 12 minutes, turning once. When the burgers are almost ready, heat the rolls on the grill, just 1 or 2 minutes, long enough to warm them.

Set each burger in a warmed roll. Serve hot with grilled sweet potato wedges or chips, sliced tomatoes, and/or sweet and sour pickles.

Hot Tip

Dried cranberries, cherries, and strawberries are relatively new items in supermarkets. If you like, you can substitute chopped walnuts or raisins for the dried cranberries.

Grilled Quail
with Brown Sugar Butter

Yield: 6 servings

Level: Advanced

Grill: 8 to 10 minutes

At the Ready: Long-handled spatula, basting brush

Quail are available at some large supermarkets and specialty butcher shops, at many Asian markets, and from shops specializing in wild game.

12 butterflied quail, washed and patted dry
1/4 cup (50 mL) vegetable oil
1/4 cup (50 mL) soy sauce
1 tablespoon (15 mL) brown sugar
1 tablespoon (15 mL) cider vinegar

1 tablespoon (15 mL) chopped fresh thyme
1 teaspoon (5 mL) coarsely ground black pepper
1/4 cup (50 mL) golden raisins

In a bowl, whisk together the vegetable oil, soy sauce, brown sugar, garlic, and green onions. Have ready 2 large, self-sealing plastic bags. Place 6 quail into each bag. Divide marinade into 2 equal parts and pour over each bag of quail. Marinate, refrigerated, for 2 to 4 hours.

To prepare the brown sugar and raisin butter, mix together using a rubber spatula the softened butter, brown sugar, cider vinegar, thyme, black pepper, and raisins. Transfer to a small dish, and reserve.

Preheat grill to medium-high. Drain quail and discard marinade. Season quail with salt and grill 3 to 4 minutes per side until pink. Be careful not to overcook the quail, as they will become tough.

Transfer the quail to a serving platter and dollop each quail with a little of the brown sugar raisin butter. Serve with an arugula salad and grilled bread.

Hot Tip

To butterfly quail, use a pair of kitchen scissors or poultry shears to cut the backbone out of the quail. Open the quail to butterfly position, then press on the breastbone until the bone cracks and the quail lies flat. Better yet, ask the butcher to do this.

Pineapple Ginger Marinated Turkey Legs

Yield: 6 servings

Level: Intermediate

Grill: 50 to 60 minutes, or until a thermometer inserted in the thickest part of the thigh registers 180°F (82°C)

At the Ready: Long-handled tongs, apple wood chips or twigs soaked 30 minutes and drained (optional), water pan, small, sharp knife, aluminum foil, meat or instant thermometer

1 cup (250 mL) pineapple juice
1/4 cup (50 mL) soy sauce,
2 tablespoons (25 mL) chopped ginger
1/4 cup (50 mL) brown sugar
1/4 cup (50 mL) lime juice
4 green onions, trimmed and minced
4 cloves garlic, peeled and minced

1 tablespoon (15 mL) ground cumin
1/2 teaspoon (2 mL) salt
6 turkey legs, about 10 to 12 ounces (280 to 350 g) each, washed and patted dry
Chopped fresh cilantro for garnish

Put the pineapple juice in a mixing bowl. Blend in the soy sauce, ginger, brown sugar, lime juice, green onion, garlic, cumin, and salt.

Place the turkey legs in a shallow glass dish. Cover them with the pineapple ginger marinade. Cover with plastic wrap and refrigerate for 6 hours or longer.

Prepare the grill for indirect heat. When the coals are medium-hot, set the turkey drumsticks, still on a piece of aluminum foil, on the grill. Cover the grill and adjust the vents. Grill until the turkey is fork tender and the juices run clear, about 50 to 60 minutes. Turn the turkey pieces every 10 to 15 minutes. If you are using a charcoal grill, replenish the grill with lit coals at least once, or as necessary.

Serve hot with salsa and warm flour tortillas. Garnish with chopped fresh cilantro.

The Least You Need to Know

➤ Chicken is one of the most versatile foods for grilling.

➤ Turkey or chicken white meat is low in fat.

➤ Large pieces of poultry must be cooked over indirect heat.

Chapter 20

Fish

In This Chapter

- ➤ Swordfish in Buttermilk Marinade
- ➤ Tarragon-Scented Striped Bass
- ➤ Red Snapper with Olive Salad
- ➤ Halibut Steaks au Poivre
- ➤ Grilled Tuna with Spicy Fried Onions
- ➤ Bluefish Piccata
- ➤ Minted Flounder on Lime Slices
- ➤ Grilled Whole Rainbow Trout Stuffed with Sage, Onions, and Bacon
- ➤ Grilled Sea Bass Wrapped in Grape Leaves
- ➤ Grilled Pacific Salmon Steaks Teriyaki
- ➤ Barbecued Atlantic Salmon Fillets
- ➤ Red Snapper Margarita
- ➤ Atlantic Cod with Grilled Apple Slices

Fish is too often ignored among the stars of the grill. Lean, sophisticated, and flavourful, it's actually one of the best foods to grill. Thanks to modern air transportation, you can walk into your fish market and have a wide selection of everything from frozen shrimp to farm-raised trout to Alaskan halibut.

Fish generally is cooked until it "flakes"—that is, when you prod it with a fork, it begins to separate into slices. For fish to cook until it flakes does not mean that it should be dry, so be careful, because it does dry out quickly if left on the grill too long. It's best to remove the fish when it is still not quite opaque all the way through the centre. It finishes cooking after you remove it from the heat.

In general, fish requires 10 minutes of cooking time per inch (2.5 cm) of thickness. In other words, you grill a 1 inch (2.5 cm) swordfish steak for 10 minutes, a 1/2 inch (1.25 cm) whitefish fillet for 5 minutes. Obviously, this is only a general rule, since fish varies in density. You'll still need to keep an eye on it.

When grilling a long fish fillet, fold the narrow part (the tail section) under the fish. This helps even out the thickness of the fish so it cooks more uniformly.

We have used readily available fish in these recipes, but if the fish we call for is not available, or doesn't look as fresh as it should, you can substitute. Ask the fishmonger for ideas, or use the following as a guide. The fish in a given listing can all substitute for one another:

➤ Swordfish, shark, tuna, marlin

➤ Striped bass, grouper, halibut, orange roughy, rockfish, tilefish, ocean perch, red sea bass

➤ Red snapper, black sea bass, grouper, halibut, mahi mahi, rockfish

➤ Halibut, snapper, mahi mahi, yellowtail, black sea bass

➤ Orange roughy, striped bass, black sea bass, perch, sole, catfish, tilapia

➤ Bluefish, mackerel

➤ Flounder, sole, tilapia

➤ Whitefish, rainbow trout, salmon

➤ Cod, haddock, flounder

Swordfish in Buttermilk Marinade

Yield: 6 servings

Level: Intermediate

Grill: About 8 minutes

At the Ready: Long-handled spatula, oil for brushing, grill screen, brush

Swordfish has a firm texture and a mildly distinct flavour. You can substitute shark or tuna.

3 cups (750 mL) buttermilk
2 teaspoons (10 mL) Tabasco sauce

6 swordfish steaks, 3/4 inch (2 cm) thick, rinsed and patted dry

In a bowl, mix together the buttermilk and the Tabasco sauce. Divide the marinade into 2 large self-sealing plastic bags. Add 3 swordfish steaks to each bag and seal securely. Turn each bag several times. Set the bags on a flat dish and marinate in the refrigerator for 2 hours. Drain the fish and pat dry with paper towelling.

Prepare the grill for direct heat. Oil or spray a grill screen. When the coals are medium-hot, set the fish on the grill screen and set that on the cooking grid. Cover the grill and adjust the vents. Grill the fish 4 minutes. Turn and continue grilling another 4 minutes, or until the fish is opaque and flakes easily when prodded with a fork.

Remove the fish from the grill and set on individual plates.

Hot Tip

Buttermilk is a great marinade. It's acidic enough to tenderize foods, and rich enough to give them a wonderful flavour. Despite its name, it is actually low in fat.

Tarragon-Scented Striped Bass

Yield: 6 servings

Level: Easy

Grill: About 4 to 6 minutes

At the Ready: 1 cup dried tarragon or basil, soaked in water 5 minutes and drained (optional), vegetable oil for brushing, long-handled spatula, basting brush, fresh tarragon if available

Striped bass is a low-fat, medium-firm fish with a mild flavour. You can substitute orange roughy or black sea bass in this recipe.

6 striped bass fillets, rinsed and patted
  dry
Olive or canola oil

Fresh or dried tarragon
Salt and pepper to taste
Balsamic vinegar

Prepare the grill for direct heat. Oil the cooking grid. When the coals are medium-hot, sprinkle the herbs over them. Brush the fish lightly with oil, put a few tarragon sprigs on top, and sprinkle with salt and pepper. Set the fish on the cooking grid. Cover the grill and adjust the vents. Grill the fish about 4 to 6 minutes, or until it is opaque and flakes easily when prodded with a fork.

Remove the fish from the grill with a long-handled spatula and set on individual plates. Sprinkle it with balsamic vinegar.

Don't Get Burned!

Do not turn delicate fish such as bass when grilling it; it will fall apart.

Red Snapper with Olive Salad

Yield: 6 servings

Level: Easy

Grill: About 8 minutes

Olive Salad
1/2 cup (125 mL) extra-virgin olive oil
2 tablespoons (25 mL) chopped fresh
    parsley
1 tablespoon (15 mL) lemon juice
1/3 cup (75 mL) pitted chopped olives

At the Ready: Olive oil or vegetable oil
    for brushing, grill screen, brush, long-
    handled spatula, 3 or 4 handfuls of
    dried grapevine twigs soaked in water
    30 minutes and drained (optional)

(use a mixture of flavourful black and
green olives)
6 red or Pacific snapper fillets, 6 to 7
    ounces (180 to 210 g) each, rinsed
    and patted dry

To prepare the salad, mix all the ingredients in a small glass bowl. Cover and refrigerate until ready to serve. Bring the salad to room temperature before serving.

Check the fish for any visible bones, and remove them with tweezers.

Prepare the grill for direct heat. Brush the snapper pieces on both sides with oil and arrange the fillets on an oiled or sprayed grill screen. When the coals are medium-hot, set the fish and grill screen on the cooking grid. Cover the grill and adjust the vents. Grill the fish 3 to 4 minutes, then turn with a long-handled spatula. Continue cooking for 3 to 4 minutes, or just until the fish is opaque and flakes easily when prodded with a fork. It should still be moist in the thickest part.

Transfer the fish to plates and serve with a spoonful of the olive salad. Serve hot.

Halibut Steaks au Poivre

Yield: 6 servings

Level: Easy

Grill: About 6 to 8 minutes

At the Ready: Long-handled spatula,
    grill screen, brush

*Halibut is a sweet-flavoured fish with a moderately high fat content, which makes it
especially suitable for grilling.*

2 tablespoons (25 mL) black
    peppercorns, crushed
2 tablespoons (25 mL) green
    peppercorns, crushed

2 teaspoons (10 mL) dried basil
6 halibut steaks, about 3/4 inch (2 cm)
    thick, rinsed and patted dry
Vegetable or olive oil

Put the crushed black and green peppercorns in a small bowl. Mix in the basil.

continues

197

continued

Brush the halibut steaks with oil. Sprinkle them with the peppercorn rub and press the peppercorns to adhere to the fish. Set the fish on a glass plate and cover loosely with plastic wrap. Refrigerate for 1 hour. Remove the covering.

Prepare the grill for direct heat. Oil or spray a grill screen. When the coals are medium-hot, set the halibut steaks on the grill screen, and set that on the cooking grid. Cover the grill and adjust the vents. Grill 4 minutes, then turn the fish over. Continue grilling for 2 to 3 minutes or until the fish flakes easily when prodded with a fork.

Remove the fish to individual plates. Serve hot.

Grilled Tuna with Spicy Fried Onions

Yield: 6 servings

Level: Intermediate

Grill: 5 to 6 minutes

At the Ready: Vegetable oil, long-handled spatula, barbecue tongs, fry pan

Tuna has a firm texture and a mildly distinct flavour. You can substitute swordfish, marlin, or shark.

6 tuna loin steaks, about 6 ounces (180 g) and at least 1 inch (2.5 cm) thick.
3 tablespoons (50 mL) Great Lakes seafood seasoning (page 147)
2 tablespoons (25 mL) vegetable oil
1 medium red onion, thinly sliced
1 medium white onion, thinly sliced
4 cloves garlic, chopped

6 green onions, thinly sliced
1/2 teaspoon (2 mL) cayenne pepper
Dash of hot sauce
2 tablespoons (25 mL) chopped fresh chives
1 tablespoon (15 mL) lemon juice
Salt and pepper to taste

Rub the tuna steaks with the Great Lakes seafood seasoning, making sure to push the spices into the flesh of the tuna. Cover and refrigerate until needed.

Heat the oil in a large frying pan over medium-high heat. Sauté the red onions, white onions, and garlic for 8 to 10 minutes, stirring continuously until the onions become soft. Add the cayenne pepper, hot sauce, and lemon juice and continue stir-frying for another 1 to 2 minutes. Add the green onions and chives, and season to taste with salt and pepper. Set aside to keep warm.

Preheat the grill to medium high. Grill the tuna for 2 to 4 minutes per side for medium-rare. Serve immediately with sautéed onions.

Bluefish Piccata

Yield: 6 servings

Level: Easy

Grill: 8 to 10 minutes, or until done to taste

At the Ready: Grill screen, oil for brushing, brush, long-handled spatula; 1 cup dried basil, soaked in water for 5 minutes and squeezed dry (optional)

2 tablespoons (25 mL) olive oil
3 cloves garlic, minced
1 cup (250 mL) dry white wine
1/3 cup (75 mL) lemon juice
1/4 cup (50 mL) capers, drained

1 3/4 to 2 pounds (875 g to 1 kg) bluefish, cut into 6 pieces, rinsed and patted dry
1/2 cup (125 mL) shredded Romano or Parmesan cheese

Heat the olive oil in a small frying pan over medium heat. Add the garlic and cook, stirring, until soft, about 1 to 2 minutes. Add the wine, lemon juice, and capers. Bring the mixture to a boil, stirring often. Remove from heat and allow to cool. Use the sauce at room temperature.

Brush the bluefish with oil. Prepare the grill for direct heat. Oil or spray a grill screen. When the coals are medium-hot, set the bluefish on the grill screen, then set that on the cooking grid. Grill the fish 4 minutes. Turn it over and continue cooking about 4 or 5 minutes, or until the fish is opaque, yet still moist in the thickest part, and flakes easily when prodded with a fork.

Transfer the fish to individual plates or to a platter. Spoon the sauce over the fish, sprinkle with cheese, and serve.

What's What

Nicknamed "bulldog of the ocean" for its tenacity, the bluefish is a coastal Atlantic fish with fine-grained, fatty flesh that makes it great on the grill.

Minted Flounder on Lime Slices

Yield: 6 servings

Level: Easy

Grill: 5 to 7 minutes

At the Ready: Lime slices, oil for brushing, grill screen and brush, food processor or blender, long-handled fork

6 flounder fillets, about 6 to 8 ounces (180 to 210 g) each
Fresh mint sprigs

Mint Butter
1/2 cup (125 mL or 1 stick) butter, at room temperature

1/4 cup (50 mL) fresh mint sprigs, stems discarded
1 tablespoon (15 mL) crème de menthe liqueur
1 tablespoon (15 mL) grated lime peel
6 limes, cut into thin slices

Cut the butter into small pieces and place it in a food processor or blender. Add the mint, crème de menthe, and lime peel. Process until the ingredients are puréed and smooth. Spoon the butter into a small bowl or a crock and cover it with plastic wrap. If you are grilling the fish right away, leave the butter at room temperature. Otherwise, refrigerate it and bring to room temperature before serving.

Prepare the grill for direct heat. Oil or spray a grill screen. When the coals are medium-hot, put the lime slices on the grill screen. Brush the fish with oil and set a mint sprig on top of each fillet. Arrange the fish directly on the lime slices. Set the grill screen on the cooking grid. Cover the grill and adjust the vents. Grill 4 to 5 minutes, check the fish, and continue grilling until the fish flakes easily when prodded with a fork.

Remove the fish and the lime slices to individual plates. Serve the fish hot and pass the mint butter to be dabbed on the fish.

Hot Tip

Peppermint or spearmint is very easy to grow. In fact, mint can choke out your garden if you don't contain it. Chop up extra mint, put it in small self-sealing bags, and freeze it for winter use.

Grilled Whole Rainbow Trout
Stuffed with Sage, Onions, and Bacon

Yield: 4 portions

Level: Advanced

Grill: 15 to 18 minutes

At the Ready: Grill screen, nonstick cooking spray, basting brush, long-handled spatula, butcher's string, and fish-filleting knife

Ever since I can remember I have loved trout. Pan-fried, baked, or grilled it is the perfect shore lunch fish.

Four 1 1/2 pound. (750 g) fresh rainbow trout, cleaned
1 tablespoon (15 mL) Great Lakes seafood seasoning (page 147)
2 tablespoons (25 mL) butter, softened
1 medium sweet yellow onion
2 cloves garlic, minced

1 tablespoon (15 mL) chopped fresh sage
2 tablespoons (25 mL) cider or malt vinegar
6 slices bacon, cooked crisp and chopped into large bits
Salt and pepper to taste
1 lemon for squeezing

Using a fish-filleting knife, enter the belly of the trout and cut through the trout's backbone at the base of the head. Spread the trout flat and remove the backbone and rib bones. Season with seafood seasoning and set aside.

In a small bowl, mix together the butter, onions, garlic, sage, vinegar, and bacon bits. Season to taste with salt and pepper. Divide the mixture into four equal portions.

Stuff the centre of the trout with the onion mixture. Fold over the trout, making sure to keep the stuffing inside. Tie closed with a couple of pieces of butcher's twine.

Preheat grill to medium-high. Spray the grill screen and stuffed trout with the nonstick cooking spray. Place trout on grill screen and grill for 15 to 18 minutes, turning carefully four times with the spatula.

When the trout is cooked, squeeze the lemon over the trout. Season with salt and serve with steamed rice and vegetables.

Grilled Sea Bass Wrapped in Grape Leaves

Yield: 4 portions

Level: Advanced

Grill: 15 to 18 minutes

At the Ready: Jarred grape leaves in brine, grill screen, long-handled barbecue spatula, nonstick cooking spray, butcher's twine

Sea bass is a delicious fish that has a similar texture to salmon. It is firm and holds up well on the grill.

Four 6 ounce (180 g) portions of sea bass fillets, skin and bones removed
2 tablespoons (25 mL) Great Lakes seafood seasoning (page 147)
1 mango, peeled, seeded, and thinly sliced
1 small red onion, thinly sliced
1 medium red pepper, thinly sliced

1 medium yellow pepper, thinly sliced
3 tablespoons (50 mL) orange juice
2 tablespoons (25 mL) olive oil
1 tablespoon (15 mL) chopped fresh tarragon
Salt and pepper to taste
12 to 16 grape leaves, drained

Season the sea bass fillets with the seafood seasoning and set aside.

In a small bowl, mix together the mango, red onion, sweet peppers, orange juice, olive oil, and tarragon. Season to taste with salt and pepper.

Unroll the grape leaves. You will need approximately 3 to 4 leaves per portion depending on the size of the leaves. Lay 3 or 4 leaves on a flat work surface and pat dry with a paper towel.

Divide the mango onion mixture into eight. Place 1/8 the mango mixture in the centre of the grape leaves. Place one seasoned sea bass fillet on top of the mango mixture. Top the sea bass with another 1/8 the mango mixture. Starting from the bottom, fold the grape leaves over the sea bass. Fold in from both sides and then roll up to encase the sea bass. Secure the bundle with some butcher's twine. Repeat for the remaining portions. (These can be made up to 6 hours ahead and stored in the refrigerator.

Preheat the grill to medium-high. Spray the grill screen and the sea bass bundles with nonstick cooking spray. Place bundles on the grill and cook for 6 to 8 minutes per side, carefully turning once.

Remove from grill and cut the string off each bundle. Gently unwrap each bundle and serve with fresh lemon or orange slices.

What's What

Grape leaves can be found jarred in brine in most grocery stores. Look in the ethnic food section.

Grilled Pacific Salmon Steaks Teriyaki

Yield: 6 servings

Level: Intermediate

Grill Time: 8 to 10 minutes

At the Ready: Grill screen, nonstick cooking spray, basting brush, long-handled barbecue spatula

Canada is fortunate to have an abundance of salmon from the Pacific Ocean and the many rivers of British Columbia. The Pacific salmon's delicate flavour is prized throughout the world.

Six 6 ounce (180 g) salmon steaks
2 tablespoons (25 mL) Great Lakes
seafood spice (page 147)
1 cup (250 mL) soy sauce
1/2 cup (125 mL) sake (Japanese rice wine) or mirin (Japanese sweet cooking wine)

4 tablespoons (60 mL) brown sugar
4 cloves garlic, minced
1 tablespoon (15 mL) ginger, minced
1 teaspoon (5 mL) sesame oil
1 tablespoon (15 mL) sesame seeds
2 green onions, finely chopped
Salt and pepper to taste

Rub the salmon steaks with the seafood seasoning mix and place in a glass dish.

In a medium bowl, whisk together the soy sauce, sake, brown sugar, garlic, ginger, sesame oil, sesame seeds, and green onions. Season to taste with salt and pepper. Pour half of the soy mixture over the salmon steaks (reserving remaining mixture for basting) and marinate refrigerated for 2 hours.

Preheat grill to medium-high. Spray the grill screen with nonstick cooking spray and place on grill. Remove salmon from marinade, discarding remaining marinade. Grill salmon steaks for 4 to 5 minutes per side, basting frequently with reserved marinade until salmon is just cooked. Salmon is best when cooked to medium-rare.

Serve salmon steaks with remaining basting sauce and a cucumber and dill salad.

Barbecued Atlantic Salmon Fillets

Yield: 6 servings

Level: Intermediate

Grill: About 8 to 10 minutes

At the Ready: grill screen, long-handled spatula, basting brush

Atlantic salmon is Canada's other salmon. It is succulent and loaded with rich flavour.

Six 6 ounce (180 g) Atlantic salmon fillets
2 tablespoons (25 mL) barbecue spice (page 146)
1 bottle beer
2 tablespoons (25 mL) butter

2 cloves garlic, chopped
1/2 cup (125 mL) honey
1 1/4 cups (300 mL) barbecue sauce
1 tablespoon (15 mL) Worcestershire sauce
2 green onions, finely chopped

Rub the salmon fillets with the barbecue seasoning and place in a glass dish. Pour 1/2 bottle of beer over the fillets, cover, refrigerate, and let marinate for 2 hours.

In a small sauce pot, melt the butter over medium-high heat. Sauté the garlic for 2 minutes until tender. Add the remaining 1/2 bottle of beer (if you haven't drank it) and bring to a boil. Reduce the beer by half and then add the honey, barbecue sauce, Worcestershire sauce, and green onions. Bring to a boil and let simmer for 5 minutes. Remove from the stove and let cool.

Preheat the grill to medium-high. Spray the grill screen with the nonstick cooking spray.

Grill the salmon for 4 to 5 minutes per side, basting frequently with the barbecue sauce until the salmon is cooked to medium-rare. Serve with any extra barbecue sauce.

What's What

Salmon is a coldwater fish from both the Atlantic and Pacific oceans. The salmon of the Northwest has five species, with sockeye, chinook, and coho being the most popular varieties. These days, most salmon in markets is farm-raised.

Red Snapper Margarita

Yield: 6 servings

Level: Easy

Grill: About 8 minutes

At the Ready: Lime wedges, oil for brushing, grill screen, brush, long-handled fork, 3 cups (750 mL) mesquite chips soaked in water 30 minutes and drained (optional)

Six 6 to 8 ounce (180 to 240 g) red or Pacific snapper fillets, washed and patted dry

Margarita Marinade
3/4 cup (175 mL) orange juice

concentrate, thawed (don't add water)
1/4 cup (50 mL) tequila
1/2 cup (125 mL) lime juice
2 tablespoons (25 mL) olive oil
1 clove garlic, peeled and smashed

In a bowl, combine the orange juice concentrate, tequila, lime juice, olive oil, and garlic. Put the fish in a flat glass dish or 2 large self-sealing plastic bags. Cover with marinade. Cover and marinate for 1 hour in the refrigerator. Drain.

Prepare the grill for direct heat. Oil or spray a grill screen. When the coals are medium-hot, set the fish on the grill screen and set that on the cooking grid. Cover the grill and adjust the vents. Grill the fish for 4 minutes, then turn it over and grill it another 4 minutes, or until it flakes easily when prodded with a fork. Remove the fish to a serving platter. Serve hot with lime or orange wedges. This is good with salsa and grilled asparagus.

Hot Tip

To make an easy orange or pineapple salsa, use your favourite salsa recipe and substitute chopped orange or pineapple for the tomatoes.

Atlantic Cod with Grilled Apple Slices

Yield: 6 servings

Level: Intermediate

Grill: 6 to 8 minutes

At the Ready: Grill screen, oil for brushing, brush, long-handled spatula

Snapper can be substituted for the cod in this recipe. While the apples are grilling, you can sprinkle them with a small amount of sugar, mixed with cinnamon for additional flavour.

Six 6 to 8 ounce (180 to 240 g) cod fillets, rinsed and patted dry
2 oranges, thinly sliced
4 large Granny Smith apples, peeled,

cored, and sliced
Melted butter or margarine for brushing apple slices
Sage and nutmeg

Prepare the grill for direct heat. Brush the scrod pieces on both sides with oil. Oil or spray a grill screen. When the coals are medium-hot, set the orange slices on the grill screen. Set it on the cooking grid 4 to 6 inches (10 to 15 cm) from the heat, then set the fish atop the orange slices. Cover the grill and adjust the vents. Grill about 6 minutes. Continue cooking until the fish turns opaque and flakes easily when prodded with a fork. It should remain moist in the thickest part. While the fish is cooking, brush the apple slices with butter and set them on the screen. Grill the apples on both sides until they are tender and just beginning to brown.

Serve the fish on individual plates surrounded with grilled apples. Sprinkle both lightly with sage and nutmeg. Serve hot.

The Least You Need to Know

➤ Lean yet flavourful, fish is one of the best choices for grilling.

➤ Cook fish for 10 minutes per inch of thickness, or until it begins to flake.

➤ When a particular fish is unavailable, you usually can easily substitute another variety.

Shellfish

Sweet and nutty or deliciously briny, shellfish are irresistible on the grill. Like other varieties of fish, shellfish are usually low in fat and calories, easy to eat, quick to cook, easy to clean up after, and absolutely delicious. Shellfish, along with fish, are indeed the food of the future.

To impart an intriguing flavour to shellfish, toss a half cup of dried herbs of your choice, soaked and drained, onto the coals. For a bit more wake-up flavour, try serving shellfish with lime wedges rather than the usual lemon.

Shellfish such as shrimp, lobster, and clams overcook and toughen very quickly. So watch carefully, and don't leave the grill unattended. Crustaceans such as shrimp are done when they turn opaque; shellfish in the shell are done as soon as the shells pop open.

Some shellfish, such as many crabs, whole lobsters, and most mollusks, are sold live. They're very perishable. Shellfish that are not alive, such as shucked oysters, cleaned crabs, and lobster that the fishmonger has butterflied for you, are even more perishable and should be kept very cold and cooked the same day you buy them. Always thaw frozen shellfish in the refrigerator.

Grilled Shrimp and Scallops with Orange Horseradish Marmalade

Yield: 4 servings

Level: Intermediate

Grill: 6 to 8 minutes

At the Ready: Grill screen, long metal skewers, nonstick cooking spray, barbecue tongs, basting brush

For the love of shrimp and scallops, this sweet and hot marmalade is a perfect match.

16 large shrimp (around 1 1/4 lbs. or 625 g)
12 large sea scallops, (around 1 lb. or 500 g)
2 tablespoons (25 mL) chopped fresh ginger
1 teaspoon (5 mL) ground cumin
1 tablespoon (15 mL) chopped fresh dill
1/2 cup (125 mL) orange juice
1/4 cup (50 mL) vegetable oil
Freshly ground black pepper to taste

Orange Horseradish Marmalade
2 tablespoons (25 mL) butter
2 cloves garlic, chopped
1/4 cup (50 mL) freshly grated horseradish (jarred can be used instead, but drain it first)
1/2 cup (125 mL) orange juice
1/2 cup (125 mL) orange marmalade
Salt and pepper to taste

Peel and devein the shrimp. Skewer the shrimp and scallops onto the metal skewers, alternating the shrimp and scallops, 4 shrimp and 3 scallops per skewer.

Place the shrimp in a glass dish. Whisk together the cumin, dill, orange juice, and vegetable oil. Season with black pepper and pour mixture over the skewers. Marinate for 1 hour.

In a small saucepot, melt the butter. Sauté the garlic for 2 to 3 minutes until tender. Add the horseradish and orange juice and cook until 1/2 the liquid has evaporated. Add the marmalade and whisk until incorporated. Season with salt and pepper and transfer to a serving dish.

Preheat grill to medium-high. Spray the grill screen with the nonstick cooking spray and place on grill. Grill shrimp for 4 to 5 minutes per side until the shrimp and scallops are opaque and cooked. Serve drizzled with the orange horseradish marmalade.

Don't Get Burned!

Be careful when you seed and chop hot peppers like jalapeños. Wash your hands thoroughly afterwards, and be careful not to rub your eyes; the capsaicin in pepper is a powerful irritant. Some people prefer to wear latex or rubber gloves when handling chiles.

Digby Bacon-Wrapped Scallop Kebabs

Yield: 4 servings

Level: Intermediate

Grill: 8 to 10 minutes

At the Ready: Grape vine skewers or metal skewers or bamboo skewers, barbecue tongs

On the the Bay of Fundy lies the small port of Digby, Nova Scotia. Digby is famous for its scallop fishermen. The tender white meat of the scallop is sweet and delicious. When buying scallops for this recipe, look for large scallops—roughly 8 to 10 pieces per pound. Most scallops are bought frozen, but if you can get fresh, buy them and cook them right away.

24 large scallops (around 3 lbs. or 1.5 kg), 6 pieces per skewer
2 tablespoons (25 mL) Great Lakes seafood seasoning (page 147)
12 slices of bacon

Marinade
1 cup (250 mL) grapefruit juice
3 cloves garlic, minced
1/2 cup (125 mL) cup honey
2 tablespoons (25 mL) grain mustard
1 tablespoon (15 mL) chopped fresh cilantro
Salt and pepper to taste

If using grapevine or bamboo skewers, remember to soak them in hot water for at least 1 hour before skewering.

Season the scallops with seafood seasoning and set aside.

In a large frying pan, cook the bacon halfway, just to the point of turning a little crisp. Remove the bacon from the pan and pat excess fat from bacon on paper towels. Cut each slice of bacon in half. Wrap each seasoned scallop in a 1/2 slice of bacon and skewer onto the skewers, 6 bacon-wrapped scallops per skewer. Place the skewers in a large glass dish.

Mix together the grapefruit juice, garlic, honey, mustard, and cilantro. Season to taste with salt and pepper. Pour half of this mixture over the scallop skewers, cover, and refrigerate for 1 hour.

continues

continued

Preheat grill to medium-high. Remove scallops from marinade and discard marinade. Grill scallops for 4 to 5 minutes per side, basting frequently with the remaining marinade, until the bacon is crisp and the scallops are just cooked.

Note: With scallops and most other shellfish, overcooking will make them tough.

Don't Get Burned!

Metal skewers can get hot on the grill. Have a pot holder or heatproof gloves handy when you're ready to turn the kebabs.

Soft-Shell Crabs on the Grill

Yield: 6 servings

Level: Easy

Grill: 6 to 8 minutes

At the Ready: Oil for brushing, long-handled spatula, 6 long metal skewers

Grilled soft-shell crabs are one of our favourite foods, and a real treat when in season.

12 cleaned soft-shell crabs (have the
   fishmonger clean them)
1/2 cup (125 mL or 1 stick) butter,

melted and cooled
2 lemons or limes, sliced

Brush the crabs with a little of the melted butter and thread 2 crabs lengthwise on each skewer.

Prepare the grill for direct heat. When the coals are medium-hot, set the threaded crabs on the grill, 4 to 6 inches (10 to 15 cm) from the heat. Grill the crabs, uncovered, for 3 minutes, turn them over, and continue to grill until they turn reddish, about 3 to 4 minutes longer. Serve the crabs hot with the remaining melted butter, lemon or lime slices, cornbread, and a salad.

What's What

Wonderfully sweet soft-shell crabs, which are available from May to October, are regular East Coast blue crabs that are gathered right after they molt (shed their shells). The crunchy new shell is completely edible and, as a bonus, is rich in calcium

Don't Get Burned!

Soft-shell crabs are sold live. It's easiest to let the fishmonger clean them (remove the face portion, gills, and sand receptacle under the mouth), but be sure to serve them the same day you buy them. They spoil very quickly.

Grilled Garlic Jumbo Shrimps Skewered on Lemongrass

Yield: 4 servings, 3 shrimp per person per serving

Level: Intermediate

Grill: 8 to 10 minutes

At the Ready: Basting brush, barbecue tongs

For this recipe, use the largest jumbo shrimp you can find. You can find lemongrass in the produce section of most grocery stores or in Asian markets. Skewering the shrimp onto lemongrass adds flavour and also makes for great presentation. If you cannot find lemongrass, you can use sugar cane or wooden or metal skewers.

12 large jumbo shrimp, (around 1 1/2 lbs. or 750 g)
2 tablespoons (25 mL) barbecue seasoning (page 146)
6 stalks lemongrass
12 cloves garlic, minced
1/4 cup (50 mL) lemon juice

1/2 cup (125 mL) butter
1 tablespoon (15 mL) chopped cilantro
Salt and pepper to taste
1/2 cup (125 mL) breadcrumbs
1/4 cup (50 mL) Parmesan cheese
2 tablespoons (25 mL) vegetable oil

Peel and devein the jumbo shrimp. Using a sharp knife, make a small incision in the thickest part of the shrimp. Cut the lemongrass stalks in half lengthways. Trim

continues

continued

the thickest end of the lemongrass into a point. Thread the shrimp, starting at the end with the incision, onto the lemongrass skewer. Season with the barbecue seasoning Set aside.

In a small saucepot, mix together the garlic, lemon juice, butter, and cilantro. Slowly heat the sauce mix until the butter is melted. Season to taste with salt and pepper. Turn heat to low to keep warm.

In a small bowl, mix together the breadcrumbs and Parmesan cheese. Set aside.

Preheat the grill to medium-high. Rub the shrimp with the vegetable oil. Place the shrimp on the grill and grill for 3 minutes per side, basting with the garlic/butter sauce. Remove the shrimp and dip into the garlic/butter sauce; then roll them in the breadcrumb/Parmesan mixture to make a crust. Return the shrimp to the grill and continue to cook for another 2 minutes per side until crisp and slightly charred. Serve immediately with remainder of the butter sauce.

Lobster Tails with Sherry Sauce

Yield: 6 servings   **Grill**: 6 minutes

Level: Easy   **At the Ready**: Basting brush, lobster forks

Lobster tails usually arrive frozen at the market. Defrost them in the refrigerator before grilling. You will notice that the lobster shell colour can vary from a mottled brown to dark red.

3/4 cup (175 mL or 1 1/2 sticks) butter, at room temperature, cut in pieces
1/4 cup (50 mL) half-and-half
1/4 cup (50 mL) dry sherry

1/4 teaspoon (1 mL) ground nutmeg
1/4 teaspoon (1 mL) ground cinnamon
6 lobster tails

Reserve about 1/4 cup (50 mL) of the butter to brush the lobster tails. Put the remaining softened butter in a mixing bowl. With the back of a wooden spoon, mash the butter until soft. Stir in the half-and-half, sherry, nutmeg, and cinnamon. Spoon the flavoured butter into a serving crock or shallow dish. Cover and let stay at room temperature for up to 1 hour, or refrigerate for later use. Bring to room temperature before serving.

Using scissors or a small, sharp knife, cut through and remove the tough outer membrane from the lobster tail meat. Brush the lobster tails with softened butter.

Prepare the grill for direct heat. When the coals are medium-hot, put the lobster tails, shell side up, on the cooking grid. Cover the grill and adjust the vents. Grill the tails 6 to 8 minutes, or until the meat is opaque and starts to separate from the shell. Do not overcook the lobster, as the meat will toughen.

Set each tail on a dinner plate. Pass the flavoured butter at the table for guests to help themselves. Serve with lobster forks.

Whole P.E.I. Lobsters

Yield: 4 servings

Level: Easy

Grill: 8 to 10 minutes

At the Ready: Basting brush, disposable bib for each guest, lobster crackersand picks, damp finger towels

Buy the lobsters within an hour or two of when you will grill them. Have the fishmonger split each lobster lengthwise (butterfly it) and clean out the stomach and intestinal vein. Keep them very cold until grilling. If you cannot grill them until later, you'll have to buy the lobsters whole and cut and clean them yourself (see Chapter 13).

1 cup (250 mL or 2 sticks) butter, at
    room temperature, cut into pieces
2 tablespoons (25 mL) lemon juice or
    lime juice
2 tablespoons (25 mL) finely grated

lemon or lime peel
2 tablespoons (25 mL) finely minced
    fresh parsley
4 P.E.I. lobsters, about 1 1/2 pounds
    (750 g) each

Reserve about 3 to 4 tablespoons (25 to 50 mL) of the butter to brush the lobsters. Put the remaining softened butter in a mixing bowl. With the back of a wooden spoon, smash the butter to soften it. Stir in the juice, peel, and parsley. Spoon the flavoured butter into a serving crock or shallow dish. Cover and let stay at room temperature for up to 1 hour, or refrigerate until needed, then let stand 30 minutes to warm up before serving.

Brush the cut side of each lobster with butter. Prepare the grill for direct heat. When the coals are medium-hot, place the lobsters, shell side up, on the cooking grid. Cover the grill and adjust the vents. Grill the lobsters 8 to 10 minutes, or until the meat is opaque and just starts to separate from the shell. Do not overcook them.

Remove the lobsters from the grill and serve immediately with the citrus butter. Garnish with lemon or lime wedges. Use bibs, lobster crackers, picks, and finger towels. Serve with grilled corn and garlic bread.

Hot Tip

If you have a choice, buy a hard-shelled lobster as opposed to a soft-shelled lobster because the hard one has more meat. The female lobsters are more flavourful because of the roe (eggs).

Seaweed Steamed Clams with Spicy Butter Sauce

Yield: 4 servings

Level: Intermediate

Grill: 5 to 8 minutes

At the Ready: Large bucket of dried pine needles, spray bottle of water, barbecue tongs

If you happen to be by the ocean, you can easily get some seaweed when the tide goes out. But for those in the city, ask your fishmonger to get you about 3 pounds (1.5 kg) of fresh seaweed. The seaweed adds a wonderful saltiness to the clams.

6 cloves garlic, minced
1/2 pound (250 g) butter
1/4 cup (50 g) hot sauce
1/4 cup (50 mL) cup lemon juice
5 pounds (2.2 kg) fresh clams (cherrystone manila) cleaned of any

external sand
1/4 cup (50 g) Prairie Dust barbecue seasoning (page 146)
3 pounds seaweed
6 green onions, finely chopped

Put the garlic and butter in a saucepot and melt the butter over medium heat. Add the hot sauce and lemon juice. Stir to incorporate. Reduce heat to low.

Preheat the grill to very high. In a large bowl, season the clams with the barbecue seasoning. Place the clams on the hot grill and cover with the seaweed. Close the lid on the grill and let the clams steam/grill for 8 to 10 minutes, until all the clams have opened. Remove the seaweed and discard. Carefully remove the clams from the grill to a serving platter, discarding any unopened clams.

Drizzle with the warm spicy butter sauce, garnish with the chopped chives, and serve.

If you don't like clams, try this recipe with mussels or oysters.

What's What

Just what are prawns, anyway? The term can refer to several creatures. One is a member of the lobster family, and another is a mostly freshwater crustacean that looks like a cross between a shrimp and a lobster. Chances are, though, that the "prawns" in your supermarket are just jumbo shrimp.

Prawns with Honey Brushing Sauce

Yield: 6 servings

Level: Easy

Grill: About 8 minutes

1 cup (250 mL) orange juice
3 tablespoons (50 mL) honey
1 tablespoon (15 mL) vegetable oil

At the Ready: Oil for brushing, grill screen, long-handled spatula, 3 cups oak, maple, or hickory chips soaked 30 minutes and drained (optional)

2 teaspoons (10 mL) grated white horseradish, or to taste
24 prawns, shelled and deveined

In a small bowl, stir together the orange juice, honey, oil, and horseradish. Wash the prawns and pat dry. With a small paring knife, cut partway through the underside of each prawn. Do not cut all the way through. Flatten them into a slight butterfly shape, then brush the prawns with the sauce.

Prepare the grill for direct heat. Oil or spray a grill screen. When the coals are medium-hot, scatter the drained chips over them. Put the prawns on the grill screen and set it on the cooking grid. Cover the grill and adjust the vents. Grill the prawns about 3 to 4 minutes, then turn them over. Continue grilling another 4 to 5 minutes, until the prawns are opaque but not overcooked.

Put the hot prawns on individual plates and serve immediately.

Coastal Shrimp in Beer

Yield: 6 servings

Level: Easy

Grill: 5 to 6 minutes

2 pounds (1 kg) extra-large shrimp, shells left on (and deveined if preferred)
2 cans (12 oz. or 340 g each) light beer

At the Ready: Long-handled spatula, grill screen, oil for brushing, basting brush, barbecue sauce (see Index), empty bowls for shells, finger wipes

Vegetable oil
2 teaspoons (10 mL) celery seed
1 teaspoon (5 mL) cayenne

Wash the shrimp and pat it dry. Pour the beer into a deep bowl and add the shrimp. Cover and marinate for 1 hour in the refrigerator. Drain.

Prepare the grill for direct heat. Oil or spray a grill screen. Brush the shrimp with oil. Mix the celery seed and cayenne together in a small bowl. Sprinkle the shrimp with the spice mixture. When the coals are medium-hot, put the shrimp on the grill screen and set it on the grid, 4 to 6 inches (10 to 15 cm) from the heat. Cover the grill and adjust the vents. Grill 5 to 6 minutes, turning once, or until opaque. Do not overcook.

continues

continued

Serve immediately. Have empty bowls on the table for the shells, and provide moist paper wipes. Serve with barbecue sauce (use one of the sauce recipes in this book, or your favourite bottled sauce) for dipping.

Seaside Clambake

Yield: 4 servings

Level: Easy

Grill: About 12 minutes for corn, 8 minutes for onions, and 5 minutes for clams (have the gas grill on high for the clams)

At the Ready: Oil for brushing, grill screen, long-handled spatula

Organization is critical in this recipe. Make sure you have the corn, onions, and clams together at the grill.

4 ears of corn, shucked and cut into three pieces each

2 large white onions, peeled and cut in 1/2 inch (1 cm) slices

3 dozen medium clams, washed

1 cup (250 mL or 2 sticks) melted butter

Lemon wedges

Prepare the corn and onions and wash the clams, discarding any open ones.

Prepare the grill for direct heat. Oil or spray a grill screen. When the coals are medium-hot, set the grill screen on the cooking grid. Brush the corn and onions with some of the melted butter and set them on the screen. Cover the grill and adjust the vents. Grill the onions about 8 minutes or until golden, turning once. Grill the corn about 12 minutes, rotating every 3 minutes; it will char slightly. Arrange the clams on the screen. Cover and grill about 5 minutes. Lift the cover to see if the clams have popped open. If not, cover and grill a few minutes longer until they have opened. Discard any clams that won't open.

Serve the corn, onions, and clams with melted butter, lemon wedges, garlic bread, and coleslaw.

Tasty Tidbit

A traditional clambake is a delicious experience. First you dig a pit in the sand and heat the charcoal in that. Then you grill the corn, potatoes, clams, and lobsters. Everyone eats messily and happily, drinking beer and enjoying the cool seabreeze.

Grilled Malpeque Oysters Stuffed with Snow Crab and Bacon

Yield: 4 servings

Level: Intermediate

Grill: 10 minutes

At the Ready: Oyster knife, heavy kitchen towel, grill screen, barbecue tongs

Malpeque oysters are found off the coast of Prince Edward Island in Malpeque Bay. When buying them, purchase ones that are quite large and have relatively deep shells. This will make it easier to stuff and grill.

16 fresh Malpeque oysters
1/2 pound (250 grams) snow crab meat, thawed and drained
6 slices of bacon, cooked crisp and diced
1/2 cup (125 mL) crumbled blue cheese
2 cloves garlic, minced

1 small onion, finely chopped
1 tablespoon (15 mL) chopped dill
1 tablespoon (15 mL) lemon juice
Dash of hot sauce
Salt and pepper to taste
1/2 cup (125 mL) barbecue sauce

In a bowl, mix together the crabmeat, bacon, blue cheese, garlic, onion, dill, and lemon juice. Season to taste with hot sauce, salt, and pepper.

To open an oyster, grip it flat side up in a folded kitchen towel. Find a small opening between the shells near the hinge and pry open with an oyster knife. This is called shucking. Be careful to remove the top shell without damaging the oyster meat. Being careful not to lose the oyster liquor, loosen the oyster from the shell by running the oyster knife underneath the body. Remove the oyster from the shell and place it on some paper towels to drain. Be gentle, and do not throw out the bottom shell. Do this with each oyster.

Take the oyster liquor and add it to the crab mixture. Place one heaping tablespoon of crab mixture into the base of the reserved oyster shell bottoms. Place one oyster on top of each crab mixture.

Preheat the grill to medium-high. Place the stuffed oysters on the grill screen. Top each oyster with a tablespoon of barbecue sauce. Place on the grill, close the grill lid, and cook 10 to 12 minutes until the barbecue sauce and stuffing is hot. Carefully remove from the grill and serve

The Least You Need to Know

➤ Most shellfish are low in fat and calories.

➤ Be careful not to overcook shellfish, which will quickly turn tough.

➤ Shellfish are highly perishable and should be cooked as soon as possible after you purchase them.

Vegetables and Grains

This chapter, which runs the gamut from pizza to baby artichokes with rosemary, is one of our favourites. Not only do we love vegetables, but we feel they're vastly underused on the grill. Grilling vegetables and grains opens a world of creativity. For example, you can use the pizza crust recipe, or buy a prepared crust, and grill assorted toppings—whatever your family likes—to go on it.

Another of our favourite "tricks" is to grill vegetables that are in season, personal favourites, and/or complementary to the rest of the meal, and toss them with cooked pasta (tortellini or ravioli is especially nice) and a little salad dressing.

If you're grilling meat as the main course, it's downright silly not to throw some vegetables or bread on the grill as well. Grilling gives vegetables and breads such as pizza those wonderfully smoky undertones. Although nearly any vegetable can be grilled, starchy and/or "meaty" vegetables or those with some sweetness do best over charcoal.

Pizza Crust

Yield: 2 crusts, about 10 to 12 inches each

Level: Advanced

Grill: About 6 to 10 minutes (may take a few minutes longer on the gas grill)

At the Ready: Food processor or electric mixer with dough hook

For a taste sensation, try adding 1/2 cup (125 mL) pesto sauce to the finished dough, perhaps 2 or 3 tablespoons (25 to 50 mL) of chili powder, or 3 or 4 tablespoons (50 to 60 mL) of crumbled dried oregano, basil, or rosemary.

2 3/4 cups (675 mL) all-purpose flour, divided
1 scant cup (250 mL) warm water

1 package quick-rising yeast
2 tablespoons (25 mL) warm olive oil
1/2 teaspoon (2 mL) salt

In a food processor, combine 2 1/2 cups (625 mL) of the flour, the yeast, and the salt. With the machine running, pour the warm water and olive oil through the feed tube. The dough will come together into a ball in about 8 seconds.

Alternatively, you can mix the dough with an electric mixer fitted with a dough hook. Mix the dough on low speed for 3 to 4 minutes, or until it forms a smooth ball.

Remove the dough from the bowl and place on a lightly floured cloth or board using the remaining 1/4 cup (50 mL) of flour. Knead until smooth, a few minutes. Set the dough in a bowl, cover with a damp, warm towel, and let the dough rise in a warm area of the kitchen for 30 minutes or until it has doubled in size. Punch the dough down and divide it in half. You are now ready to roll out the pizza dough. See the next recipe for instructions on shaping the dough and one idea for pizza— but remember, when it comes to pizza, your personal tastes are of the utmost importance, so use what you like, and improvise.

This dough can be made ahead of time and refrigerated for up to 24 hours, or frozen for up to 3 months. If it's refrigerated, let it stand at room temperature for about 2 to 3 hours, or until doubled. If frozen, let it stand at room temperature for about 4 to 6 hours, or until it doubles.

Hot Tip

If time or lack of skill is a problem, use defrosted frozen bread dough. It is available at large supermarkets in the frozen food section. Or just use a prepared pizza crust. Add the toppings and warm the pizza on the grill (with the baking tiles set on a pan or a grill screen and with the grill covered).

Asparagus and Mushrooms with Sage Brushing Sauce

Yield: 6 servings

Level: Easy

Grill: About 4 to 8 minutes

At the Ready: Grill screen, oil for brushing, basting brush, long-handled spatula, and 1/2 cup (125 mL) dried sage leaves soaked in water 5 minutes and drained (optional)

1/4 cup (50 mL) olive oil
3 tablespoons (25 mL) balsamic, red wine, or tarragon vinegar
2 cloves garlic, peeled and minced
1 teaspoon (5 mL) grainy mustard
1 tablespoon (15 mL) minced fresh sage or 1 1/2 teaspoons (7 mL) dried crumbled sage

Salt and pepper
1 1/2 pounds (750 g) asparagus, ends snapped off, washed
1 pound (500 g) white, brown, or Portobello mushrooms, cleaned
6 large plum tomatoes, seeded and chopped
1 small onion, peeled and chopped

In a small bowl, whisk together the oil, vinegar, garlic, mustard, sage, 1/2 teaspoon (2 mL) salt, and 1/2 teaspoon (2 mL) pepper. Prepare the vegetables and brush them liberally with the sauce. Set aside.

Toss together the tomatoes and onion in a bowl. Season with salt and pepper to taste. Set aside.

Prepare the grill for direct heat. Oil or spray a grill screen. When the coals are medium-hot, set the marinated vegetables on the grill screen and place them on the cooking grid. Grill the asparagus and the mushrooms, uncovered, for 2 or 3 minutes on each side, brushing them again with sauce as you turn them. Continue grilling until they are done to taste, another few minutes on each side.

Remove the vegetables to a serving platter and sprinkle them with the chopped tomato and onion mixture. Serve hot.

Buffalo Cheese and Tomato Sauce Pizza

Yield: 8 servings, enough for 2 pizzas

Level: Intermediate

Grill: About 3 minutes for the crust and 5 to 6 minutes with the topping

At the Ready: Baking tiles for the grill, grill screen, cornmeal, pizza paddle (or use the back side of a cookie sheet sprinkled with cornmeal), olive oil for brushing, brush

It is perfectly natural to cook a pizza on the barbecue grill. After all, for centuries pizzas were cooked over wood—and they still are in many restaurants or bakeries.

Tomato-Herb Sauce
1 can (28 oz. or 800 mL) crushed tomatoes, drained
1/4 cup (50 mL) tomato paste
2 tablespoons (25 mL) crumbled dried oregano
1 tablespoon (15 mL) crumbled dried

basil
1/4 teaspoon (1 mL) pepper
1 recipe basic pizza crust (page 220)
1 pound (500 g) buffalo milk mozzarella cheese, sliced thin
1/4 cup (50 mL) grated Asiago or other sharp cheese

To make the sauce, put the drained tomatoes in a bowl. Mix in the tomato paste, oregano, basil, and pepper. Taste, and adjust the seasonings.

Roll out each half of the dough to a 10 or 12 inch (25 to 30 cm) circle.

Prepare the grill for direct heat. When the coals are medium-hot, set the tiles on a grill screen (or on a cookie sheet) and place on the cooking grid. Preheat the tiles for about 5 minutes.

Brush the dough lightly with olive oil. Transfer the pizza crust (on a paddle sprinkled with cornmeal or on the back of a cookie sheet sprinkled with cornmeal) to the tiles or to a second oiled grill screen set on the tiles (the grill screen makes it easier to lift the pizza from the grill).

Grill the crust for about 3 minutes. Remove the crust. Brush it again with olive oil, and lay the mozzarella slices over it. Drizzle with the tomato sauce and sprinkle with the Asiago cheese. Return the pizza to the grill screen. Cover the grill and adjust the vents. Grill the pizza for about 3 minutes, then rotate it a half-turn to ensure even cooking. Continue grilling for about 2 to 3 minutes or until the topping is heated through and the crust is firm. Cut and serve the pizza while it is hot.

Don't Get Burned!

Be sure to rotate the pizza during grilling so that it will cook evenly.

Mixed Grilled Vegetables in a Pita Pocket

Yield: 6 servings

Level: Intermediate

Grill: About 6 to 10 minutes

At the Ready: Grill screen, oil for brushing, basting brush, long-handled spatula, aluminum foil

2 large red bell peppers, seeded and cut in 1/2 inch (1 cm) strips
2 large green or yellow bell peppers, seeded and cut in 1/2 inch (1 cm) strips
2 large, ripe tomatoes, cut in 1/2 inch (1 cm) slices

1 large onion, cut in 1/2 inch (1 cm) slices
6 pita breads
2 jalapeño peppers, seeded and chopped
1 clove garlic, peeled and minced
1/4 cup (50 mL) cider vinegar

Prepare the grill for direct heat. Oil or spray a grill screen. When the coals are medium-hot, set the grill screen on the cooking grid. Brush the bell peppers, tomatoes, and onion with oil and set them on the grill. Grill the vegetables, uncovered, 3 to 4 minutes on each side or until they are tender. The tomato will warm and cook first. The bell peppers and onions will take a few minutes longer, and should be removed when they are tender and beginning to brown.

Warm the pita breads on the grill about 1 minute on each side or only until warm. Cut in half.

Place the vegetables in a mixing bowl. Toss them with the jalapeño peppers, garlic, and cider vinegar. Using a large spoon, gently stuff the warm pita bread with the grilled vegetable mixture or serve the vegetables with the pita bread on the side. Serve immediately.

Hot Tip

Grilled vegetables are fine as a side dish, but for an even more fun lunch or first course, stuff them into pitas, wrap them in tortillas, or roll them up in a big deli wrap.

Tortellini Vegetable Salad

Yield: 6 servings

Level: Intermediate

Grill: 20 minutes (cover a gas grill for the eggplant; leave it uncovered if you like for the remaining vegetables)

At the Ready: Grill screen, oil or nonstick cooking spray, brush, long-handled spatula

3/4 cup (175 mL) red wine
Olive oil
3 shallots, minced
1 tablespoon (15 mL) chopped fresh mint or 1 1/2 teaspoons (7 mL) dried mint
1 medium-small eggplant, trimmed and thinly sliced lengthwise
18 cherry tomatoes, trimmed and washed
1 red onion, peeled and cut in 1/2 inch (1 cm) slices

1 cup (250 mL) sliced salami
1 pound (500 g) tortellini, cooked according to package directions
2 teaspoons (10 mL) minced fresh thyme
1 teaspoon (5 mL) minced fresh marjoram
1 teaspoon (5 mL) minced fresh mint
1/4 cup (50 mL) chopped fresh parsley
3/4 cup (175 mL) stuffed green olives

Prepare the dressing by putting the wine in a small bowl. Whisk in 1/2 cup (125 mL) olive oil, a few drops at a time, then the shallots and mint. Cover and refrigerate until ready to serve. Whisk again before serving.

Prepare the grill for direct heat. Oil or spray a grill screen. When the coals are medium-hot, set the grill screen on the cooking grid. Brush the eggplant with olive oil and place it on the grill screen. Cover the grill and adjust the vents. Grill for 10 to 12 minutes, turning once. Brush the remaining vegetables with oil. Uncover the grill and add the tomatoes, onion slices, and salami to the grill screen (do not remove the eggplant). Grill the vegetables, uncovered, allowing another 8 to 10 minutes for the eggplant and 3 to 4 minutes per side for the tomatoes and onions. The vegetables should be tender and beginning to brown. The salami needs to cook only for a minute or two per side, just to warm it.

Rewarm the cooked tortellini under hot running water. Put it in a serving bowl. Toss it with the thyme, marjoram, mint, parsley, eggplant, tomatoes, onions, salami, olives, and dressing. Serve immediately.

New Potatoes with Garlic and Cilantro

Yield: 6 servings

Level: Easy

Grill: About 10 minutes

At the Ready: Grill screen, vegetable oil for brushing, basting brush, long-handled spatula

2 to 2 1/4 pounds (1 to 1.2 kg) new potatoes, scrubbed
4 cloves garlic, peeled and minced

Olive oil
1/4 cup (50 mL) minced fresh cilantro

Cook the potatoes in boiling water or in the top of a vegetable steamer just until fork tender, about 13 to 15 minutes. Remove, drain, and cool the potatoes. Cut them in half. Brush them with olive oil and sprinkle with the garlic.

Prepare the grill for direct heat. Oil or spray a grill screen. When the coals are medium-hot, set the grill screen on the cooking grid. Arrange the potatoes on the screen. Cover the grill and adjust the vents. Grill the potatoes until they are hot and browned, turning once or twice. This should take about 10 minutes, or longer if you like them browner.

Remove the potatoes to a serving bowl and sprinkle with the cilantro. Serve hot.

What's What

New potatoes are very young, small, unblemished potatoes. You'll find them at farmers' markets and some supermarkets and natural food stores, usually in the spring. Stores often label small potatoes "new potatoes," but genuine new potatoes are tiny and tender.

Mixed Greens Topped with Grilled Vegetables

Yield: 6 servings

Level: Easy

Grill: About 8 to 10 minutes (if using a gas grill, cook uncovered)

12 cups (3 L) torn mixed salad greens, such as red leaf lettuce, Boston lettuce, and arugula
2 tablespoons (25 mL) chopped fresh tarragon or 1 tablespoon (15 mL) dried tarragon
Salt and black pepper to taste

Cider Vinegar Dressing
1/4 cup (50 mL) olive oil

At the Ready: Grill screen, oil for brushing, brush, long-handled spatula, salad spinner

1/4 cup (50 mL) cider vinegar
3 tablespoons (50 mL) orange juice
1 tablespoon (15 mL) honey mustard
3 cloves garlic, peeled and smashed
2 medium zucchini, washed, trimmed, and cut lengthwise into thin slices
18 cherry tomatoes, trimmed and washed
1 bunch green onions, trimmed
Olive oil

Wash and spin dry the mixed salad greens and place them in a salad bowl. Sprinkle with the fresh tarragon, salt, and pepper. (If you're using dried tarragon, add it to the dressing.) Set aside.

In a small bowl, whisk together the oil, vinegar, orange juice, and mustard. Stir in the garlic and the tarragon (if you're using the dried herb). Set aside.

Prepare the grill for direct heat. Oil or spray a grill screen. When the coals are medium-hot, set the grill screen on the cooking grid. Brush the zucchini, tomatoes, and green onions with oil and arrange them on the grill screen. Grill the vegetables, uncovered, for 2 or 3 minutes. As they cook, turn them over as necessary. The onions will take the longest to grill, and the zucchini will cook the quickest. Remove the vegetables as they become tender and begin to brown.

Decoratively arrange the grilled vegetables over the salad and serve immediately. Pass the dressing on the side.

Hot Tip

For no more tears, slice onions under cold running water. It also helps to refrigerate the onions first, or pop them in the freezer for 15 minutes just before cutting if they are at room temperature.

Baked Potatoes with Vidalia Onions

Yield: 6 servings

Grill: About 1 hour

Level: Intermediate

At the Ready: Aluminum foil, olive oil for brushing, brush

Other sweet onions, such as Walla Walla, Maui, or Texas 1015, may be substituted.

6 large Vidalia onions or other sweet onions, peeled and sliced thin
3 tablespoons (50 mL) olive oil
1/2 cup (125 mL) dried cherries, currants, or dark raisins
1/4 cup (50 mL) packed light-brown

sugar
1/2 teaspoon (2 mL) salt
1/4 teaspoon (1 mL) black pepper
6 baking potatoes, washed, poked several times with a paring knife
Additional olive oil

Early in the day, prepare the onions. Heat the oil in a nonstick frying pan over medium heat. Add the onions and reduce the heat to medium-low. Continue cooking, stirring occasionally, until the onions are softened but not yet browned. Stir in the dried cherries, brown sugar, salt, and pepper. Continue cooking, slowly, until the onions are a golden colour. Remove from the heat and allow to cool. If the rest of the recipe is not to be prepared for several hours, place the onion mixture in a bowl, cover with plastic wrap, and refrigerate. Reheat to serve.

Rub each potato with oil and double-wrap the potatoes individually in aluminum foil.

Prepare the grill for direct heat. When the coals are medium-hot, set the potatoes directly on the coals (if using charcoal) or on the cooking grid (if using gas). Cover the grill and adjust the vents. Using long-handled tongs, turn the potatoes every 10 or 15 minutes. Cook about 1 hour, or until they are fork tender. If you're using a charcoal grill, replenish the grill with lit coals as necessary.

Carefully remove the foil from each potato, and set a potato on each plate. Slit the potato lengthwise, squeeze it open, and spoon the hot glazed onions over the top. Serve immediately.

Tasty Tidbit

The Vidalia, a very sweet, mild onion, is available in the spring. These onions grow in south-eastern Georgia, and the name "Vidalia" can be used only by the thirteen counties between Macon and Savannah and parts of seven other counties. The Vidalia gets its name from the first county from which this onion was shipped.

Grilled Tomatoes and Green Onions

Yield: 6 servings

Level: Easy

Grill: About 4 to 6 minutes

At the Ready: Long-handled spatula, olive oil

6 medium tomatoes, cut in half
   crosswise
Olive oil

12 green onions, trimmed
2 tablespoons (25 mL) snipped fresh dill
   or basil

Brush the cut side of the tomatoes and the onions with olive oil. Sprinkle the tomatoes and onions with the dill or basil.

Prepare the grill for direct heat. Oil or spray a grill screen. When the coals are medium-hot, set the grill screen on the cooking grid. Place the tomatoes and green onions on the screen. Leaving the grill uncovered, grill the tomatoes about 4 minutes and the onions for 3 minutes on each side. The onions should be tender and starting to brown, and the tomatoes should soften but not be mushy. Remove the vegetables from the grill and serve.

What's What

The slender "green onions" sold in supermarkets often are really scallions. True green onions are slightly bulbous on the bottom (and often are larger than scallions), while scallions are straight up and down. We use the term "green onion" rather than "scallion" throughout this book because that's the way they're labelled in supermarkets.

Baby Artichokes with Rosemary

Yield: 6 servings

Level: Easy

Grill: 10 to 12 minutes

At the Ready: Dressing, long-handled tongs, 1/2 cup (125 mL) dried mint soaked for 5 minutes and drained (optional)

12 fresh baby artichokes
1/4 (1 mL) teaspoon pepper
3 tablespoons (50 mL) lemon juice
2 tablespoons (25 mL) chopped fresh
    rosemary

1/4 cup (50 mL) olive oil
1 teaspoon (5 mL) minced garlic
3 tablespoons (50 mL) red wine vinegar

Trim the stems from the artichokes, cut the artichokes in half lengthwise, and immediately place them in a large bowl of cold water to which you've added the lemon juice. Let them soak for 15 minutes.

In a bowl, mix together the olive oil, vinegar, pepper, rosemary, and garlic. Drain the artichokes, pat them dry, and toss them with the dressing. Let the artichokes marinate for 1 hour, then drain.

Prepare the grill for direct heat. When the coals are medium-hot, set the artichokes directly on the cooking grid. Grill them, uncovered, for 10 minutes, turning once, or until cooked through.

The Least You Need to Know

➤ Vegetables are too seldom chosen for the grill, and can inspire great creativity.

➤ To make full use of the fired-up grill, put some vegetables on the grid alongside the meat main course.

➤ Starchy and/or "meaty" vegetables fare best on the grill.

Chapter 23

Sweet Stuff

In This Chapter

➤ Glazed Mixed Fruit Grill

➤ Blueberry-Apple Cobbler on the Grill

➤ Wine-Brushed Pears

➤ Warm Apple Cinnamon Slices with Cheddar Cheese

➤ Fruit Kebabs on Grilled Chocolate Pound Cake

➤ Campfire-Style S'Mores

➤ Apricots Topped with Raspberries and Raspberry Sherbet

➤ Honeyed Papaya Strips with Warm Brie

➤ Grilled Angel Food Cake and Pineapple

Now that you've fired up the grill for the rest of your meal, why not grill the dessert as well? After the coals have begun to cool down from the main course, they're the perfect temperature for grilling nearly any fruit, and even cake.

The taste of slightly burnt sugar is irresistible. Just ask any kid (or adult) who's eaten roasted marshmallows. However, the sugar content is also the reason that fruits and other sweet foods can scorch easily on the grill. When you're grilling your dessert, don't get distracted and wander off.

For a really simple dessert, grill wedges of papaya or cantaloupe, top with a scoop of vanilla yogurt, and sprinkle with granola.

Glazed Mixed Fruit Grill

Yield: 6 servings

Level: Easy

Grill: About 4 minutes

At the Ready: Oiled grill screen, long-handled spatula

Vary the fruits according to your taste and seasonal availability. Peeled and cored fresh pineapple is available at most large supermarkets.

3 large peaches
3 to 4 tablespoons (50 to 60 cm) brandy (optional)
1/4 cup (50 mL) peach jam
2 to 3 tablespoons (25 to 50 mL) water
6 medium bananas

Melted butter
1/2 cup (125 mL) packed dark-brown sugar, or to taste
1 fresh peeled and cored pineapple
6 scoops peach ice cream or pineapple sherbet

Peel the peaches, cut them in half, and discard the pits. Sprinkle with the brandy if desired. Melt the jam in a small pan with the water, stirring constantly until the jam melts. Brush the peach halves with the cooled, melted jam. Set on a plate.

Peel the bananas and leave them whole. Brush them lightly with melted butter and sprinkle with half of the sugar. Drain the pineapple and if it is not already sliced, cut it into 1/2 inch (1 cm) slices. Sprinkle the pineapple slices with the remaining sugar.

After you have grilled your meal and while the coals are still hot, place the fruit on an oiled grill screen and set it on the grid. Grill the fruit, uncovered, for just a few minutes, until it is warmed through and beginning to brown. Remove each piece of fruit as it is done. Divide the warm fruit among dessert plates and set a scoop of ice cream or sherbet in the centre. Serve immediately.

Don't Get Burned!

Make sure you cook your dessert on a clean grid. Chocolate pound cake just doesn't go with barbecue sauce or flecks of fish skin. To ensure your dessert is pristine, place it on a clean grill screen, then set that atop the grid. You may also want to give the grid a quick once-over with a wire brush to remove any of the larger bits of the previous course.

Hot Tip

To peel peaches, let them soak in boiling water for 30 seconds to 1 minute, then plunge them into a bowl of ice water. Remove the peaches with a slotted spoon. You should be able to easily pull or rub the skin off.

Blueberry-Apple Cobbler on the Grill

Yield: 6 servings

Level: Intermediate

Grill: 20 to 30 minutes

At the Ready: Large pot holders, baking tiles

For extra crunch and flavour, add 3/4 cup (175 mL) chopped pecans to the topping. For a faster cobbler, you can use a can of apple pie slices or peach pie slices.

5 large Granny Smith or Golden
  Delicious apples
3 cups (750 mL) fresh blueberries
2 tablespoons (25 mL) lemon juice
1/2 cup (125 mL or 1 stick) butter, at

  room temperature
1/2 cup (125 mL) sugar
1 cup (250 mL) all-purpose flour
3/4 cup (175 mL) regular rolled oats
1 teaspoon (5 mL) ground cinnamon

Butter a 9 inch (2.5 L) cast iron frying pan. Peel and core the apples and thinly slice them. You should have about 6 cups of apples. Wash and pick over the blueberries, discarding any shrivelled ones.

In a large bowl, toss together the blueberries and the apples. Sprinkle with the lemon juice and toss the fruit again. Set aside.

Cut the butter into 1/2inch (1 cm) pieces. Using a food processor or a bowl and a fork, mix together the butter, sugar, flour, oats, and cinnamon to make moist crumbs. Arrange the fruit on the bottom of the prepared pan. Sprinkle the crumbs over the fruit.

While the coals are cooling but still hot, set the baking tiles on a grill screen and set it on the grid. Place the frying pan on the tiles. Cover the grill, adjust the vents, and grill for about 20 to 30 minutes, or until the topping is golden and the fruit is hot. Spoon the cobbler into individual dessert bowls and top with sweetened whipped cream or vanilla ice cream.

Hot Tip

If you do not have a cast iron frying pan, you can make this cobbler in a heavy-duty 9-inch (2.5 mL) cake pan. Do not use a thin pan, or it may scorch.

Wine-Brushed Pears

Yield: 6 servings

Level: Easy

Grill: About 4 to 6 minutes

At the Ready: Oiled grill screen, pot holders or barbecue mitts, long-handled spatula, basting brush, dinner fork

Apples can be substituted for the pears. They will take slightly longer to cook. The apples, too, are done when they are fork tender.

1/2 cup (125 mL) sugar
1/2 cup (125 mL) red wine
1 cinnamon stick
6 ripe but firm pears, preferably Bosc or

Anjou
Sweetened whipped cream or vanilla frozen yogurt
Mint leaves for garnish (optional)

Mix the sugar, wine, and cinnamon together in a small saucepan. Bring to a boil over medium heat and simmer for 5 minutes. Stir occasionally. Let cool.

Peel and core the pears and cut them in half lengthwise. Brush them generously with the wine mixture.

When the coals are cooling down but still hot, set the pear halves, cut side down, on an oiled grill screen and set that on the grid. Grill the pears, uncovered, for 2 minutes, then turn them and continue grilling for 2 to 3 minutes, or until soft but not mushy. Brush the pears liberally with the wine mixture as they grill. To test for doneness, remove one pear using the pot holders or a spatula, then insert a fork. If it goes in easily, the pear is done.

To serve, set each pear on a dessert plate and top with sweetened whipped cream or vanilla frozen yogurt. Garnish with mint leaves if desired.

What's What

You'll generally see three pear varieties in your supermarket: the Bartlett, whose juicy, slightly grainy flesh is great for eating out of hand; the Bosc, which has a slender neck, russet skin, and tart-sweet flavour; and the Anjou, a firm, sweet, yellowish-green winter pear. All three varieties are good raw or cooked, but the Bosc keeps its shape best during cooking.

Warm Apple Cinnamon Slices with Cheddar Cheese

Yield: 6 servings

Level: Easy

6 large, firm apples
1/4 cup (50 mL) orange juice
1/2 cup (125 mL) sugar
1 teaspoon (5 mL) ground cinnamon
1/4 cup (50 mL) butter, melted and

Grill: About 4 minutes

At the Ready: Oiled grill screen

  cooled
1/2 pound (250 g) wedge of Cheddar
  cheese, wrapped in aluminum foil
1/2 cup (125 mL) chopped walnuts and
  or raisins

Peel and core the apples, and slice them into rounds. Put the sliced apple rounds in a bowl and sprinkle with the orange juice. Mix the sugar and cinnamon together and toss with the apples. Drizzle the butter over the apple mixture and toss again.

Wrap the Cheddar cheese in aluminum foil.

While the coals are still hot but cooling down, set an oiled grill screen on the cooking grid. Put the apples on the grill screen.

Grill the apple slices, uncovered, about 2 minutes on each side or until they're warm and beginning to brown. Set the covered cheese on the grill and cook for 1 to 2 minutes on each side. You want the cheese to be just warm and slightly softened. Remove the apples and divide them among individual dessert plates. Sprinkle with the nuts or raisins. Slice the warmed cheese and arrange it on the plates with the apples. Serve immediately.

Tasty Tidbit

Our inspiration for this recipe comes from New England, where it long has been a tradition to pair apple pie with wedges of Cheddar cheese.

Fruit Kebabs on Grilled Chocolate Pound Cake

Yield: 6 to 8 servings

Level: Intermediate

Grill: About 4 to 6 minutes

At the Ready: 6 or 8 short bamboo skewers, soaked in water and drained; oiled grill screen; pot holders; long-handled spatula; chocolate sauce

If you're pressed for time or lack baking skills, you can prepare this recipe with a store-bought pound cake and bottled chocolate sauce.

Chocolate pound cake
1 3/4 cups (425 mL) cake flour
1/3 cup (75 mL) unsweetened cocoa
1/2 teaspoon (2 mL) salt
1/2 teaspoon (2 mL) baking powder
10 tablespoons (150 mL or 1 1/4 sticks) unsalted butter, at room temperature
1 1/4 cups (300 mL) sugar
3 eggs
1 teaspoon (5 mL) vanilla
3/4 cup (175 mL) sour cream

Chocolate sauce
2 ounces (60 g) unsweetened chocolate
3/4 teaspoon (4 mL) vanilla
2 tablespoons (25 mL) unsalted butter
Regular milk as needed
1 cup (250 mL) sweetened condensed milk
Melted butter

Fruit
6 plums
3 large ripe peaches

To make the cake, first grease or spray a 9 x 5 inch (2 L) nonstick loaf pan. Preheat the oven to 350°F (180°C).

Sift the flour, cocoa, salt, and baking powder together. Set aside.

Cream the butter in the large bowl of an electric mixer until light, about 1 to 2 minutes. Add the sugar and continue beating for about 2 minutes. Add the eggs, one at a time; beat well after each addition. Mix in the vanilla. Add about one-third of the flour mixture, then half the sour cream, beating about 20 seconds after each addition. Repeat. Then add the remaining flour and beat just until it's mixed in.

Pour the batter into the prepared pan. Bake it on the centre rack of the oven for about 1 hour and 10 minutes, or until a toothpick inserted in the centre comes out dry and clean. Cool the cake on a rack for 5 minutes. Run a knife around the inside edges of the pan and turn the cake out of the pan. Cool the cake on a wire rack, right side up.

To make the sauce, coarsely chop the chocolate. Place it and the butter in a small glass microwave-proof dish. Microwave on medium-high for 45 seconds to 1 minute, stirring once. Stir until the chocolate is smooth and cooled. Using a spatula, scrape the chocolate and butter into a bowl. Mix in the condensed milk and vanilla. If the sauce is too thick, thin it with a little regular milk. Cover the sauce with plastic wrap and store it in the refrigerator until ready to serve. The sauce can be served warm or at room temperature.

Cut the plums in half and remove and discard the pits. Cut the peaches in half, remove and discard the pits, and cut each peach half into 2 or 3 wedges. Thread the fruit on the skewers and brush lightly with melted butter.

Cut 6 to 8 slices, 1/2 to 1 inch (1 to 2.5 cm) thick, from the pound cake. Brush the cake slices lightly on both sides with melted butter.

When the coals are medium-hot or cooling down, set the skewers on an oiled grill screen and set the screen on the grid. Grill, uncovered, for a few minutes on each side. You just want the fruit to warm through. While the fruit warms, grill the cake for just 1 minute on each side, being careful not to burn it, as it cooks quickly. The cake should have a slight crust.

To assemble, set a slice of cake on each dessert plate. Place a fruit kebab on top of it or to the side. Drizzle the cake and the fruit with chocolate sauce. Serve immediately.

Tasty Tidbit

Pound cake was so named because it originally was made of a pound each of flour, eggs, sugar, and butter.

Campfire-Style S'Mores

Yield: 8 servings

Level: Easy

Grill: 4 to 8 minutes

At the Ready: Lightly buttered aluminum foil, long-handled spatula

6 milk chocolate bars, 5 ounces (150 g) each

16 squares cinnamon or chocolate graham crackers

2 cups (500 mL) marshmallow fluff or 16 large marshmallows

1 cup (250 mL) good-quality peanut butter

Set half of a chocolate bar on 1 graham cracker. Set a mound of marshmallow fluff on top or use 2 marshmallows in the centre over the chocolate. Dab 1 tablespoon (15 mL) of the peanut butter on top. Press the second graham cracker into place, making a sandwich. Wrap each sandwich securely in lightly buttered aluminum foil.

After you have grilled dinner, and while the coals are still hot but cooling down, set the sandwiches on the cooking grid. Grill, uncovered, for about 2 to 4 minutes on each side. Turn them over using a long-handled spatula. Remove one s'more and carefully unwrap to check if it is done to perfection: that is, the chocolate is runny and the marshmallows are soft. Serve immediately.

Apricots Topped with Raspberries and Raspberry Sherbet

Yield: 6 servings

Level: Easy

Grill: About 4 minutes

At the Ready: Long-handled spatula, raspberries, sherbet, oiled grill screen, long-handled brush

1 1/2 cups (375 mL) fresh raspberries, rinsed

Melted butter

Sugar

6 scoops of raspberry sherbet

24 ripe apricots

Sprinkle the raspberries with a little sugar and place them at grillside. Wash the apricots, cut them in half, and remove and discard the pits.

When the coals are still hot but starting to cool down, set an oiled grill screen on the grid. Brush the apricot halves lightly with melted butter and sprinkle them with 3 tablespoons (50 mL) of sugar. Arrange them on the screen. Grill, uncovered, for about 2 minutes on each side, until they begin to brown.

Arrange the apricots on individual dessert plates and sprinkle with the raspberries. Top each serving with a scoop of raspberry sherbet and serve immediately.

Honeyed Papaya Strips with Warm Brie

Yield: 6 servings

Level: Easy

Grill: About 4 minutes

At the Ready: Oiled grill screen, long-handled spatula, cheese knife

1 ripe papaya, about 1 to 1 1/2 pounds (500 to 750 g)
1/4 cup (50 mL) honey
1/4 cup (50 mL or 1/2 stick) butter,

melted and cooled
1/2 pound (250 g) ripe Brie, or to taste
1/2 teaspoon (2 mL) cinnamon

Peel the papaya and cut it in half lengthwise. Scoop out and discard the seeds. Cut the papaya halves into lengthwise slices. Stir the butter with the cinnamon and honey. Brush the papaya slices with the mixture. Wrap the Brie securely in aluminum foil.

After you have grilled your dinner and the coals are beginning to cool down, set an oiled grill screen on the cooking grid. Arrange the papaya slices on the grill screen. Grill the papaya uncovered, about 1 to 2 minutes on each side. The papaya should be warm but not mushy, and starting to brown. Put the Brie bundle on the grill at the same time and heat about 1 to 2 minutes on each side. The Brie should be warm, soft, and beginning to run when you cut through the rind.

Serve the warm papaya slices with wedges of cheese. Grapes are good served with this dessert.

Grilled Angel Food Cake and Pineapple

Yield: 6 servings

Level: Easy

Grill: 2 minutes for the cake, 5 minutes for the pineapple

At the Ready: Oiled grill screen, melted butter, basting brush

Six 1/2 inch (1 cm) slices fresh pineapple
6 slices prepared angel food cake

Melted butter for brushing
1/4 cup (50 mL) packed dark-brown sugar

While the coals are still hot but cooling down, brush the pineapple with melted butter, set it on an oiled grill screen, and set that on the cooking grid. Grill the pineapple, uncovered, for 5 to 6 minutes, turning once. Brush the cake slices on both sides with melted butter. Grill the cake for just 1 minute on each side, being careful not to burn it as it cooks quickly. The cake should have a slight crust.

Set a slice of cake on each plate along with a slice of pineapple. Sprinkle the pineapple with brown sugar. Serve. This is good with vanilla ice cream.

Hot Tip

Instead of sprinkling pineapple with brown sugar, you can drizzle a prepared chocolate sauce over it. Pineapple and chocolate are an excellent combination.

The Least You Need to Know

➤ The ideal time to grill most desserts is after you've cooked the main course, when the coals are still hot but cooling down a bit.

➤ Sugar burns quickly, so keep an eye on sweets as they cook.

➤ Make sure the grill screen is very clean before you put your dessert on it.

Chapter 24

Smoked Foods

In This Chapter

➤ Smoked Shrimp with Chili-Orange Mopping Sauce

➤ Cedar-Planked Salmon with Green Onion Mustard Crust

➤ Dungeness Crab–Crusted Alderwood-Planked Pacific Salmon

➤ Maple Planked Honey Lemon Herb Chicken Breasts

➤ Carolina-Style Slow-Smoked Pulled Pork

➤ Smoked Beef Short Ribs

➤ Mesquite-Smoked Turkey Thighs

➤ Smoked Turkey Sausages

➤ Honey-Brushed Smoked Chicken with Mandarin Orange Sauce

➤ Smoked Pork Sandwiches with Bourbon Barbecue Sauce

Smoking—or barbecuing, if you prefer—is the long, slow cooking that makes traditional barbecued foods so justifiably famous.

It's definitely a do-ahead process. In fact, smoked foods usually taste even better after they've sat in the refrigerator for a day or two.

Because smokers can differ, follow the manufacturer's directions for setting up and cooking. Smoked foods taste much better if cooked over pure charcoal rather than briquets. Under no circumstances should you use lighter fluid or instant-lighting briquets when you're smoking foods.

To give smoked foods an intriguing flavour undertone, add aromatics such as a thinly sliced orange, lime, or lemon, or a bit of whole allspice, or chopped fresh ginger, to the water pan.

In this section we also have recipes that deal with the subject of planking. Planking is a wonderfully simple way to smoke foods quickly, and the results are delicious.

Smoked Shrimp with Chili-Orange Mopping Sauce

Yield: 6 servings

Level: Intermediate

Grill: 25 to 30 minutes

At the Ready: Short bamboo skewers

1 pound (500 g) jumbo shrimp, shelled and deveined
3 large oranges, thinly sliced
12 cherry tomatoes

soaked in water 30 minutes and drained; 3 cups of oak or hickory chips or other chips of your choice, soaked 30 minutes and drained; long-handled spatula; chili mopping sauce; oil for brushing; brush; pot holders

Chili mopping sauce
1 cup (250 g) chili sauce
1 teaspoon (5 mL) Worcestershire sauce
1/4 cup (50 mL) orange juice
1/2 teaspoon (2 mL) cumin seeds

In a small glass bowl, combine the chili sauce, Worcestershire sauce, orange juice, and cumin. Cover lightly and refrigerate until ready to use. Stir the sauce before using.

Wash the shrimp and pat dry with paper towelling. Thread the shrimp onto bamboo skewers, alternating with the orange slices and tomatoes, and putting any extra shrimp at the end.

Follow the smoker manufacturer's directions. Fill the fire pan about three-quarters full of hardwood charcoal and heat the coals until ashen. Arrange the drained chips over the hot coals. Fill the water pan of the smoker about three-quarters full with hot water, add any aromatics, and set the pan in place in the smoker carefully, using thick pot holders.

Brush the cooking grid with oil. Mop (brush) the shrimp amply with sauce. Grill the kebabs 2 to 3 minutes. Turn and mop again. Grill 2 to 3 minutes longer or until the shrimp are white in colour and just firm to the touch. Do not overcook or the shrimp will become tough.

Place one kebab on each plate and pass any remaining mopping sauce (be sure to reheat it thoroughly first). You might want to make extra sauce to pass at the table. Serve with raw vegetables such as sliced red or green bell peppers, sliced celery, sliced carrots, and green onions.

Hot Tip

You can use this recipe for an appetizer or an entrée. If you decide to use it as an entrée, double it by using long, 12-inch (30 cm) wooden bamboo skewers, soaked in water for 30 minutes and drained, and use double the amount of shrimp, tomatoes, and orange slices on each kebab.

Cedar-Planked Salmon with Green Onion Mustard Crust

Yield: 6 portions

Level: Advanced

Plank: 12 to 15 minutes

At the Ready: Cedar planks 1 inch (2.5 cm) thick by 12 inches (30 cm) long and 8 inches (20 cm) wide, spray bottle of water, barbecue tongs, spatula

Planking has been around for hundreds of years. These recipes, which were inspired by the Pacific Northwest natives, bring out the best flavour in fresh fish and game. It is truly a natural way to cook, and delicious. Salmon is the most traditional seafood to plank, but once you get the idea behind planking you can use any fish you like. Planking works best with fish that is flaky and a little fatty, such as halibut, sea bass, scallops, trout, bluefish, and monkfish.

2 cedar planks, soaked in cold water for 4 to 6 hours
Six 6 ounce (180 g) skinless fillets of Atlantic salmon, about 2 inches (5 cm) thick
2 tablespoons (25 mL) Great Lakes seafood seasoning (page 147)
1 bunch green onions, finely chopped

1 small red onion, finely chopped
1/4 cup (50 mL) chopped fresh parsley
1/4 cup (50 mL) chopped fresh dill
Juice of one lemon
2 tablespoons (25 mL) olive oil
1/4 cup (50 mL) cup grain mustard
Salt and pepper to taste

Preheat the grill to high. Season the salmon fillets with the seafood seasoning, pushing the spices into the flesh of the salmon fillets.

In a bowl, mix the green onions, red onion, parsley, dill, lemon juice, olive oil, and mustard. Season to taste with salt and pepper. Crust the top side of the salmon fillets with the green onion mixture.

Place the cedar planks on the grill, close the lid, and heat for 3 to 5 minutes until the planks start to crackle and smoke. Carefully lift the lid and place the crusted salmon fillets on hot planks, crust side up. Close the lid and plank-bake for 12 to

continues

continued

15 minutes (medium doneness). Check periodically to make sure the planks are not on fire. Use a spray bottle of water to extinguish any flames.

Carefully remove the planks from the grill and, using a spatula, transfer the salmon fillets to a serving platter. Serve immediately.

Hot Tip

Leftover planked salmon makes great salmon salad sandwiches. Add a little mayonnaise, lemon juice, onion, and celery. Mix with salmon and serve.

Dungeness Crab–Crusted Alderwood-Planked Pacific Salmon

Yield: 6 servings

Level: Advanced

Plank: 12 to 15 minutes

At the Ready: Alderwood planks, 1 inch (2.5 cm) thick by 12 inches (30 cm) long and 8 inches (20 cm) wide, spray bottle of water, barbecue tongs, spatula

Once you plank, you will find that it is truly the only way to cook salmon. You will also find that you can crust it with virtually anything. This recipe uses the sweet meat of the Dungeness crab.

2 alderwood planks, soaked in cold water for 4 to 6 hours
Six 6 ounce (180 g) skinless fillets of Pacific salmon about 2 inches (5 cm) thick
2 tablespoons (25 mL) Great Lakes seafood seasoning (page 147)
1 pound (500 g) Dungeness crabmeat

(use snow crab or bleu crab or even surimi if you can't get Dungeness)
4 shallots, finely chopped
2 cloves garlic, minced
4 green onions, finely chopped
2 tablespoons (25 mL) chopped tarragon
Juice of 1 orange
Salt and pepper to taste

Preheat the grill to high. Season the salmon fillets with the seafood seasoning, pushing the spices into the flesh of the salmon fillets.

In a bowl, mix the crabmeat, shallots, garlic, green onion, tarragon, and orange juice. Season to taste with salt and pepper. Crust the topside of the salmon fillets with the crabmeat mixture.

Place the alderwood planks on the grill, close the lid, and heat for 3 to 5 minutes until the planks start to crackle and smoke. Carefully lift the lid and place the crusted salmon fillets on hot planks, crust side up. Close the lid and plank-bake for 12 to 15 minutes (medium doneness). Check periodically to make sure the planks are not on fire. Use a spray bottle of water to extinguish any flames.

Carefully remove the planks from the grill and, using a spatula, transfer the salmon fillets to a serving platter. Serve immediately.

Try this recipe with sea bass or halibut.

What's What

Cedar planks can be found at your local hardware store or lumberyard. Note that you must use "untreated woods" for planking. If you cannot get cedar, try maple, oak, alder, hickory, peach, apple, or cherry.

Maple-Planked Honey Lemon Herb Chicken Breasts

Yield: 6 servings

Level: Intermediate

Plank: 18 to 20 minutes

At the Ready: Maple planks, 1 inch (2.5 cm) thick by 12 inches (30 cm) long and 8 inches (20 cm) wide, spray bottle of water, barbecue tongs, spatula

Planking is a fast way of smoking foods. You can add just as much smoke flavour to food by planking as you can by smoking. It is easier and produces delicious results in minutes.

1 maple plank soaked in water for 6 hours
6 large chicken breasts, skin on, 6 to 8 ounces (180 to 240 g) each
2 tablespoons (25 mL) barbecue seasoning (page 146)
1/2 cup (125 mL) lemon juice
12 cloves garlic, crushed

2 tablespoons (25 mL) chopped rosemary
2 tablespoons (25 mL) chopped thyme
2 tablespoons (25 mL) chopped sage
1/2 cup (125 mL) honey
1 teaspoon (5 mL) ground black pepper
2 tablespoons (25 mL) olive oil
Salt to taste

continues

245

continued

Rub the chicken breasts with the barbecue seasoning.

In a bowl, whisk together the lemon juice, garlic, herbs, honey, black pepper, and olive oil. Season to taste. Place the chicken breasts in a large glass dish and pour 3/4 of the marinade over top. Turn the breasts to coat completely. Cover and refrigerate for 4 to 6 hours. Reserve the last 1/4 of marinade for basting.

Preheat the grill to high. Place the maple plank on the grill, close the lid, and heat for 3 to 5 minutes until the planks start to crackle and smoke. Carefully lift the lid, place the chicken breasts on the hot plank, and close the lid. Plank-bake for 15 to 20 minutes until the skin is golden-brown and crisp and the breats are fully cooked. Baste the breasts with the reserved marinade, and serve.

Carolina-Style Slow-Smoked Pulled Pork

Yield: 8 servings

Level: Intermediate

Grill: 7 to 8 hours

At the Ready: Meat thermometer; apple or cherry chips or dry twigs, soaked in water 30 minutes and drained; barbecue mitts or large pot holders

1/4 cup (50 mL) dark-brown sugar
1 tablespoon (15 mL) chili powder
1/2 teaspoon (2 mL) salt
1 teaspoon (5 mL) ground cumin
Dash of cayenne
1 teaspoon (5 mL) ground ginger
1/2 teaspoon (2 mL) cloves
4 1/2 to 5 pound (2 to 2.2 kg) pork butt

or Boston butt
1/2 cup (125 mL) prepared mustard
1 cup (250 mL) apple juice (for basting)

Carolina sauce
1 cup (250 mL) cider vinegar
1/4 cup (50 mL) sugar
3 dashes Tabasco sauce, or to taste

To make the rub, combine the sugar, chili powder, salt, cumin, cayenne, ginger, and cloves. Brush the meat with the mustard, and then rub with the spice mixture. Put the meat in a glass bowl and refrigerate for 1 1/2 to 2 hours.

Follow the smoker manufacturer's directions. Fill the fire pan about three-quarters full of hardwood charcoal and heat the coals until the smoker reaches 225°F (107°C). Scatter the apple twigs over the hot coals. Fill the water pan of the smoker about three-quarters full with hot water and set the pan in place in the smoker, carefully using barbecue mitts or pot holders.

This is a long, slow "smoke"; figure on 8 hours or so. Set the pork butt on the oiled cooking grid, cover, and smoke until the pork registers 180°F (82°C) with an instant-read thermometer that you have inserted in the thickest part of the meat without touching bone. Wrap the pork in aluminum foil after about 6 hours, or if the outside starts to look dry. Brush it with the apple juice several times during the last hour of smoking. Replenish the charcoal and water as necessary to keep a constant heat of about 225°F (107°C).

To prepare the Carolina sauce, use a glass mixing bowl and combine the vinegar, sugar, and Tabasco. Stir well.

Remove the pork to a board, cover with aluminum foil, and let rest for 15 minutes. Discard any fat. Using two forks, pull the pork into shreds. Sprinkle a small amount of the Carolina sauce over the meat for extra flavour. Serve the pulled pork hot in a warm bun, accompanied by coleslaw and all the trimmings, including spicy baked beans and pickles.

Hot Tip

This is a good idea for a Canada Day celebration. You can even prepare the pork the day before if you like. It takes most of a day to cook this, so be prepared. Serve with coleslaw, lightly warmed buns, relish, and salad.

Smoked Beef Short Ribs

Yield: 6 servings

Level: Intermediate

Grill: 1 1/2 hours

At the Ready: Aluminum foil to wrap ribs, marinade, large pot holders or barbecue mitts, a brush, and hickory, pecan, or cherry chips or twigs soaked in water 30 minutes and drained

The smoking time depends on the thickness of the ribs, the heat of the coals, and the temperature the day that you are grilling.

5 to 6 pounds (2.2 to 3 kg) beef chuck ribs, cut into individual ribs

Pink Grapefruit Sauce
1/3 cup (75 mL) dark-brown sugar

1 1/4 cups (300 mL) pink grapefruit juice
2 cloves garlic, peeled and smashed
1 tablespoon (15 mL) dried oregano, crumbled
1 teaspoon (5 mL) ground cinnamon

To make the sauce, combine the sugar, grapefruit juice, garlic, oregano, and cinnamon in a bowl, and mix well.

Place the ribs in a glass dish and brush with the sauce. Cover and marinate for 2 hours, turning one or two times. Drain.

Follow the smoker manufacturer's directions. Fill the fire pan about three-quarters full of hardwood charcoal and heat the coals until ashen. Arrange drained chips or twigs over the coals. Fill the water pan of the smoker about three-quarters full with hot water, add any aromatics, and carefully set the pan in place in the smoker, using barbecue mitts or pot holders.

Wrap the ribs, 4 or 5 together, in a double-layer of aluminum foil, sealing the packages securely. Continue until all of the ribs have been wrapped. Set the ribs on the grill and cover. Smoke the ribs for 1 hour, replacing water and twigs as necessary. Uncover the ribs during the last 30 minutes of grilling and brush with your favourite barbecue sauce. The meat should be fork tender. Serve hot with hush puppies or corn bread.

Hot Tip

Wrapping the ribs in foil ensures they'll stay moist.

Mesquite-Smoked Turkey Thighs

Yield: 6 to 8 servings

Level: Intermediate

Smoke: About 2 hours

At the Ready: The rub, 3 cups (750 mL) soaked and drained mesquite or other chips, vegetable oil for brushing, brush

You can substitute turkey breast if you prefer.

1/4 cup (50 mL) light-brown sugar
1/4 cup (50 mL) grated lemon peel
2 teaspoons (10 mL) lemon pepper
2 teaspoons (10 mL) chili powder
2 teaspoons (10 mL) dried marjoram

2 teaspoons (10 mL) dried sage
1/2 teaspoon (2 mL) salt
3 turkey thighs, skin on, about 12 ounces (350 g) each

In a small glass bowl, mix together the sugar, lemon peel, lemon pepper, chili powder, marjoram, sage, and salt.

Wash and dry the turkey thighs with paper towels. Brush the turkey with oil and rub it all over with the spice mixture. Set the turkey in a glass dish and let stand in the refrigerator for 1 hour.

Follow the smoker manufacturer's directions. Fill the fire pan about three-quarters full of hardwood charcoal and heat the coals until ashen. Arrange the drained chips over the hot coals. Fill the water pan of the smoker about three-quarters full with hot water, add any aromatics, and carefully set the pan in place in the smoker, using barbecue mitts or pot holders.

Brush the cooking grid with oil. Set the turkey thighs on the grid, cover, and smoke for about 2 hours or until the turkey juices run clear and the meat is fork-tender. Replenish the coals and wood chips as necessary during grilling.

Remove the turkey to a cutting board. Let it stand for 15 minutes. Slice the turkey and serve hot, warm or cold. This is good with salsa and grilled vegetables, or try a black and white bean salad with chili powder seasoning.

Smoked Turkey Sausages

Yield: 6 servings

Level: Intermediate

Grill: About 40 to 50 minutes

At the Ready: 3 tablespoons (50 mL)

12 turkey sausages, regular or Italian
Yellow hot dog mustard
Ketchup
Pickles

allspice as an aromatic for the water pan, barbecue mitts or large pot holders, 3 cups (750 mL) hickory chips soaked in water 30 minutes and drained

1 can (16 oz. or 450 g) sauerkraut, drained
12 hot dog rolls

Follow the smoker manufacturer's directions. Fill the fire pan about three-quarters full of hardwood charcoal and heat the coals until ashen. Arrange the drained chips over the hot coals. Fill the water pan of the smoker about three-quarters full with hot water and add the allspice. Carefully set the pan in place in the smoker, using barbecue mitts or pot holders.

Stick the sausages with a fork several times. Set the sausages on top of the cooking grid and cover the smoker, adjusting the vents. Smoke the sausages about 40 to 50 minutes, turning twice or as necessary. The sausages will turn a golden colour and should be cooked through. Remove the sausages to individual plates. Serve with mustard, ketchup, pickles, sauerkraut, and hot dog rolls that have been warmed on the grill.

Honey-Brushed Smoked Chicken with Mandarin Orange Sauce

Yield: 6 to 8 servings

Level: Intermediate

Smoke: About 70 minutes

At the Ready: Barbecue mitts or large pot holders; dried plum twigs or other twigs or chips of your choice, soaked in water 30 minutes and drained; long-handled fork; vegetable oil for brushing

The orange sauce can be prepared ahead of time and reheated. For extra flavour, you can add 2 tablespoons (25 mL) grated orange peel or orange liqueur.

2 chickens, each 3 or 3 1/2 pounds 1.5 to 1.75 kg), cut in half (see section on butterflying chickens in Chapter 12)
3/4 cup (175 mL) wildflower or other honey
1/3 cup (75 mL) stone-ground mustard

Orange sauce
2 cans (11 oz. or 315 g each) mandarin orange segments, with the liquid
1/3 cup (75 mL) unsalted butter
1 medium onion, peeled and minced
1/2 cup (125 mL) chicken broth
1/2 teaspoon (2 mL) salt
5 tablespoons (75 mL) sugar

Wash the chickens and pat dry with paper towelling. In a small bowl, mix the honey with the mustard. Brush the chickens with the mixture on all sides. Refrigerate the chickens until the smoker is ready.

Follow the smoker manufacturer's directions. Fill the fire pan about three-quarters full of hardwood charcoal and heat the coals until ashen. Arrange the drained twigs over the hot coals. Fill the water pan of the smoker about three-quarters full with hot water, add any aromatics, and carefully set the pan in place in the smoker, using barbecue mitts or pot holders.

Set the chickens on the oiled cooking grid. Cover and smoke for about 70 minutes, or until the chicken legs move easily and the juices run clear. Replenish the charcoal and drained wood chips as necessary during smoking.

While the chicken is smoking, prepare the orange sauce. Purée the orange segments with their juice in a food processor fitted with the steel blade. Set aside. Heat the butter and cook the onions over medium heat until soft, about 5 minutes. Stir in the orange purée, chicken broth, salt, and sugar. Simmer over medium heat for 10 to 15 minutes or until the sauce thickens slightly. Taste and adjust the seasonings. Reheat before serving.

Remove the chickens to a cutting board. Let stand for about 10 minutes. Cut the chicken if desired. Serve hot and pass the sauce.

Tasty Tidbit

In southern Illinois, pork is often smoked with apple twigs and apple cider for its unique flavour.

Hot Tip

For extra flavour, use 2 cups (500 mL) of apple juice in the water pan, or add 1/2 cup (125 mL) crumbled bay leaves to the water.

Smoked Pork Sandwiches with Bourbon Barbecue Sauce

Yield: 6 servings

Level: Intermediate

Smoke: About 2 hours

At the Ready: Long-handled fork; 3 cups (750 mL) apple twigs or hickory chips soaked in water 30 minutes and drained; meat or instant thermometer

1/4 cup (50 mL) peanut oil or canola blend oil
3/4 cup (175 mL) apple cider
1 tablespoon (15 mL) chili powder
1/2 teaspoon (2 mL) garlic powder
2 to 2 1/2 pounds (1 to 1.25 kg) pork

loin roast, trimmed of excess fat
Canadian whiskey barbecue sauce (page 148), made with bourbon instead of whiskey
8 sliced sesame seed hamburger buns or other sandwich rolls

Combine the oil, cider, chili powder, and garlic powder. Pour into a glass dish large enough to hold the pork loin. Place the pork in the marinade and turn several time so that all surfaces are coated with the marinade. Cover, and refrigerate. Marinate the pork for 5 to 6 hours, turning occasionally. Drain.

While the pork is marinating, prepare the sauce and refrigerate it.

Follow the smoker manufacturer's directions. Fill the fire pan about three-quarters full of hardwood charcoal and heat the coals until ashen. Arrange the drained chips over the hot coals. Fill the water pan of the smoker about three-quarters full with hot water, add any aromatics, and carefully set the pan in place in the smoker, using barbecue mitts or pot holders.

Set the pork on the lowest rack. Brush it lightly with the sauce. Cover, adjust the vents, and smoke the pork for about 2 hours. Rotate it 2 or 3 times and brush it with the sauce during the last 15 minutes of smoking. Check for doneness after 1 1/2 hours. The pork is done when the juices run clear when meat is cut, and an instant read thermometer registers 180°F (82°C) when inserted in the thickest part of the meat.

Transfer the pork to a cutting board and let it stand 5 minutes. Thinly slice the meat. Arrange the sliced pork in heated rolls and drizzle with the remaining sauce. Serve the pork sandwiches hot, accompanied by baked beans, hush puppies, and coleslaw.

The Least You Need to Know

➤ Smoking is the process by which most famous barbecued foods are cooked.

➤ Smoked foods improve in flavour as they "age."

➤ It's best to use real charcoal rather than briquets when smoking foods.

What's Wrong, and How to Fix or Prevent It

Burner flame on gas grill is too yellow.

➤ If the burner is new, it's probably just burning off machine oil. Don't worry.

➤ If it's not new, consult the owner's manual or call the manufacturer. You may need to adjust something.

Gas grill makes noise.

➤ A bit of a "whoosh" as the gas flows in is normal.

➤ Ticking and slight pinging are normal as the elements expand and contract with heat.

➤ Excessive rattling or vibrating may mean something's loose. Consult the owner's manual, or call the manufacturer.

Ignition sparks, but burner(s) on gas grill won't light.

➤ Burners may be clogged. Bend a paper clip straight, and dig out any crud in the burner holes.

➤ If that doesn't work, consult the manufacturer.

Charcoal won't light.

➤ Use a charcoal chimney.

➤ Use an electric fire starter.

➤ Use solid starters.

➤ Use kindling—crumpled newspaper, twigs, pine cones—under the charcoal. Add a teaspoon of vegetable oil to the newspaper to help it catch.

Charcoal won't stay lit or burns slowly.

➤ Make sure it's piled in a pyramid shape.

➤ Open the grill vents.

It's windy.

➤ Use the lid to shield the grill as much as possible.

➤ Use a charcoal chimney, electric starter, or solid starters to get the coals lit.

➤ Be sure the grill is covered during cooking.

➤ If fire flares, close the bottom vents.

It's raining.

➤ Forget cooking in the pouring rain. Put everything in the oven or under the broiler.

➤ If it's drizzling, allow extra time for lighting charcoal and preheating the grill, and for cooking. Cover the grill during cooking.

Fire keeps flaring up.

➤ Trim fats from food before cooking.

➤ Move the food so it's not directly over the coals.

➤ Cover the grill.

➤ Close the bottom vents.

Food drops into the coals.

➤ Put the food on a grill screen, or a piece of oiled foil with holes punched in it.

Food sticks.

➤ Clean the cooking grid.

➤ Make sure the grid and/or the food is oiled. If you're cooking fish, both the grill and the fish need to be oiled.

➤ "Preheat" the grid by putting it over the coals a few minutes before you put the food on it.

Food is nicely browned on outside, still raw on inside.

➤ Coals are too hot. They should be covered with a layer of ash before you start cooking.

➤ Food hasn't cooked long enough. Before you remove foods from the grill, insert an instant-read thermometer or cut into a slice to be sure it's cooked through.

➤ The sugar in the sauce burned. When you're using a sugary sauce, baste with it toward the end of the cooking time, or turn the food frequently.

➤ To salvage food in this condition, finish cooking it in the microwave. Cut off any burnt parts, and serve the food with a sauce.

Food is burnt and/or dry.

➤ The coals are too hot.

➤ It was cooked too long.

➤ To salvage burnt food, cut off the burnt parts, slice, and cover with a sauce.

➤ Next time, don't answer the phone while you're grilling.

Food is "grimy" looking.

➤ Clean the grill.

➤ Use separate sets of tongs for food and for charcoal.

➤ Use a better grade of charcoal.

➤ When you lift the lid up, pull it to the side rather than straight up.

Food doesn't brown nicely.

➤ The coals are too cool. They should be covered with ash, but still faintly glowing.

Meat is tough (applies to slow-cooking cuts like brisket or ribs).

> ➤ Food needs to be cooked longer.
> ➤ Coals are too hot—keep the temperature for slow-smoked foods at about 225°F (107°C).

Food tastes smoky and bitter.

> ➤ Use fewer wood chunks or chips.
> ➤ Use a milder smoking wood (for example, pecan instead of mesquite).

Food has an unpleasant chemical flavour.

> ➤ Don't use lighter fluid.
> ➤ If you do use it, let the coals burn to ash with the grill lid open, so volatile fumes can escape.

Glossary

Anjou A firm, sweet, yellowish-green winter pear.

Aromatic A herb, spice, or other ingredient that you sprinkle onto the coals or into the drip pan to perfume the smoke and enhance a food's flavour.

Ash catcher A metal tray or container that is attached to the bottom of a charcoal grill to collect ashes.

Ashen See *Medium hot coals*.

Barbecue Often used broadly to mean cooking over wood or out of doors. But serious barbecuers use it to mean slow-cooking meats over a low fire. See also *Grill and Smoke*.

Bartlett A pear variety with juicy, slightly grainy flesh.

Baste To brush or drizzle a sauce or other liquid on a food during cooking. It helps keep food moist.

Big Green Egg Trade name for a charcoal grill made of ceramic. It is inspired by the Japanese *kamado*.

Bluefish A coastal Atlantic fish with fine-grained, fatty flesh that makes it great on the grill.

Boil To cook a liquid on medium-high or high heat until the liquid is very active, with large bubbles breaking the surface.

Boning knives Knives with thin, curved blades designed to cut meat off the bone.

Bosc A slender-necked, russet pear with a sweet-tart flavour.

Briquets A mixture of charcoal and other substances, molded into uniform pillow shapes that are designed to catch fire easily.

Buffalo wings Chicken wings that are marinated in a spicy rub, grilled, and served with a blue cheese dip. Named for Buffalo, New York, where they originated.

Burner The heating element in a gas grill. Burners commonly are made of stainless steel, and often are shaped like an "H."

Butterfly To cut a food most, but not all of the way through, so that it can be flattened, like butterfly wings. Butterflied meats and poultry absorb marinade better and cook faster on the grill.

Carving knives Knives with very long, fairly thin blades that are strictly for slicing.

Charcoal Often used as a generic term for any fuel made of burnt wood. But true charcoal is actually hardwood that has been burned down to eliminate volatile gases and reduce its water content so that it doesn't smoke.

Charcoal chimney A large metal can that has a heatproof handle, an interior plate to hold charcoal, and a ventilated bottom. You put coals in the pan and light it from the bottom; the bottom coals ignite, and in turn ignite the other ones.

Chef's knives All-purpose chopping and slicing utensils with thick, heavy blades.

Chop To roughly cut food into fairly small pieces, using a chef's knife or food processor. To chop onions, peppers, and similar vegetables, lift and drop the blade of the knife rapidly, using a bit of a rocking motion.

Coals Generic grilling term that refers to the heat source, whether it's briquets, true charcoal, or gas-heating elements. See also *Medium hot coals; Red hot coals*.

Cooking grid The wire rack in the grill that you put food on.

Core To remove the woody or seedy centre of a fruit, such as a pear, apple, or pineapple. If you don't have a special tool called a corer, the easiest way to do this usually is to cut the fruit in half lengthwise and cut out the core.

Crustaceans Ocean and freshwater creatures that wear their skeletons on the outside of their bodies. Popular edible crustaceans include lobster, shrimp, prawns, and crawfish.

Dice To cut a food into little cubes, about 1/2 inch (1 cm) or smaller. It's neater than chopping and is often used for hard foods such as carrots. To dice, you slice the food one way, then the other way to make small squares.

Direct heat A method in which the food is cooked right over the heat source. It is used with most foods, unless they are very thick or large pieces.

Dressed Scaled, gutted, and ready to cook (as applied to fish).

Drip pan A pan put directly under the food when cooking by indirect heat or smoking. Usually you partly fill it with water or another liquid.

Dust A fine, powdery rub.

Elephant garlic A relative of the leek that looks like giant garlic and tastes like mild garlic. It's a good choice for the grill.

Finishing sauce A barbecue sauce or other liquid that is served alongside the meat at the table, and may also be used to baste the meat in the last few minutes of cooking. Also called table sauce.

Firebox, fire pan The part of the grill that holds the charcoal, wood, or briquets. In most wood-fired smokers, the firebox is separate from the cooking chamber.

Flake As applied to fish, to separate into sections. When fish is cooked through, it flakes when you prod it gently with a fork.

Gas grill A grill that is fuelled by propane or, less often, natural gas.

Glowing See *Red hot coals*.

Grate To shred a food such as ginger or cheese by rubbing it against the holes in a grater. Used interchangeably with *shred*.

Grill To cook foods relatively quickly over a medium-hot fire. It's a quicker process than barbecuing or smoking.

Grilling basket Hinged, long-handled flat wire baskets into which you put delicate foods, such as fish or vegetables, to make turning them on the grill easier.

Grill roasting See Indirect heat.

Grill screen A portable metal grid designed to sit atop the grill's cooking grid. It has mesh or small holes to keep foods such as sliced onions and shrimp from falling through the wires of the grid.

Hardwood The solid, compact wood of various trees. Hardwoods commonly used in grilling include oak, cherry, maple, hickory, and mesquite (which is actually a shrub).

Hardwood charcoal See *Charcoal*.

Heat distributors The "briquets" or bars in a gas grill that help spread the heat from the burners. They can be made of metal, pumice stone, or ceramic.

Heterocyclic amines (HCAs) Chemicals that are formed when protein foods are cooked over high heat. They may be harmful to human health.

Hibachi A rectangular tabletop grill with a stand, rather than legs, so it won't tip over, and a fairly heavy cooking grid that's often adjustable.

Indirect heat A method in which food is placed away from the heat source, so that it cooks more slowly. This is the grilling equivalent of roasting, and is usually used with larger cuts of meat or poultry that is whole.

Jerk A seasoning mixture traditionally used in Jamiaca to flavour slow-cooked pork. Its ingredients vary, but it always contains Jamaican pimento, or allspice. Other common ingredients include chiles, ginger, thyme, and garlic.

Kamado In Japan, a bell-shaped grill made of ceramic. In the United States, it's a trademarked name for a similar ceramic grill, modelled after the Asian type.

Kettle A round grill with a dome-shaped bottom and lid. Developed and sold by the Weber-Stephens Company, it is the most commonly sold form of charcoal grill.

Lemongrass A citrusy herb that looks a bit like a tough scallion. It is widely used in marinades and sauces in Southeast Asia.

Marinade An acid-containing liquid in which raw foods are soaked. See also *Marinate*.

Marinate Traditionally, to tenderize and flavour meats by soaking them in a liquid, usually a mixture of acid and oil, for a long time—anywhere from an hour to overnight. We use the term "marinate" a bit more broadly, to also include foods that are rubbed with a spice mixture and allowed to stand.

Meats See *Medium*; *Medium-rare*; *Medium-well*; *Well done*.

Medium As applied to meats, pinkish in the centre, with an internal temperature of 155°F (68°C).

Medium-hot coals Coals that have burned, then become covered with a fairly thick layer of ash. Most foods are grilled over ashen, or medium-hot, coals.

Medium-rare As applied to meats, still quite pink in the centre, but warm, with an internal temperature of 145°F (63°C).

Medium-well As applied to meats, brown in the centre, but still juicy, with an internal temperature of 160°F (71°C).

Mince To chop into very fine pieces. Garlic, ginger, and herbs are often minced.

Mollusks Spineless creatures that live inside hard shells. Popular edible mollusks include clams, oysters, scallops, and mussels.

Mop A small utensil with a cotton string top. It's designed for applying a thin sauce to foods. As a verb, *mop* is the same as *baste*.

Mopping sauce A liquid added to foods to add moisture and flavour. Also called *basting sauce* or *sopping sauce*.

New potatoes Very young, small, unblemished potatoes.

Oil or spray To rub the cooking grid lightly with a vegetable oil (use a brush or a paper towel for this), or to spray it with a nonstick cooking spray.

Orzo Rice-shaped pasta.

Paella A Spanish rice dish with many variations. It usually includes seafood, poultry, and meats, and is flavoured with saffron.

Paring knives Knives with short blades suitable for peeling and other detail work.

Peel To remove the skin of a fruit or vegetable. The easiest way to peel hard vegetables such as carrots or potatoes is with a vegetable peeler. The easiest way to peel soft fruits such as peaches or tomatoes is to put them in boiling water briefly (see Chapter 14). We also use peel to refer to the coloured part of the rind in citrus fruits.

Pig pickin' The classic barbecue style in the Carolinas. Slow-cooked pork is pulled into shreds, then moistened with a vinegary sauce and served on buns.

Pit To remove the large seed in a fruit such as a plum or peach. Cut the fruit in half lengthwise, then pry out the seed.

Polycyclic aromatic hydrocarbons (PAHs) Substances formed when the fatty juices from meat drip into the heat source. They may be dangerous to human health.

Portobello, Portabella An extra-large, cultivated brown mushroom. The caps are often cooked on the grill.

Prawns A broad term that can refer to a member of the lobster family or to a freshwater crustacean. Most seafood labelled "prawns" is actually jumbo shrimp.

Process To grind, chop, or blend foods in a blender or food processor.

Propane A colourless, flammable gas that's a component of petroleum and natural gas. It burns more cleanly than gasoline and is the most common fuel used to run gas grills.

Rare As applied to meat, still red in the centre and soft to the touch, with an internal temperature of 130 to 135°F (54 to 57°C).

Red-hot coals Coals that are still burning brightly orange. At this point, they may have only a thin coating of ash. Charcoal at this temperature is suitable for searing meats and for quickly cooking shellfish.

Rotate To turn food clockwise or counterclockwise without turning it over.

Rotisserie A long rotating rod, or spit, with prongs on either end to hold the food in place. At one end is a small motor, which rotates the rod with the food on it so that larger cuts of meat and poultry can cook more evenly.

Rub A mixture of spices used to flavour meats for barbecuing. It forms an oily crust that helps seal in juices.

Salmon A coldwater, fatty fish that's very popular for grilling. It comes from both the Atlantic and Pacific oceans, but these days most of the salmon in the markets is farm-raised.

Sear To quickly brown over high heat. Searing meats and poultry helps form a crust on the surface, sealing in the juices.

Simmer To cook foods at just below a boil. The liquid will have small bubbles coming to the surface, but will be "calmer" than a boiling liquid.

Skewer A thin metal or wooden rod that's used to hold chunks of food.

Slice To cut crosswise or lengthwise through a food to make thin, fairly large pieces.

Smoke To cook foods very slowly over a low fire, with wood chips or chunks added to produce fragrant smoke.

Smoker A specialized grill fired by wood, charcoal, gas, or electricity. The food sits far away from the heat source, so that it cooks very slowly and absorbs more of the flavour from the cooking wood or the wood chunks or chips added to the coals. The water smoker is a common variant.

Smoking woods Chips or chunks of unburnt wood that are soaked and scattered onto the charcoal (or heat diffusers in a gas grill) to produce an aromatic smoke.

Soft-shell crabs Regular East Coast blue crabs that are gathered right after they molt (shed their shells). The crunchy new shell is eaten right along with the meat.

Softwoods The resinous woods of conifer trees such as pine, spruce, fir, and cedar. They are unsuitable for cooking or smoking woods, but fine for kindling.

Solid starter Squares of a nontoxic wax that sit under the briquets. As they burn, they ignite the charcoal.

Trim To cut off and discard parts of a food that you don't normally eat. That includes such things as the woody bottoms of asparagus, the ends of green beans, or the fat and gristle on meats.

Trout Various species of a freshwater fish that are commonly grilled. Most of the rainbow trout in markets is farm-raised.

Turn To use a spatula or tongs to flip a food onto its other side.

Vent An opening on the top, side, or bottom of a grill or smoker that's designed to let air in and smoke out. Adjusting the vents can change the cooking temperature.

Water smoker A tall, cylindrical grill with a firebox, a water pan, and one or two cooking grids. The food sits above the water pan, which is between it and the heat source, allowing the food to cook slowly.

Well done As applied to meats, completely brown through the center, with little juice and an internal temperature of 165°F (74°C).

Resources

Information

Here's where you can learn all you want to, and probably more, about barbecue. Consider this a bibliography as well; many of these Web sites were used as research resources for this book.

Weber-Stephen Products Co.
1333 Ester Drive
Burlington
Ontario
L7P 1L2
e-mail: t.stahl@sympatico.ca
Phone 905-336-5700, fax 905-336-7272
Weber Grill-Line1-800-GRILL-OUT toll free for North America (1-800-474-5568)
www.weberbbq.com
Makers of charcoal and gas grills and accessories. The company's superb Web site offers tons of information about grilling and entertaining.

Barbecue'n
www.barbecuen.com
Excellent, comprehensive Web site devoted to grilling and barbecuingóbut mostly the latter. Also includes extensive lists of grill manufacturers, and on-line shopping for accessories.

The Lexington Collection
www.ipass.net/~lineback/lex.htm
All about Southern barbecue and Carolina pig pickin'.
U.S. Department of Agriculture
Food Safety and Inspection Service

Meat and Poultry Hot Line
1-800-535-4555
www.fsis.usda.gov
îLiveî Monday to Friday, from 10 a.m. to 4 p.m., Eastern Time. Recorded messages the rest of the time.
Agency responsible for meat and poultry safety.

U.S. Food & Drug Administration
Center for Food Safety and Applied Nutrition
Food Information and Seafood Hot Line:
1-800-FDA-4010 (or 202-205-4314 in the Washington, D.C., area)
îLiveî noon to 4 p.m. Eastern Daylight Time, Monday through Friday; recorded messages the rest of the time.
www.vm.cfsan.fda.gov
Agency responsible for general food safety and seafood safety.

Barbecue Industry Association (BIA)
710 East Ogden, Suite 600
Naperville, IL 60563-8603
(630) 369-2404
www.bbqind.org
Trade association that keeps track of grilling trends and statistics.

Bibliography

In addition to most of the Web sites mentioned above, we also relied on these books and articles for information:

Bennett, Bev, and Virginia Van Vynckt. *The Dictionary of Healthful Food Terms*.

Barron's Educational Series, 1997.

Grunes, Barbara. *The Beef Lover's Grill Book*. Contemporary Books, 1991.

Grunes, Barbara, and Phyllis Magida. *Poultry on the Grill*. Dell Publishing, 1989.

Grunes, Barbara, and Phyllis Magida. *The Complete Fish on the Grill*. Contemporary Books, 1994.

Herbst, Sharon Tyler. *The New Food Lover's Companion*, 2d ed. Barron's Educational Series, 1995.

Jamison, Cheryl Alters, and Bill Jamison. *Texas Home Cooking*. Harvard Common Press, 1993.

Lawrence Livermore National Labs. "Marinating and Heterocyclic Amines" www-bio.llnl.gov/mutagens/html/fd.marinade.html (World Wide Web). Cited August 25, 1998.

Product Information and Mail Order

Equipment and Accessories

Barbecue Renew
Moss Bay Commerce Center
731 Kirkland Ave.
Kirkland, WA 98033
(425) 828-0637
www.grillparts.com
On-line tips and ordering of gas grill parts.

Barbeques Galore
15041 Bake Parkway, Suite A
Irvine, CA 92618
1-800-GRILL-UP
www.bbggalore.com
Chain of barbecue equipment superstores in the United States and Australia. Call or visit the Web site to find out if there is a store in your area.

Big Green Egg
3414 Clairmont Road
Atlanta, GA 30319
(404) 321-4658
www.biggreenegg.com
Makers of a charcoal grill/smoker made of ceramic.

Char-Broil
PO Box 1300
Columbus, GA 31902-1300
1-800-241-8981 (orders)
1-800-252-8248 (customer service)
www.grilllovers.com
Makers of gas, charcoal, and electric grills.

Chef's Catalog
3215 Commercial Ave.
Northbrook, IL 60062-1920
(847) 480-9400
1-800-338-3232 (orders only)
www.chefscatalog.com
Purveyor of a wide variety of kitchen tools, cookware, and utensils.

Frontgate
2800 Henkle Dr.
Lebanon, Ohio 45036-8899
1-800-626-6488 (orders)
1-800-537-8484 (questions)
www.frontgate.com
Upscale grills and accessories for entertaining. Offers a grilling-specific catalogue in addition to the main catalogue.

Grill Parts Distributors
6150 49th St. North
St. Petersburg, FL 33709
1-800-4GRILLS
www.gasgrills.com
Company that specializes in supplying parts for over 20 brands of gas grills.

The Kamado Company
2224 Rice Ave.
West Sacramento, CA 95691
1-888-KAMADOS
www.kamado.com
Makers of a charcoal grill/smoker made of ceramic.

Peoples Woods
75 Mill Street
Cumberland, RI 02864
1-800-729-5800, or (401) 725-2700 (in Rhode Island)
www.peopleswoods.com
Manufacturers and purveyors of Nature's Own pure hardwood charcoal, as well as a variety of smoking woods, some exotic. Available in kitchenware and natural-foods stores, or by mail order.

Traeger Industries
1385 E. College St.
P.O. Box 829
Mt. Angel, OR 97362
1-800-872-3437, or (503) 845-9234
www.traegerindustries.com
Manufacturers of wood pellet grills.

Foodstuffs

American Spoon Foods
1668 Clarion Ave.
P.O. Box 566
Petoskey, MI 49770-0566
1-888-735-6700 (orders)
1-800-222-5886
www.spoon.com
Barbecue and marinating sauces, chutneys and relishes, and other condiments.

Culver Duck Farms
12215 County Road 10
Middlebury, IN 46540
1-800-825-9225, or (219) 825-9537
www.culverduck.com
Sells ducks and duck parts, including boneless breasts.

Mo Hotta Mo Betta
P.O. Box 4136
San Luis Obispo, CA 93403
1-800-462-3220
www.mohotta.com/index2.html
Wide selection of spicy barbecue sauces, salsas, and marinades.

Penzeys, Ltd.
W19362 Apollo Dr.
Muskego, Wisconsin 53150
(414) 679-7207
www.penzeys.com
Wide variety of spices and seasonings, including various barbecue rubs.

Peppers
2009 Highway One
Dewey Beach, DE 19971
1-800-998-FIRE, or (302) 227-4608
www.peppers.com
Restaurant with "the world's largest collection of hot sauces," and online catalogue and ordering of spicy marinades and sauces, mustards, and other condiments.

Index

About the Authors

Chef **TED READER**, Cottage Country Television barbecue chef extraordinaire, has had a love of cooking since childhood. As the host of Cottage Country Television (recently signed to air on PBS across the USA) for the past 8 years, appearing in over 100 episodes, Ted has a flair for making barbecuing easy and entertaining.

Throughout his career, Ted has worked as an Executive Chef for some of Toronto's finest restaurants. He was the chef of the Skydome Hotel, and most recently was the Executive Chef for President's Choice®. There he was a product developer as well as chef. He helped develop such products as the PC® Tournament Ribs and PC® Thick and Cheesy Burgers along with the development of the recipes in the *Dave Nichol Cookbook* and the *PC® Barbecue Cookbook*. His newest book releases have been the *Cottage Cooking Cookbook* and the *Sticks and Stones Cookbook*.

Ted is a chef with a lot on the go. He not only works as a much-sought-after consultant to companies for product and recipe development, but has recently joined Patrick Racing of the C.A.R.T. Racing Series as Team Chef for Drivers Adrian Fernandez and Roberto Moreno.

BARBARA GRUNES has established a national reputation as a food writer, food historian, cooking teacher, and television guest cook. She specializes in grilling and developing nutritionally aware recipes, and is the author or coauthor of more than thirty cookbooks, including ten volumes dedicated to grilling. Among the titles are: *Kabobs on the Grill*, *Appetizers on the Grill*, *Skinny Grilling*, *The Beef Lover's Great Grill Book*, *Fish on the Grill*, and *Grill Cookbook for Williams-Sonoma*. She lives near Chicago with her husband, Jerry.

VIRGINIA VAN VYNCKT is the author or coauthor of five previous books on food and nutrition, including *Feed Your Kids Right the Lazy Way* (Alpha Books). She is a freelance food writer and editor living in Colorado, where she can use her barbecue grill nearly year-round.

G